Centering Women of Color in Academic Counterspaces

Race and Education in the Twenty-First Century

Series Editor: Kenneth Fasching-Varner, Louisiana State University, Roland Mitchell, Louisiana State University, and Lori Martin, Louisiana State University

This series asks authors and editors to consider the role of race and education, addressing question such as "how do communities and educators alike take on issues of race in meaningful and authentic ways?" and "how might education work to disrupt, resolve, and otherwise transform current racial realities?" The series pays close attention to the intersections of difference, recognizing that isolated conversations about race eclipse the dynamic nature of identity development that play out for race as it intersects with gender, sexuality, socio-economic class, and ability. It welcomes perspectives from across the entire spectrum of education from Pre-K through advanced graduate studies, and it invites work from a variety of disciplines, including counseling, psychology, higher education, curriculum theory, curriculum and instruction, and special education.

Titles in the Series

Big Box Schools: Race, Education, and the Danger of the Wal-Martization of Public Schools in America, by Lori Latrice Martin

The Journey Unraveled: African American Students' Career and College Readiness, edited by Jennifer R. Curry and M. Ann Shillingford

Race and Pedagogy: Creating Collaborative Spaces for Teacher Transformations, by Susan R. Adams and Jamie Buffington-Adams

Asian Americans and Education: A Critical Analysis of the "Model Minority" as Perpetrators and Victims of Crime, edited by Daisy Ball and Nicholas D. Hartlep

Centering Women of Color in Academic Counterspaces: A Critical Race Analysis of Teaching, Learning, and Classroom Dynamics, by Annemarie Vaccaro and Melissa J. Camba-Kelsay

Centering Women of Color in Academic Counterspaces

A Critical Race Analysis of Teaching, Learning, and Classroom Dynamics

Annemarie Vaccaro and
Melissa J. Camba-Kelsay

LEXINGTON BOOKS
Lanham • Boulder • New York • London

PublishedbyLexingtonBooks
AnimprintofTheRowman&LittlefieldPublishingGroup,Inc.
4501ForbesBoulevard,Suite200,Lanham,Maryland20706
www.rowman.com

UnitA,WhitacreMews,26-34StannaryStreet,LondonSE114AB

BritishLibraryCataloguinginPublicationInformationAvailable

ThehardbackeditionofthisbookwaspreviouslycatalogedbytheLibraryofCongressas
follows:

LibraryofCongressCataloging-in-PublicationDataAvailable

Names:Vaccaro,Annemarie,author.|Camba-Kelsay,Melissa,author.
Title:Centeringwomenofcolorinacademiccounterspaces:acriticalraceanalysisofteaching,
    learning,andclassroomdynamics/AnnemarieVaccaroandMelissaCamba-Kelsay.
Description:Lanham:LexingtonBooks,[2016]|Series:Raceandeducationinthetwenty-first
    century|Includesbibliographicalreferencesandindex.
Identifiers:LCCN2016032892(print)|LCCN2016039643(ebook)
Subjects:LCSH:AfricanAmericanwomeninhighereducation.|Discriminationinhighereducation-
    -UnitedStates.|Blacks--Raceidentity--UnitedStates.
Classification:LCCLC2781.V332016(print)|LCCLC2781(ebook)|DDC378.1/982996073--
    dc23
LCrecordavailableathttps://lccn.loc.gov/2016032892

ISBN978-1-4985-1710-2(cloth:alk.paper)
ISBN978-1-4985-1712-6(pbk.:alk.paper)
ISBN978-1-4985-1711-9(electronic)

♾™ Thepaperusedinthispublicationmeetstheminimumrequirementsof American
NationalStandardforInformationSciencesPermanenceofPaperforPrintedLibrary
Materials,ANSI/NISOZ39.48-1992.

PrintedintheUnitedStatesofAmerica

Contents

Series Foreword   vii
Kenneth Fasching-Varner, Roland Mitchell, and Lori L. Martin

Acknowledgments   ix

Preface   xi

Introduction   xvii

1   Sister Stories: "Not your typical class."   1

2   Microaggressions on Campus: "We still have a long way to go."   27

3   What Are Counterspaces and Why Do We Need Them?: "It's a refuge on campus."   49

4   Student Interactions in a Counterspace: "It's complicated."   69

5   Silence and Self-Censoring: "Telling my story . . . *or* not."   89

6   Learning about Identity: "Who am I?"   111

7   My Body, My Looks: "I'm never gonna look like that."   131

8   Becoming an Inclusive Leader: "Everyone has a voice."   151

Conclusion   171

Appendix   189

Index   195

About the Authors   201

Series Foreword

Kenneth Fasching-Varner, Roland Mitchell, and Lori L. Martin

DuBois some one hundred-plus years ago suggested that "the world problem of the twentieth century is the problem of the color line." Despite claims of a twenty-first-century evolution into a post-racial society, the reality of our times suggests that systemic oppression, marginalization, and alienation continues to play out along color lines. The Race and Education series asks authors and editors to consider "what is the role of race and education?," "how do communities and educators alike take on issues of race in meaningful and authentic ways?," and "how might education (from womb to tomb) work to disrupt, resolve, and otherwise transform current racial realities?"

While much scholarly attention has been paid to race over the last one hundred years, very little substantive and systemic change seems to occur. Simultaneously in non-academic settings, the election of the nation's first president of color has prompted many to suggest that we have achieved racial nirvana—that the Obama era has ushered in a post-racial reality. The vast majority of children of color continue to live in poverty, attend largely re-segregated public schools, are taught by predominantly white teachers, and have little supported access to institutions of higher education. If we live in a post-racial moment, the highlights of those times include intensified segregation with little opportunity to openly dialogue about the realities, opportunities, and challenges of race. This series is a necessary addition to the literature because it 1) works to understand race through inter-disciplinary lenses, 2) draws on educational perspectives across the entire spectrum of education from Pre-K through advanced graduate studies, and 3) confronts the contributions between the articulation of being post-racial and the very racial realities of the times.

The Race and Education series covers a broad range of educational perspectives and contexts, drawing upon both qualitative/quantitative and empirical/theoretical approaches to understanding race and education. Further, the series will contextualize the relationship between race and education not just in the United States, but also in a variety of trans-national settings. Disciplines such as counseling, psychology, higher education, curriculum theory, curriculum and instruction, and special education all contribute to the larger dialogue in the series. The series pays close attention to the intersections of difference, recognizing that isolated conversations about race eclipse the dynamic nature of identity development that play out for race as it intersects with gender, sexuality, socio-economic class, and ability (among others). Consequently, the series provides readers with multiple opportunities to examine the importance of race in both breadth and depth as it plays out in the human experience.

What happens when historically disadvantaged groups are moved from the margins and become the center of teaching and learning in classrooms in colleges and universities all across the United States of America? *Centering Women of Color in Academic Counterspaces* challenges scholars, students, administrators, and the general public to think about the unique experiences of undergraduate women of color within a predominately White university with a critical lens. The thoroughly researched book, which was five years in the making, challenges readers to resist conventional approaches to understanding the experiences of historically disadvantaged groups. Conventional approaches to understanding the experiences of people of color, particularly women of color, often give very little consideration to the multilevel and multidimensional contexts of their lives. Narratives from the instructor, teaching assistants, and undergraduate mentor for a course where women of color are the focus and not a footnote offer insight into the goals and methods for creating an affirming classroom counterspace. *Centering Women of Color in Academic Counterspaces* also sheds light on other important topics related to the experiences of undergraduate women of color, including microaggressions on- and off-campus, self-censoring, and beauty and body image. *Centering Women of Color in Academic Counterspaces* identifies challenges faced by undergraduate women of color, which have the potential to create a hostile environment in a space far too many faculty, students, and administrators view as race- and gender-neutral. The book also shows with great clarity how higher education is a social institution and is subject to all of the same -isms that impact the broader society, including racism and sexism, systems of oppression, which are by no means mutually exclusive. Fortunately, *Centering Women of Color in Academic Counterspaces* provides recommendations for anyone, which should include everyone, concerned about making colleges and universities more welcoming and equitable environments.

Acknowledgments

We are thankful for this opportunity to write *Centering Women of Color in Academic Counterspaces* and would like to acknowledge those who helped to make this book a reality. First, we thank the students of Sister Stories, whose strength, honesty, and resilience served as inspiration and motivation to us. The success of the course would not have been possible without the voices and partnership of Elsiecheyenne Amoo, Margarida DaGraca, Michelle Rosa, and Isaura Dos Santos. The beautiful artwork for the cover was designed by Tenneh Jerricka Wilkins. We want to acknowledge her talent and thank the University of Rhode Island Center for Student Leadership Development for granting us permission to use this classic Sister Stories image.

Many friends, colleagues, and students offered us their expertise, enthusiasm, and encouragement. We thank colleagues who attended our conference presentations and provided feedback and ideas. Specifically, we thank Melissa Boyd-Colvin for her guidance and support. We would also like to thank Natalie Sabino, Nicki Toler, and Sarah Couch for their keen eyes on the final drafts of the manuscript.

Finally, we offer our deepest appreciation to our family members, both two-legged and four: Sarah Couch, Donna Vaccaro, Chloe, Maddie, Gilbert and Cecilia Camba, Brian Camba, Dan Kelsay, Austin Camba-Kelsay, Rover, Charlie, Maeby and Lucy. Without their support, encouragement, patience (and naptimes!), this book would not have been possible.

Preface

MELISSA J. CAMBA-KELSAY

I am a child of immigrants.
I am Asian.
I am Filipina.
I am American.
I am lumpia, longanissa, tocino, pancit palabok, rice, corned beef, and spam.
I am a twin sister.
I am an educator.
I am a wife.
I am a mother.
I am strong.
I am resilient.
I am enough.

In truth, I never thought I'd be writing a book. So, in introducing myself to the readers and sharing the story of how this book came to be, I find myself introducing myself in the same way I do in the class: by sharing my story.

My parents were born, grew up, and college-educated in the Philippines. When they speak of "home," that is where they mean. And my extended family considers it my home as well, though I've only visited three times in my life. My mom is one of five kids and my dad is one of thirteen. I come from a big family from the other side of the world, most of whom I barely know. Thus, I also consider my Titos and Titas, fellow immigrants with my parents, and those of us in the first generation born and raised here in the United States to be my family; my uncles, aunts, and cousins.

My brother and I were born in Queens, New York and lived there for our first five years. We then moved out to a predominantly White community on Long Island. Though there were few people who looked like us, and I always knew I was different, I don't recall ever feeling like an outsider. I attribute this to assimilation and to being included in groups because my brother and I excelled at sports. Plus, friends were always jealous of our awesome tans. The first significant moment I had of feeling different was not until I visited the Philippines when I was twelve.

My mom was about to haggle the price of something in a flea market. She turned to me and my brother and told us not to say anything except "no," or "hindi," which is "no" in Tagalog, otherwise the seller would know we were American and try to take advantage of this. It would be years later before I would internalize this—in the Philippines, I'm American, but in America, I'm Filipino.

I've experienced issues of internalized racism more so than anything else—this concept of being seen by others, and being seen by myself, as not Asian enough, Filipino enough, brown enough. I've had other people of color tell me to my face that I was not one of them, because my story was different. It was years before I started to deal with my internalized racism, and it is something I still struggle with at times.

Exploring my racial identity deeper coincided with my graduate education at Colorado State University (CSU) where I studied Student Affairs in Higher Education. My values about education, instilled in me by my parents, drove me to seek a career as an educator, and from my undergraduate experiences, I knew I wanted to work with college students. As I learned more about myself, I also learned more about issues of oppression and privilege, and soon, social justice became both a personal and professional value. My twelve-plus years of professional experience have included staff positions in offices of multicultural affairs at multiple institutions, as well as working with diverse college students through other functional areas, including student activities, college union administration, residence life, and leadership development.

It was at CSU where I met Dr. Linda Ahuna-Hamill and Dr. Blanche Hughes, two women of color who held higher administration positions and who also taught our Inclusive University course in the graduate program. Early in the semester when I was taking their course, I met with the two of them and they encouraged me to speak up more often in class. They told me that my voice was valuable and deserved to be heard by others, advising me to speak up, "or we'll kick you in the butt." This threat, I believe to this day, was real. Linda and Blanche became my mentors and were two of the first people I ever felt validated by. They always saw me as "enough." In looking back, I realize how significant this validation was for my development and self-worth, and it is something I have always tried to do with my students.

My current role as coordinator in the Center for Student Leadership Development at the University of Rhode Island allows me to infuse social justice values into leadership education, both inside and outside of the traditional classroom. A major piece that drew me to this position was the opportunity to teach students in the leadership studies minor. When I started planning the Sister Stories course in my first year, Annemarie and I talked about doing focus groups in order for me to get feedback about students' experiences in the course. I thought it was a great idea—I'd get some comments on teaching style, assignments, and whether students had fun. What I did not expect was learning how much impact the course would have on these students. Chapter 1 details my experiences with course planning.

I can write about the importance this book can have for fellow educators, trainers, or consultants in multiple fields. But here's the heart of it: I believe this book is important because it showcases real students' voices. Like my mentors saw in me, I see that these voices deserve to be heard, validated, and honored. This is particularly important in a world where many of these students are often silenced, ignored, or unseen. These students and their stories are honest. If their words inspire us to make changes in our curricula, enhance training programs, and improve campus climate, these are ways we can truly honor them.

ANNEMARIE VACCARO

I am a middle-class, White, queer, cisgender, bisexual woman who is not religious and does not have a disability. Over the course of my life, these social identities have meant different things to me and those around me. I grew up in a working-class, White neighborhood with a younger brother and two parents who were educators. My parents always told me that I could achieve anything I set my mind to. Those affirmational messages helped me persevere as I waded through overt and covert societal messages about beauty, body image, and appropriate career trajectories for women. Unfortunately, I also got a hefty dose of racist, heterosexist, and homophobic socialization throughout my young life. Homophobic and heterosexist messaging from loved ones, peers, and media kept me in the closet until well after college.

My feminist mother was always open-minded and inclusive of people from diverse backgrounds. Yet, many other relatives told racist, sexist, and homophobic jokes. They believed and perpetuated stereotypes about people of color, lesbian, gay, bisexual and transgender (LGBT) people, and people from lower-class backgrounds. As a young person, I knew there was something wrong with these perspectives, but I never had the courage, or knowledge, to speak up. So, I resorted to walking away or saying, "That's not funny" or "That's not right."

It was not until I enrolled in multicultural education courses, participated in social justice workshops, and encountered socially just supervisors that I gained the knowledge and skills to confront oppression. This was not an easy task. As many scholars have noted (Case & Cole, 2013; Goodman, 2011; Watt, 2007), people with privilege often resist learning about issues of diversity and social justice. My family, friends, and fellow students were no different. They resisted my efforts to engage them in conversations about inequality and privilege. Some even mocked my attempts by referring to me as "diversity girl." It took decades for me to glean the skills to effectively confront some loved ones. Family resistance, however, prepared me for difficult dialogues about diversity and social justice in my roles as a student affairs professional and faculty member.

Being a social justice educator requires deep self-awareness. I am on a life-long journey of making meaning of my privileged (race, class, ability) and minoritized (gender, sexual orientation) identities and the intersections among them. As a researcher, part of my journey has included learning about, and adopting, critical perspectives. My scholarly work is informed by queer, feminist, critical race, and critical race feminist perspectives. These are the lenses through which I understand myself and the world around me.

Early in my scholarly career, writings by feminist scholars (e.g., Reinharz, 1992) about androcentric bias in research opened my eyes to the social injustice that occurs when people with privilege conduct research with minoritized populations. I also noticed how research about LGBT people was often steeped in deficit perspectives. I often wondered how the sexual orientation and gender identities of researchers influenced their approach to research with LGBT people and topics. Bias in research impacted me personally as a queer-identified, bisexual woman. Of course, I began to realize that as a privileged White researcher, I could potentially engage in biased and harmful research with people of color (and other minoritized groups). Enter critical race theory (CRT) and mentors who pushed me to delve deeply into what it meant to do ethical, inclusive, and socially just research as a White person. Was it even possible? One of my favorite articles is by Bergerson (2003) who asked, "Is there room for White scholars in fighting racism in education?" My answer: it depends on the cultural competency (i.e., racial awareness, knowledge, and skills) of the researcher (Pope, Reynolds & Mueller, 2004). As Helms (1993) argued:

> If a researcher is unable to examine the effects of her or his own racial development on her or his research activities, then the researcher risks contributing to the existing body of racially oppressive literature rather than offering illuminating scholarship. (p. 242)

Throughout my career, I have taken this quote to heart. I seek learning opportunities to explore all of my intersecting social identities. I have also developed relationships with social justice scholars with whom I have candid conversations about privilege, racial identity, and the ways those factors influence my scholarship.

As Melissa mentioned in the prior section, the seeds for *Centering Women of Color in Academic Counterspaces* began when she invited me to evaluate Sister Stories. This initial invitation turned into a collaborative, multi-year research project where students and instructors shared powerful stories about microaggressions, counterspaces, identity, beauty, body image, leadership, and resiliency. Their stories touched me deeply. I hope readers will also be inspired by these narratives and use key findings to effect change in their personal and professional spheres of influence.

REFERENCES

Bergerson, A. A. (2003). Critical race theory and white racism: Is there room for white scholars in fighting racism in education? *International Journal of Qualitative Studies in Education, 16*(1), 51–63.

Case, K. A., & Cole, E. R. (2013). Deconstructing privilege when students resist: The journey back to the community of engaged learners. In K. A. Case (Ed), *Deconstructing privilege: Teaching and learning as allies in the classroom* (pp. 34–48). New York, NY: Routledge.

Goodman, D. J. (2011). *Promoting diversity and social justice: Educating people from privileged groups* (2nd ed). Thousand Oaks, CA: Sage.

Helms, J. E. (1993). I also said, "White racial identity influences White researchers." *The Counseling Psychologist, 21*(2), 240–43.

Jones, S. R., Torres, V., & Arminio, J. (2014). *Negotiating the complexities of qualitative research in higher education: Fundamental elements and issues*. New York, NY: Routledge.

Pope, R. L., Reynolds, A. L., & Mueller, J. A. (2004). *Multicultural competence in student affairs*. San Francisco, CA: Jossey-Bass.

Reinharz, S. (1992). *Feminist methods in social research*. New York, NY: Oxford.

Watt, S. K. (2007). Difficult dialogues, privilege and social justice: Uses of privileged identity exploration framework in student affairs practice. *The College Student Affairs Journal, 26*(2), 114–26.

Introduction

Imagine centering the lives of women of color in a higher education classroom. How would faculty design and teach such a course? How would undergraduate women of color respond to a course for and about them? What would happen if a small number of White students or men of color joined the course? How would teaching, learning, and classroom dynamics change as the racial and gender demographics changed? What would students learn about oppression, identity, and leadership in such a course? These are just a few of the questions we answer in *Centering Women of Color in Academic Counterspaces*.

Centering Women of Color in Academic Counterspaces is based upon an intensive five-year case study of an undergraduate course about the historical and contemporary experiences of women of color. Throughout the book we refer to the course by the pseudonym Sister Stories, and in chapter 1, we provide a detailed description of the course and the study. This introductory chapter is intended to provide a theoretical and empirical roadmap for the rest of the book. All of the concepts mentioned in the Introduction are expanded upon later in the text. First, we begin with a note on language and terminology. Then, we offer a short overview of contemporary oppression in the United States, focusing on the intersection of race and gender. Next, we introduce readers to the concept of microaggressions. This brief synthesis of the literature is followed by an overview of the critical race theory (CRT) and critical race feminist (CRF) frameworks that informed our work. This introductory chapter concludes with an overview of the book.

LANGUAGE AND TERMINOLOGY

Throughout this book, we use an array of academic concepts which we define at the time of use. However, there are some key terms and phrases we use regularly that must be clarified from the outset. First, we use both the terms *race* and *ethnicity* throughout the book. While they are sometimes used interchangeably, they are not the same thing.

> The word ethnicity derives from the Greek word ethnos, meaning a nation. Ethnicity is a multi-faceted quality that refers to the group to which people belong, and/or are perceived to belong, as a result of certain shared characteristics, including geographical and ancestral ori-

gins, but particularly cultural traditions and languages. The characteristics that define ethnicity are not fixed or easily measured, so ethnicity
is imprecise and fluid. (Bhopal, 2004, p. 441)

Both ethnicity and race are social constructions, but race is a construction
based upon the categorization of individuals into distinct social groups
using phenotypic characteristics such as skin color, eye shape, hair tex-
ture, and body size as well as a person's ancestry—regardless of whether
or not an individual has been socialized into, or has adopted, their cultural heritage.

The 2010 U.S. census used the following racial categories: 1) White; 2)
Black or African American; 3) American Indian and Alaska Native, 4)
Asian; and 5) Native Hawaiian and other Pacific Islander. Subsumed by
each of these racial categories are a variety of ethnicities. For instance,
individuals categorized as Asian can be Filipino, Chinese, Korean, Japanese, Vietnamese, or "other Asian" ethnic backgrounds (U.S. Bureau of
the Census, n.d). Latinos/as or Hispanic people may come from a range
of racial backgrounds. In fact, those who identify as Hispanic may identify with any race on the U.S. census. They are also asked to name their
"Hispanic, Latino or Spanish Origin," which can include the following
ethnicities: Mexican, Mexican American, Chicano, Puerto Rican, Cuban,
or other (U.S. Bureau of the Census, n.d.). Complicated terminology regarding Latinos/as emerged quite frequently in Sister Stories. Many students in the course referred to themselves as "Spanish" instead of Hispanic or Latino/a. Melissa taught about terminology and distinguished
between people whose families were from Spain and Latinos from other
areas of the world. Despite these conversations, many students continued
to refer to themselves as "Spanish" even though they may have categorized themselves as Puerto Rican or Mexican American on the Sister Stories demographic form. We believe it is important to honor students' self-
identifications. As such, we kept the word "Spanish" in student quotes,
even if they noted a different ethnic heritage (e.g., Mexican, Mexican
American, Chicano, Puerto Rican, Cuban) on their demographic form.
We do this because we believe that centering women of color means
honoring the words they use to describe themselves.

CONTEMPORARY OPPRESSION: CONTEXT FOR SISTER STORIES

When thinking about inequality in society in general, or higher education
in particular, the term that best captures the complex phenomenon is
oppression. Bell (2007) defined oppression as "the fusion of institutional
and systemic discrimination, personal bias, bigotry, and social prejudice
in a complex web of relationships and structures that shade most aspects
of life in our society" (p. 3). In U.S. society, oppression is experienced by

members of certain social groups, sometimes referred to as marginalized or minoritized social identity groups (Harper, 2013). A social identity group is a categorization of people who share a socially constructed identity such as race, gender, sexual orientation, ability, social class, or religion. In the United States, women and people of color are considered minoritized, because they experience oppression. Harper (2013) explained how minoritized, or oppressed, social identity groups are subjected to "social construction of underrepresentation and subordination in U.S. social institutions, including colleges and universities" (p. 207). We explicate this reality throughout *Centering Women of Color in Academic Counterspaces*.

Bell (2007) described six defining features of oppression. First, oppression is restrictive, meaning it restricts life opportunities and chances for people from minoritized social identity groups. Second, oppression is hierarchical with minoritized social identity groups experiencing oppression while others reap privileges. Privilege is a term used to describe a set of unearned benefits and advantages afforded to individuals because of a social identity such as race, gender, sexual orientation, social class, religion, ability, or age. Peggy McIntosh's (1988) classic work on privilege describes it as an invisible backpack of unearned assets (e.g., tools, maps, provisions, assurances, relationships) that White people and men can cash in on every day, but remain oblivious to their existence. Privilege also confers dominance, giving members of some social identity groups permission to exert control over life experiences of others (e.g., women, people of color) (Johnson, 2006; McIntosh, 1988). Third, oppression can be internalized, which means that harmful stereotypes about social identity groups that we belong to can become deeply ingrained into our psyches. The fourth characteristic is that different isms (e.g., racism, sexism, heterosexism) share common (and divergent) patterns and manifestations. For instance, being stereotyped as inferior, or outside of societal norms, are common manifestations of racial and gender oppression. Yet, sexual objectification is more commonly associated with gender oppression. The fifth characteristic of oppression is that it is complex, multiple, and cross-cutting. Every individual has multiple social identities (e.g., race, gender, social class, sexual orientation, ability, age). Some of these social identities may be privileged in society while others may be oppressed. For instance, women of color experience oppression based upon both their gender and race. Men of color experience racial oppression and gender privilege. The sixth characteristic is that oppression is pervasive in society.

Building upon these six characteristics, scholars have noted how social identities intersect to shape peoples' lived realities (Cho, Crenshaw & McCall, 2013; Crenshaw, 1989; Combahee River Collective, 1977/1995; Hill Collins, 1991, 2000; Solórzano, 1997, 1998; Wing, 2003). In *Centering Women of Color in Academic Counterspaces*, we explicate how race and gender oppressions intersect to shape the lived realities of women of color. The Sister Stories course focused on the convergence of these two particular oppressions and so does *Centering Women of Color in Academic Counterspaces*. Of course, other social identities (e.g., social class, sexual orientation) were occasionally discussed in the course. However, the racial and gender identities and experiences of women of color were the focus of the course and, thus, are the most pronounced themes in *Centering Women of Color in Academic Counterspaces*.

In the following pages, we provide a very brief introduction to racial and gender oppression, paying special attention to how these isms manifest in collegiate environments. A comprehensive review of those topics is well beyond the scope of this book. Nonetheless, it is important to begin *Centering Women of Color in Academic Counterspaces* with an introduction to contemporary oppression. Throughout the book, we revisit and expand upon these topics during our analyses of student quotes.

Even though many people would like to believe that we live in a post-racial (and post-gender) society, oppression is a reality in the contemporary United States (Wise, 2009). In fact, a recent book by Arminio, Torres, and Pope (2012) is titled *"Why Aren't We There Yet?"* These authors lament how college campuses are not yet welcoming and inclusive spaces for students from minoritized social identity backgrounds. Arminio et al. also explained how many people believe racism and sexism are vestiges of the past. The reality, however, is that inequality is pervasive in contemporary U.S. society and on college campuses. Hurtado and Guillermo-Wann (2013) argued, "Students continue to experience negative cross-racial interactions, discrimination and bias, and harassment along multiple social identities (e.g., race, class, gender, age, sexual orientation) but rarely report it to campus authorities" (p. vii). Under-reporting only perpetuates the myth that inequality is no longer a widespread problem. In fact, one of the Sister Stories students wrote about this cycle in a reflection paper. Lena said,

> Such awful things actually happen on campus! . . . It is important to report them when they do happen so that they can hopefully happen less. Not to mention, it is important to educate the people in our community about what is considered to be offensive to women of color in order to prevent them from speaking ignorantly about us.

As Lena argued, it is important for people to be educated about what is offensive to women of color. Indeed, scholars argued that manifestations of oppression experienced by women of color are qualitatively different from the sexism experienced by White women and racism by men of color (Cho et al., 2013; Crenshaw, 1989; Combahee River Collective, 1977/1995; Hill Collins, 1991, 2000; hooks, 1981, 2000; Moraga & Anzaldúa, 1981, 2002; Solórzano, 1998; Wing, 2003). Hill Collins (1991, 2000) used the term *matrix of domination* to highlight the interlocking systems of racial, gender, and social class oppression experienced by women of color. hooks (1981) referred to the interconnections of racial, gender, and social class oppression as White supremacist capitalist patriarchy. In 1991, Essed used the term *gendered racism* to describe concurrent racial and gender oppressions faced by women of color. Others have used *intersectionality* as a "heuristic term to focus attention on the vexed dynamics of difference and the solidarities" to expose "how single-axis thinking [i.e., racism, sexism] undermines . . . struggles for social justice" (Cho et al., 2013). Throughout *Centering Women of Color in Academic Counterspaces*, we use various terminology such as gendered racism, gendered racist microaggressions, and intersectionality when most appropriate, and sometimes interchangeably.

Microaggression Taxonomies

The oppression of women and people of color can manifest as intentional and overt acts such as racial or gender slurs, rape, and other forms of violence. But, oppression *also* occurs as unintentional acts by well-meaning people and social institutions—a phenomenon called microaggressions. Microaggressions are "subtle and commonplace exchanges that somehow convey insulting or demeaning messages to people" from minoritized social identity groups (Constantine, 2007, p. 2). The term *microaggression* was first used in the early 1970s by Chester Pierce to show how racism manifested in subtle everyday exchanges. Seminal microaggression works focused on racial microaggressions (Sue et al., 2007), while more recent research acknowledges the presence of microaggressions for a host of minoritized populations such as women, LGBTQ people, and people from lower socioeconomic statuses (Capodilupo et al., 2010; Nadal et al., 2011; Nadal, Whitman, Davis, Erazo & Davidoff, 2016; Sue, 2010a, 2010b).

Foundational microaggression literature builds upon taxonomies that divided microaggressions into multiple categories and types (Sue, 2010b; Sue et al., 2007). The original racial microaggression taxonomy, as described by Sue et al. (2007), included eight categories. In the bulleted list below, we directly cite the eight taxonomy titles (Sue et al., p. 276), but paraphrase their descriptions.

- *Alien in own land* where people of color, especially Latinos/as and Asian Americans are assumed to be immigrants;
- *Ascription of intelligence* where people of color are assumed to have lower intelligence than Whites;
- *Colorblindness* where individuals refuse to acknowledge race or racism;
- *Assumptions of criminal status* where people of color are assumed to be deviant or criminal;

- *Denial of individual racism* where White people refuse to recognize personal racist thoughts and behaviors;
- *Myth of meritocracy* where Whites focus on merit and blame people of color for failure instead of recognizing the role racism plays in "success";
- *Pathologizing cultural values and communication styles* whereby the cultural norms, values and communication styles of people of color are deemed abnormal in comparison to White, Eurocentric standards;
- *Second class citizen* where people of color are denied service or given sub-standard treatment compared to Whites.

The taxonomy of gender microaggressions described by Capodilupo et al. (2010) contains three themes that mirror this racial taxonomy: second-class citizen; assumptions of inferiority; and men's denial of sexism. In a recent analysis of multiple research studies, Nadal, Davidoff, Davis, Wong, Marshall, and McKenzie (2015) found that women of color most commonly experienced three types microaggressions: exoticization, assumptions of inferior status, and spokespersons for diversity. The similarities between the microaggression taxonomies for people of color (Sue, 2010), women (Capodilupo et al., 2010), and women of color (Nadal et al., 2015) reinforce Bell's (2007) point about shared characteristics between different forms of oppression. However, the differences *also* confirm Bell's (2007) argument that each type of ism has unique characteristics. For instance, women are exoticized and sexually objectified. Sexual objectification "occurs when women are treated as though they were objects at men's disposal" (Sue, 2001b, p. 34). The notion of sexual objectification builds upon the feminist concept of objectification—a term that describes the phenomenon whereby women are treated as objects as opposed to human beings with value and a sense of agency (Fredrickson & Roberts, 1997). Sexual objectification encompasses behaviors ranging from innuendos, to cat calling, to sexual violence. While all women experience sexual objectification, it manifests for women of color as an intersection of racism and sexism when women are deemed to be exotic (i.e., non-normative or non-White) sexual objects. For instance, scholars have long documented how women of color are portrayed as hypersexual beings in comparison to supposedly chaste and virginal White women (hooks, 1981, 2000; Harris-Perry, 2011; Hill Collins, 1991, 2000). The "Jezebel, whore, or sexually aggressive woman" were listed by Hill Collins (1991) as common stereotypes used to degrade Black women (p. 77). Other scholars have noted how Asian American women are either stereotyped as submissive and/or exotic sex objects like mail order brides or dangerous dragon ladies who spread venereal diseases (Shah, 1997). Latinas are stereotyped as sexually available (McCabe, 2009) or hot mammas who are always pregnant (López & Chesney-Lind, 2014). Native American women are excluded to the point of invisibility. When they are visible, Native American women are typically portrayed as victims of domestic violence at the hands of alcoholic Native American men or romanticized as demure, spiritual women who should be saved by White men — think Pocahontas (Ono & Buescher, 2001). Such stereotypical images can have a profound impact on the ways women of color think about themselves. Hanna, a Sister Stories student, noted:

> I actually learn about women of color from what I see in the media — the stereotypes. . . . Latinas are perceived to be maids. And then, I'm African American. We are perceived to be aggressive, or the baby mamas, or angry, or single mothers. . . . Why can't we see [ourselves] in the media as professional or successful? We're downgraded for no reason.

We delve much more deeply into the effects of objectification on women of color in chapter 7.

Another gender-specific microaggression taxonomy category is the assumption of traditional gender roles (Capodilupo et al., 2010). Women are often praised for engaging in domestic tasks such as cooking and cleaning. They are expected to take on careers in fields dominated by women such as education, nursing, and fashion. It is also assumed that women should be proper, feminine, and caring. These expectations are intensified for women of color as they experience racist manifestations of this microaggression. Hill Collins (1991) described dual stereotypical images of Black women as mammies — "faithful, obedient, domestic servants" — or the matriarch who is an "overly aggressive mother figure in Black homes" (pp. 71–73). Hill Collins's work highlights the power of intersectionality by showing how gender roles for women of color are simultaneously shaped by sexism and racism and, in turn, transform into unique manifestations of oppression.

ENVIRONMENTAL AND INTERPERSONAL MICROAGGRESSIONS

Both racial and gender microaggression taxonomies distinguish between microaggressions that emanate from a setting (i.e., environmental) and those perpetrated by individuals (i.e., interpersonal). In this section, we describe environmental microaggressions and then delve into three types of interpersonal microaggressions.

Environmental microaggressions are "the numerous demeaning and threatening social, educational, political or economic cues that are communicated individually, institutionally or societally to marginalized groups" (Sue, 2010b, p. 25). The higher education literature is rife with descriptions of unwelcoming or hostile campus climates for women and people of color (Feagin, Vera & Imani, 1996; Fleming, 1983; Hall & Sandler, 1984; Harper, 2008; Howard-Hamilton, Morelon-Quainoo, Johnson, Winkle-Wagner & Santiague, 2009; Hurtado, 1992, 2002; Hurtado & Guillermo-Wann, 2013; Vaccaro, 2010, 2012, 2014; Watson, Terrell, Wright & Associates, 2002). While many of these higher education scholars do not use the term *environmental microaggressions*, the descriptions of campus climate and environmental microaggressions are strikingly similar. Rankin and Reason (2008) described climate as the prevailing standards, behaviors, and attitudes of people on campus. More recent work on campus climate affirms how formal and informal institutional policies, practices, and curricula (e.g., the environment) shape the campus climate in profound ways (Hurtado & Guillermo-Wann, 2013).

A variety of institutional cues lead to hostile, unwelcoming, and chilly campus climates for women of color. Some of these include under-representation of women of color in the student body and faculty as well as invisibility of women of color in curricula. Environmental microaggressions can also come in the form of official or unofficial campus policies, practices, or administrative action (or inaction) which result in differential effects for minoritized populations. For instance, Smith and Freyd (2014) coined the term *institutional betrayal* to describe how colleges and universities betray women's trust with victim-blaming practices, administratively taxing reporting processes, and inaction in response to reported campus sexual assaults. In chapter 2, a conversation between Laura, Diana, and Nicole explicates environmental microaggressions in the form of differential treatment by campus police and a discriminatory university policy that required campus organizations for students of color to pay for security for social events, while predominantly White Greek organizations were not required to do so. Environmental microaggressions can also manifest in visual cues that suggest a campus is not inclusive. Examples can include campus buildings named after White men, statues of Confederate soldiers on campus, sexually objectifying images of women in advertisements for campus programs, lack of visible racial and gender diversity in campus publications and websites, or mascots that co-opt Native American symbols or portray them as cartoonist images.

Interpersonal microaggressions come in three forms: microinsults, microinvalidations, and microassaults. The first two forms, microinvalidations and microinsults, are typically perpetrated without conscious awareness while microassaults are intentional. In the following paragraphs, we offer a brief summary of these complex forms of microaggressions. For more detailed information on microaggressions, we recommend a number of foundational writings (c.f., Sue 2010a, 2010b; Sue et al., 2007).

Microinvalidations are "communications that exclude, negate, or nullify the psychological thoughts, feelings or experiential reality" of a person from a minoritized social identity group (Sue, 2010b, p. 29). Examples can include: assuming a person of color is not a U.S. citizen and asking them where they are from; claiming to be colorblind or gender blind while treating women and people of color differently; arguing that people succeed solely on merit while disregarding the realities of racism and sexism; and denying that one's actions are racist or sexist despite claims otherwise.

Microinsults are any form of communication that disrespects or dishonors a person's ethnic heritage or gender. They are largely perpetrated unknowingly. Microinsults include a variety of subtle comments or behaviors rooted in stereotypes and myths about women and people of color. Examples might include: believing women and people of color are not as intelligent or qualified as Whites and men; assuming people of color are criminals; viewing women as too emotional or weaker than men or portraying women of color as domineering and matriarchal (Hill Collins, 1991, 2000); ignoring women's strengths and achievements while focusing on their looks; and viewing a person's communication style (e.g., language, speech patterns, dialects, eye contact, tone, volume) as abnormal.

The third form of interpersonal microaggression is called a microassault and most closely resembles "old fashioned racism" or sexism (Sue, 2010b, p. 29) because it typically involves intentional actions meant to harm others. These might include racist or sexist slurs or physical/sexual violence directed at women and people of color. Microassaults, like the recorded racist chant sung by fraternity brothers at one university, make national news. However, as we show in chapter 2, more subtle and pervasive forms of microaggressions (i.e., microinvalidations, microinsults, environmental) happen regularly on college campuses, and often receive little attention from media or campus administrators.

THEORETICAL FRAMEWORKS

Two overlapping theoretical frameworks informed our work: critical race theory (CRT) and critical race feminism (CRF). Critical race theory is a perspective that "seeks to identify, analyze, and transform those structural and cultural aspects of society that maintain the subordination and marginalization of People of Color" (Solórzano, 1997, p. 6). While this theoretical paradigm emerged from the legal field, CRT scholars often pull from multiple professions and disciplines and critique racist policies and practices well beyond the justice system.

In 1997, Solórzano named five central themes that emerged from critical race theory writings in education. Those included:

1. The centrality and intersectionality of race and racism
2. The challenge to dominant ideology
3. The commitment to social justice

4. The centrality of experiential knowledge
5. The interdisciplinary perspective. (Solórzano 1997, pp. 122–23)

Since that article was published, those five themes (or versions of them), as well as new concepts, appear in critical race writings. In the following paragraphs, we synthesize key foci from seminal and contemporary critical race and critical race feminist literature in education.

CRT consciously places race and racism at the center of analyses (Bernal, 2002; Love, 2004; Lynn & Adams, 2002; Solórzano, 1997; Solórzano & Yosso, 2001; Solórzano & Ornelas, 2004; Villapando, 2003). Through a CRT lens, racial oppression is understood as endemic to society. It manifests consciously and unconsciously at micro (individual) and macro (institutional) levels (Solórzano, 1997) and impacts the lives of people of color in profound ways. Although race is central, contemporary critical race scholars acknowledge the intersections of race and other social identities, such as gender and class (Solórzano, 1997; Solórzano & Yosso, 2001).

CRT exposes and challenges dominant ideologies such as meritocracy, race neutrality, colorblindness, and equal opportunity (Bergerson, 2003; Harper, Patton & Wooden, 2009; Solórzano, 1997; Solórzano & Yosso, 2001). Dominant ideologies take the form of majoritarian narratives that silence or distort the lived realities of people of color (Solórzano & Yosso, 2001). To counter these distortions, critical race theorists "make central the voices and experiences of those who have historically existed within the margins of mainstream institutions" (Darder, Baltodano & Torres, 2003, p. 14). CRT scholars draw attention to the realities of contemporary racism, as well as the resiliency of people of color, to debunk dominant ideologies and deficit-based stereotypes.

Solórzano (1997) argued CRT is a tool for anyone who seeks social justice by ending oppression of people of color and other marginalized social groups. Although Whites can become critical race scholars (Bergerson, 2003) who work for social justice, some CRT authors warn that White people work for racial equality only when it benefits them. Bell (1980) referred to this phenomenon as interest convergence. Milner (2008) explained that "interest convergence stresses that racial equality and equity for people of color will be pursued and advanced when they converge with the interests, needs, expectations, and ideologies of Whites" (p. 333).

Critical race feminism (CRF) is a smaller and more focused body of writing that emerged from CRT and feminist literature. CRF utilizes *and* critiques basic tenets of critical legal, critical race, and feminist paradigms (Wing, 2003). Critical race feminists support many of the foundational tenets of CRT (as described above). They also push the bounds of classic critical legal and CRT writings which were largely authored by men and do not adequately address the intersections of race, gender, and social class. In fact, CRF scholars described how single-identity "paradigms have permitted women of color to fall between the cracks, so that they become, literally and figuratively, voiceless and invisible" (Wing, 2003, p. 2).

CRF scholars might agree with inclusive definitions of feminism such as those by hooks (2000), who defined it as "a movement to end sexism, sexist exploitation and oppression" (p. viii). Yet, critical race feminists have also critiqued the abundance of feminist literature written from a White worldview (Crenshaw, 1989; Wing, 2003). In an effort to more accurately represent the intersections of race and gender for women of color, CRF scholars utilize concepts such as intersectionality and multiplicative identity to document and analyze the lives of "women of color who face multiple discrimination on the basis of race, gender, and class as well as other identities . . . within a system of white male patriarchy and racist subordination" (Wing, pp. 7–8). Critical race feminists have been at the leading edge of exploring how multiple systems of oppression intersect to influence women's lives (Crenshaw, 1989; McCall, 2005; Shields, 2008). As such, CRF literature has informed the ways scholars, like ourselves, make meaning of the academic and interpersonal experiences of women of color in college.

Counterstories

Both CRT and CRF scholars centralize the experiences and voices of those who have been marginalized by dominant ideologies and oppressive social institutions (Darder et al., 2003; Solórzano, 1997, 1998) through the use of controversial narratives or counter storytelling (Darder et al., 2003; Wing, 2003). To reflect the diversity of terminology used in various CRT writings, we use the terms *counter narratives* and *counterstories* interchangeably throughout the book.

Delgado and Stefancic (2000) described counter narratives as "questioning comfortable liberal premises, and leading the search for new ways of thinking about our nation's most intractable, and insoluble problem—race" (p. xvi). Counter storytelling is a vehicle by which marginalized voices can be heard and new societal realities forged. More specifically, they can provide women of color an opportunity to "document experiences of struggle, survival, and resistance within the context of oppressive institutional structures and interpersonal events" (Pérez Huber & Cueva, 2012, pp. 396–97). Counterstories also challenge dominant ideologies of meritocracy, equal opportunity, colorblindness, and the myth that racism is a vestige of the past (Delgado, 1989; Pérez Huber & Cueva, 2012; Solórzano & Yosso, 2001). Delgado and Stefancic (2000) explained how counterstories simultaneously honor the lived experiences of people of color while challenging dominant narratives:

Critical race theory's challenge to racial oppression and the status quo sometimes takes the form of storytelling in which writers analyze the myths, presuppositions, and received wisdoms that make up the common culture about race and that invariably renders [B]lacks and other minorities one-down . . . these scholars set out to construct a different reality. (p. xvii)

Through the counter storytelling process, women of color have an opportunity to share experiences that are typically ignored, invalidated, or suppressed by dominant and oppressive narratives that permeate U.S. society. In predominantly White and male-dominated educational settings, counter storytelling serves a similar purpose. Through counter narratives, women of color are afforded the opportunity to debunk deficit notions and focus on cultural wealth (e.g., cultural resources and assets) (Pérez Huber & Cueva, 2012; Yosso, Smith, Ceja & Solórzano, 2009). This process can be validating, affirming, and empowering for women of color who have spent their formative years navigating racist and sexist educational systems.

CRITICAL RACE CRITIQUES IN EDUCATION

While CRT and CRF originated in the legal profession as critiques of racist (and sexist) policies and practices (Delgado, 1989), these perspectives have been adopted by scholars as a tool to expose inequalities embedded in U.S. systems of education (Gildersleeve, Croom & Vasquez, 2011; Love, 2004; Pérez Huber, 2010; Smith, Yosso & Solórzano, 2007; Solórzano, 1998; Solórzano, Ceja & Yosso, 2000; Yosso et al., 2009). Just as CRT and CRF are used to debunk dominant ideologies (e.g., colorblindness, equal opportunity, meritocracy) in society, they are also vehicles to critique manifestations of these ideologies in education (Solórzano, 1997). Bergerson (2003) explained, "When people of color continue to be systematically excluded from education and the opportunities it provides, it becomes clear that although merit is an espoused American value, it operates under the burden of racism, which limits its applicability to people of color" (p. 54). Additionally, Pérez Huber (2010) argued that dominant ideologies inappropriately "suggest educational institutions are neutral systems that function in the same ways for all students" (p. 78).

CRT and CRF scholars have shown that educational institutions are replete with systemic forms of oppression. Women of color are marginalized by educational systems and processes and by educators who perpetrate and/or refuse to challenge racial and gender inequities (Charleston, George, Jackson, Berhanu & Amechi, 2014; Harris, Haywood, Ivery & Shuck, 2015). Many studies emphasize how educational institutions in general, and faculty in particular, are guided by deficit stereotypes about the academic abilities of students of color (Dancy & Brown, 2008; Gilder-sleeve et al., 2011; Harris et al., 2015; Smith et al., 2007; Solórzano, 1998; Solórzano, et al., 2000; Yosso et al., 2009). Dominant ideologies of meritocracy and equal opportunity fuel deficit and other stereotypical images of women of color, who are blamed for lack of success, or assumed to fail, despite their achievements. Throughout *Centering Women of Color in Academic Counterspaces*, we offer compelling quotes from women of color explicating these oppressive realities.

CRT scholars also provide rich documentation about the ways oppressive forces shape the daily lives of college students. Solórzano et al. (2000) argued that students of color are all too familiar with their "voices being silenced in the classroom discourse or with having their personal and/or group experiences and beliefs discounted" (p. 71). In response, students from minoritized backgrounds often seek counterspaces where they can discuss their experiences with people who understand them (Pérez Huber & Cueva, 2012; Solórzano et al., 2000; Yosso et al., 2009). Counterspaces are environments where students from similar social identities (e.g., race, gender) can "vent frustrations and cultivate friendships with people who share many of their experiences" (Yosso et al., 2009, p. 677). Extra-curricular (e.g., multicultural centers, women's centers, student organizations) and academic (e.g., ethnic studies, women's studies) counterspaces can serve as communities of empowerment and healing for women of color (Butler & Walter, 1991; Grier-Reed, 2010; Nuñez, 2011; Pérez Huber & Cueva, 2012; Solórzano et al., 2000; Solórzano & Villalpando,1998; Stewart, 2011; Yosso, 2006; Yosso et al., 2009). In counterspaces, the counter narratives of women and people of color are centered and affirmed. The focus on storytelling in counterspaces can be affirming for students, and aligns with the CRT theme of affirming the voices and experiences of people of color (Darder et al., 2003; Solórzano, 1997, 1998). In chapters 1 and 3, we explicate how Sister Stories was an academic counterspace designed by and for women of color.

Throughout this book, we delve into the teaching, learning, and student dynamics in one academic counterspace situated within one predominantly White institution. The Sister Stories course was a counterspace that centered the lived experiences of women of color via storytelling, counter narratives, and other first-person accounts. *Centering Women of Color in Academic Counterspaces* offers CRT and CRF analyses of the rich counterstories shared by students, alumni, faculty, and teaching assistants over a five-year time period.

OVERVIEW OF THE BOOK

This book has three sections that build upon one another. In each chapter, we offer readers a brief synopsis of relevant literature. Within this scholarly context, we situate rich student counter narratives as evidence of learning and classroom dynamics in a counterspace centered on the lives of women of color.

Part 1 sets the context for the course, study, and concepts discussed throughout the book. In chapter 1, we provide an in-depth description of the course, highlighting details about the carefully chosen curriculum and pedagogical methods. Narratives from the instructor, teaching assistants, and undergraduate mentor offer insight into their goals and methods for creating an affirming classroom counterspace. In chapter 2, we draw upon classic and cutting-edge research to provide a brief overview of microaggressions in higher education. This growing body of research provides a framework within which we contextualize participant accounts of microaggressions on and off campus. Chapter 3 is about counterspaces. What are they? Why do students from minoritized social identities need and desire them? We use contemporary literature and student narratives to answer these questions.

Part 2 contains two chapters that focus on the interpersonal dynamics in the Sister Stories counterspace. Chapter 4 offers a divergent perspective from the traditional CRT literature which largely emphasizes the benefits of counterspaces. "It's complicated" highlights how intersectionality as well as differences in personalities and perspectives shaped student assumptions, perceptions, and counterspace dynamics. In chapter 5, we contrast the instructor's goals to elicit student counterstories with the realities of self-censorship and silence. The chapter summarizes the complicated reasons students gave for self-censoring their contributions or refusing to divulge personal narratives.

The three chapters that constitute Part 3 summarize what students learned in the counterspace. We draw upon focus group reflections and student assignments to provide evidence of student learning in Sister Stories. Gleaned largely from assignments titled "I Am" and "My story," chapter 6 offers vignettes that highlight how students' racial and ethnic identities were shaped by Sister Stories curriculum and conversations. In chapter 7, we delve into topics of beauty and body image, noting how women of color internalized negative images throughout their lives. We also highlight the ways women of color were empowered to love themselves and their bodies and to serve as role models to others. In chapter 8, we detail how students learned about inclusive leadership. The chapter also contains inspirational stories about the specific ways students drew upon their critical race–inspired leadership learning to incite change on campus and in their families.

This book is designed to serve as a resource to students, teachers, and trainers. In the Conclusion, we pull together major concepts that emerged from *Centering Women of Color in Academic Counterspaces* and offer CRT and CRF analyses of those themes. We also provide tangible recommendations for faculty, trainers, college administrators, and students who want to apply key themes from this book to their everyday lives.

REFERENCES

Arminio, J., Torres, V., & Pope, R. L. (2012). *Why aren't we there yet? Taking personal responsibility for creating an inclusive campus.* Sterling, VA: Stylus.

Bell, D. A. (1980). Brown v. Board of Education and the interest convergence dilemma. *Harvard Law Review, 93*(3), 518–33.

Bell, L. A. (2007). Theoretical foundations for social justice education. In M. Adams, L. A. Bell, & P. Griffin (Eds.), *Teaching for diversity and social justice: A sourcebook* (2nd ed., pp. 1–14). New York: Routledge.

Bergerson, A. A. (2003). Critical race theory and white racism: Is there room for white scholars in fighting racism in education? *Qualitative Studies in Education, 16*(1), 51–63.

Bernal, D. D. (2002). Critical race theory, and critical race-gendered epistemologies: Recognizing students of color as holders and creators of knowledge. *Qualitative Inquiry, 8*(1), 105–27.

Bhopal, R. (2004). Glossary of terms relating to ethnicity and race: For reflection and debate. *Journal of Epidemiology and Community Health, 58*(6), 441–45.

Butler, J. E., & Walter, J. C. (1991). *Transforming the curriculum: Ethnic studies and women's studies.* Albany, NY: SUNY Press.

Capodilupo, C. M., Nadal, K. L., Corman, L., Hamit, S., Lyons, O. B., & Weinberg, A. (2010). The manifestation of gender microaggressions. In D. W. Sue (Ed.), *Microaggressions and marginality: Manifestation, dynamics, and impact* (pp. 193–216). Hoboken, NJ: Wiley.

Charleston, L. J., George, P. L., Jackson, J. F., Berhanu, J., & Amechi, M. H. (2014). Navigating underrepresented STEM spaces: Experiences of black women in U.S. computer science higher education programs who actualize success. *Journal of Diversity in Higher Education, 7*(3), 166–76.

Cho, S., Crenshaw, K. W., & McCall, L. (2013). Toward a field of intersectionality studies: Theory, applications, and praxis. *Signs, 38*(4), 785–810.

Combahee River Collective (1977/1995). Combahee River Collective statement. In B. Guy-Sheftall (Ed.), *Words of fire: An anthology of African American feminist thought* (pp. 232–40). New York: New Press (original work published 1977).

Constantine, M. G. (2007). Racial microaggressions against African American clients in cross-racial counseling relationships. *Journal of Counseling Psychology, 54*(1), 1–16.

Crenshaw, K. (1989). Demarginalizing the intersection of race and sex: A black feminist critique of antidiscrimination doctrine, feminist theory and antiracist politics. *University of Chicago Legal Forum,* 139.

Dancy, T. E. E., & Brown, M. C. (2008). Unintended consequences: African American male educational attainment and collegiate perceptions after Brown v. Board of Education. *American Behavioral Scientist, 51*(7), 984–1003.

Darder, A., Baltodano, M., & Torres, R. D. (2003). Critical pedagogy: An introduction. In A. Darder, M. Baltodano & R. D. Torres (Eds.). *The critical pedagogy reader* (pp. 1–21). New York: Routledge.

Delgado, R. (1989). Storytelling for oppositionists and others: A plea for narrative. *Michigan Law Review, 87*(8), 2411–41.

———, & Stefancic, J. (Eds.) (2000). *Critical race theory: The cutting edge.* Philadelphia, PA: Temple University Press.

Essed, P. (1991). *Understanding everyday racism: An interdisciplinary theory.* Thousand Oaks: Sage.

Feagin, J. R., Vera, H., & Imani, N. (1996). *The agony of education: Black students at white colleges and universities.* New York: Routledge.

Fleming, J. (1983). Black women in black and white college environments: The making of a matriarch. *Journal of Social Issues, 39*(3), 41–54.

Fredrickson, B. L., & Roberts, T. A. (1997). Objectification theory. *Psychology of Women Quarterly, 21*(2), 173–206.

Gildersleeve, R. E., Croom, N. N., & Vasquez, P. L. (2011). "Am I going crazy?!": A critical race analysis of doctoral education. *Equity & Excellence in Education, 44*(1), 93–114.

Grier-Reed, T. L. (2010). The African American student network: Creating sanctuaries and counterspaces for coping with racial microaggressions in higher education settings. *Journal of Humanistic Counseling, Education, and Development, 49*(2), 181–88.

Hall, R. M., & Sandler, B. R. (1984). *Out of the classroom: A chilly climate for women?* Washington, DC: Association of American Colleges, Project on the Status and Education of Women.

Harper, S. R. (Ed.) (2008). *Creating inclusive campus environments for cross-cultural learning and student engagement.* Washington, DC: NASPA.

——— (2013). Am I my brother's teacher? Black undergraduates, racial socialization, and peer pedagogies in predominantly white postsecondary contexts. *Review of Research in Education, 37,* 183–211.

———, Patton, L. D., & Wooden, O. S. (2009). Access and equity for African American students in higher education: A critical race historical analysis of policy efforts. *The Journal of Higher Education, 80*(4), 389–414.

Harris, J. C., Haywood, J. M., Ivery, S. M., & Shuck, J. R. (2015). "Yes, I am smart!": Battling microaggressions as women of color doctoral students. In J. L. Martin (Ed.), *Racial battle fatigue: Insights from the front lines of social justice advocacy* (pp. 151–62). Santa Barbara, CA: Praeger.

Harris-Perry, M. V. (2011). *Sister citizen: Shame, stereotypes, and Black women in America.* New Haven, CT: Yale University Press.

Hill Collins, P. (1991, 2000). *Black feminist thought: Knowledge, consciousness, and the politics of empowerment.* New York: Routledge.

hooks, b. (1981). *Ain't I a woman: Black women and feminism.* Cambridge, MA: South End.

——— (2000). *Feminist theory: From margin to center.* London: Pluto Press.

Howard-Hamilton, M. L., Morelon-Quainoo, C. L., Johnson, S. D., Winkle-Wagner, R., & Santiague, L. (Eds.) (2009). *Standing on the outside looking in: Underrepresented students' experiences in advanced degree programs.* Sterling, VA: Stylus.

Hurtado, S. (1992, September/October). The campus racial climate: Contexts of conflict. *Journal of Higher Education, 63*(5), 539–69.

——— (2002). Creating a climate of inclusion: Understanding Latina/o college students. In W. A. Smith, P. G. Altback & K. Lomotey (Eds.), *The racial crisis in American higher education: Continuing challenges for the twenty-first century* (rev. ed., pp. 121–36). New York: SUNY Press.

———, & Guillermo-Wann, C. (2013). *Diverse learning environments: Assessing and creating conditions for student success—Final Report to the Ford Foundation.* University of California, Los Angeles: Higher Education Research Institute.

Johnson, A. G. (2006). *Privilege, power and difference* (2nd ed.). Boston, MA: McGraw Hill.

López, V., & Chesney-Lind, M. (2014). Latina girls speak out: Stereotypes, gender and relationship dynamics. *Latino Studies, 12*(4), 527–49.

Love, B. J. (2004). Brown plus 50 counter storytelling: A critical race theory analysis of the "majoritarian achievement gap" story. *Equality and Excellence, 37,* 227–46.

Lynn, M., & Adams, M. (2002). Introductory overview to the special issue: Critical race theory and education: Recent developments in the field. *Equality and Excellence, 35*(2), 87–92.

McCabe, J. (2009). Racial and gender microaggressions on a predominately White campus: Experiences of Black, Latina/o and White undergraduates. *Race, Gender and Class, 16,* 133–51.

McCall, L. (2005). The complexity of intersectionality. *Signs, 30*(3), 1771–1800.

McIntosh, P. (1988). *White privilege and male privilege: A personal account of coming to see correspondences through work in women's studies. Working Paper No. 189.* Wellesley, MA: Wellesley Centers for Women.

Milner, H. R. (2008). Critical race theory and interest convergence as analytic tools in teacher education policies and practices. *Journal of Teacher Education, 59*(4), 332–46.

Moraga, C., & Anzaldúa, G. (Eds.) (1981, 2002). *This bridge called my back* (3rd ed.). Berkeley, CA: Third Women's Press.

Nadal, K. L., Davidoff, K. C., Davis, L. S., Wong, Y., Marshall, D., & McKenzie, V. (2015). A qualitative approach to intersectional microaggressions: Understanding influences of race, ethnicity, gender, sexuality, and religion. *Qualitative Psychology, 2*(2), 147.

Nadal, K. L., Issa, M. A., Leon, J., Meterko, V., Wideman, M., & Wong, Y. (2011). Sexual orientation microaggressions: "Death by a thousand cuts" for lesbian, gay, and bisexual youth. *Journal of LGBT Youth, 8*(3), 234–59.

Nadal, K. L., Whitman, C. N., Davis, L. S., Erazo, T., & Davidoff, K. C. (2016). Microaggressions toward lesbian, gay, bisexual, transgender, queer, and genderqueer people: A review of the literature. *The Journal of Sex Research, 53*(4–5), 488–508.

Nuñez, A. M. (2011). Counterspaces and connections in college transitions: First-generation Latino students' perspectives on Chicano studies. *Journal of College Student Development, 52*(6), 639–55.

Ono, K. A., & Buescher, D. T. (2001). Deciphering Pocahontas: Unpackaging the commodification of a Native American woman. *Critical Studies in Media Communication, 18*(1), 23–43.

Pérez Huber, L. (2010). Using Latina/o critical race theory (LatCrit) and racist nativism to explore intersectionality in the educational experiences of undocumented chicana college students. *Educational Foundations, 24*, 77–96.

———, & Cueva, B. M. (2012). Chicana/Latina testimonios on effects and responses to microaggressions. *Equity and Excellence in Education, 45*(3), 392–410.

Pierce, C. (1974). Psychiatric problems of the Black minority. In S. Arieti (Ed.), *American Handbook of Psychiatry* (pp. 512–23). New York: Basic Books.

Rankin, S., & Reason, R. (2008). Transformational tapestry model: A comprehensive approach to transforming campus climate. *Journal of Diversity in Higher Education, 1*(4), 262–74.

Shah, S. (Ed.) (1997). *Dragon ladies: Asian American feminists breathe fire.* Boston, MA: South End.

Shields, S. A. (2008). Gender: An intersectionality perspective. *Sex Roles, 59*(5–6), 301–11.

Smith, C. P., & Freyd, J. J. (2014). Institutional betrayal. *American Psychologist, 69*(6), 575.

Smith, D. G. (2009). *Diversity's promise for higher education: Making it work.* Baltimore, MD: Johns Hopkins University Press.

Smith, W. A., Yosso, T. J., & Solórzano, D. G. (2007). Racial primes and Black misandry on historically white campuses: Toward critical race accountability in educational administration. *Educational Administration Quarterly, 43*(5), 559–585.

Solórzano, D. G. (1997). Images and words that wound: Critical race theory, racial stereotyping, and teacher education. *Teacher Education Quarterly, 24*(3), 5–20.

——— (1998). Critical race theory, race and gender microaggressions, and the experience of Chicana and Chicano scholars. *Qualitative Studies in Education, 11*(1), 121–36.

———, Ceja, M., & Yosso, T. J. (2000). Critical race theory, racial microaggressions, and campus racial climate: The experiences of African American college students. *The Journal of Negro Education, 69*(1/2), 60–73.

———, & Ornelas, A. (2004). A critical race analysis of Latina/o and African American advanced placement enrollment in public high schools. *High School Journal, 87* (3), 15–27.

———, & Villalpando, O. (1998). Critical race theory, marginality and the experience of students of color in higher education. In T. Mitchell & C. A. Torres (Eds.), *Sociology of education: Emerging perspectives* (pp. 181–210). Albany, NY: SUNY Press.

———, & Yosso, T. J. (2001). Critical race and LatCrit theory and method: Counterstorytelling. *International Journal of Qualitative Studies in Education, 14*(4), 471–95.

Stewart, D. L. (Ed.) (2011). *Multicultural student services on campus: Building bridges, revisioning community.* Sterling, VA: Stylus.

Sue, D. W. (Ed.) (2010a). *Microaggressions and marginality: Manifestations, dynamics and impact.* Hoboken, NJ: Wiley.

——— (2010b). *Microaggressions in everyday life: Race, gender and sexual orientation.* Hoboken, NJ: Wiley.

———, Capodilupo, C. M., Torino, G. C., Bucceri, J. M., Holder, A. M. B., Nadal, K. L., & Esquilin, M. (2007). Racial microaggressions in everyday life: Implications for clinical practice. *American Psychologist, 62,* 271–86.

U.S. Bureau of the Census, Population Estimates Program (PEP). Updated annually. www.census.gov/popest/estimates.html.

———, *The 2010 Census Questionnaire: Informational Copy,* 2010.census.gov/2010census/pdf/2010_Questionnaire_Info_Copy.pdf.

Vaccaro, A. (2010). What lies beneath seemingly positive campus climate results: Institutional sexism, symbolic racism, and male hostility toward equity initiatives. *Equity and Excellence in Education, 43*(2), 202–15.

——— (2012). Campus microclimates for LGBT faculty, staff, and students: An exploration of the intersections of social identity and campus roles. *Journal of Student Affairs Research and Practice, 44*(4), 429–46.

——— (2014). Campus climate for diversity: Current realities and suggestions for the future. *Texas Education Review, 2*(1), 129–37.

Villapando, O. (2003). Self-segregation or self-preservation? A critical race theory and Latina/o critical theory analysis of a study of Chicana/o college students. *International Journal of Qualitative Studies in Education, 16*(5), 619–46.

Watson, L., Terrell, M. C., Wright, D., & Associates (2002). *How minority students experience college: Implications for planning and policy.* Sterling, VA: Stylus.

Wing, A. K. (2003). *Critical race feminism: A reader* (2nd ed.). New York: New York University Press.

Wise, T. (2009). *Between Barack and a hard place: Racism and white denial in the age of Obama.* San Francisco, CA: Open Books.

Yosso, T. (2006). *Critical race counterstories along the Chicano/Chicana educational pipeline.* New York: Routledge.

———, Smith, W., Ceja, M., & Solórzano, D. (2009). Critical race theory, racial microaggressions, and campus climate for Latina/o undergraduates. *Harvard Educational Review, 79*(4), 659–69.

ONE

Sister Stories

"Not your typical class."

Throughout *Centering Women of Color in Academic Counterspaces*, student narratives yield rich insight into the ways women of color made meaning of the Sister Stories course materials and interacted with peers in the classroom. Before delving into the impact of the course, this chapter provides a brief overview of the history, outcomes, foci, and demographics of Sister Stories.

We consistently heard students say that Sister Stories was unlike any other course they had ever taken. Students such as Mindy said about the class: "It wasn't your typical!" What made Sister Stories unique? The demographics—mostly women of color—certainly differentiated Sister Stories from other courses at the predominantly White university. We also contend five foci, rooted in critical race theory (CRT) and critical race feminist (CRF) theoretical perspectives, contributed to its uniqueness. Sister Stories focused on: 1) diversity and intersectionality, 2) validating and empowering stories from women of color, 3) reflection on, and application of, course materials, 4) role models, networks, and mentors, and 5) setting a tone of trust and respect. While each of these foci is described separately, they are certainly not unrelated. In fact, there is quite a bit of overlap between them. For instance, many of the students' reflections about identity and intersectionality were based upon validating and empowering stories from women of color—many of whom students considered role models. Despite the interconnections between foci, they are addressed one at a time in this chapter for brevity and clarity.

In the first section of this chapter, I (Melissa) provide a brief overview of the Sister Stories curriculum, paying special attention to these five foci. Then, we (Annemarie and Melissa) describe our five-year case study of

1

Sister Stories, which supplied most of the rich student narratives used in this book. Finally, we detail student demographics to show how Sister Stories was not a "typical" course at the predominately White university.

THE EVOLUTION OF SISTER STORIES

Sister Stories started because one woman of color began to ask tough questions about the lack of diversity at the predominantly White university. In the mid-1990s, an undergraduate student noticed there was a high number of Latinas leaving the university during their first year. She brought her concerns to the attention of the Women's Center staff, and a group was formed to provide support for first-year Latinas at the university. Soon after the first few meetings, it was hypothesized that if many Latinas were having difficulties adjusting to the predominately White campus environment, women from other historically marginalized racial groups might be having similar experiences. Therefore, the concept of support for first-year Latina women was expanded to include all women of color. Over the years, the extra-curricular program evolved to include professional, academic, and social support for all women of color. Yet, women of color wanted more opportunities for support. The university's Leadership Development Center (LDC), Multicultural Center, and bridge program for first-generation college students joined the Women's Center to strategize about expanding programs for women of color. In 2001, a formalized mentor program was initiated. That was still not enough. In order to create something with depth, consistency, and long-lasting effects, faculty, staff, and students decided an academic component was necessary. A credit-bearing academic course, Sister Stories, was first offered in the fall of 2005. The curriculum development and delivery of the academic class became the primary responsibility of the LDC. The LDC is an office within the division of student affairs that works in conjunction with the academic department of human development and family studies to offer an interdisciplinary minor in leadership studies.

As a staff member in the LDC, I (Melissa) am responsible for teaching one introductory course in the leadership studies minor and at least one elective option. Given my personal and professional interests, I was offered the opportunity to teach the Sister Stories course when I arrived at the university. As such, anytime "I" is used in this section of the chapter, it is in reference to me (Melissa).

The official university course description for Sister Stories reads:

> This elective is designed for students who are interested in an exploratory and introspective look at the issues affecting women of color. Students will explore cultural identity and leadership theories through readings and other media, as well as learn about a variety of issues,

including historical perspectives, which continue to affect women of color today. (University website, n.d.)

When I took on the responsibility for Sister Stories from the prior instructor, I was afforded the flexibility of doing almost anything I wanted with the course. However, I was not allowed to alter the learning outcomes. Learning outcomes for Sister Stories included:

- Students will show knowledge of historical issues pertaining to women of color
- Students will show knowledge of current issues pertaining to women of color
- Students will show knowledge of models of racial identity development
- Students will show knowledge of models of leadership theory
- Students will show knowledge and demonstrate application of principles of mentoring and networking

When I was hired, I had access to several years of past syllabi. These documents provided a picture of what prior semesters were like. I retained some content and assignments from previous semesters, but I was excited by the opportunity to make the course my own. Over the years, I have adopted new readings, revised assignments, introduced new media, and honed my teaching style. A detailed account of these changes are beyond the scope of this chapter, and frankly, probably would not be very exciting for readers. In thinking about what readers should know about Sister Stories, I decided to share five overarching and interrelated foci that, I believe, make Sister Stories unique: 1) diversity and intersectionality, 2) validating and empowering stories, 3) reflection on, and application of, course materials, and 4) role models, networks, and mentors, and 5) setting a tone of trust and respect. In the following pages, I summarize these five foci and provide short quotes from students regarding these topics.

DIVERSITY AND INTERSECTIONALITY

As an instructor, I crafted the course so that all materials and assignments would reflect the diversity among women of color as well as intersectionality. In truth, part of my reasoning for emphasizing the diversity among women of color was selfish: as an Asian American woman, I never saw myself reflected in curricula. I rarely could relate to, or felt validated by, examples in my classes from elementary school through my undergraduate studies. Whenever the topic of "diversity" came up, it was almost always specifically about the Black/White binary. Where was I in this conversation? As a teacher, I quickly learned I was not alone; many of my students of color also felt left out of curricula. For instance, Vera found examples, activities, and information in other classes to be irrelevant to her life: "because they don't include people that look like me. And it's still like that. As a junior, I still go into class and examples they use have nothing to do with me." It was important that Sister Stories be different, more inclusive. When I had the opportunity to make Sister Stories my own, I wanted students to examine a wide array of perspectives from diverse women of color so that *all* woman of color who took the course could find something to relate to. I wanted Sister Stories students to think: "I'm *not* the only one." To my delight, that is what happened. Laura spoke about the feelings engendered by Sister Stories compared to other classes at the predominantly White university:

> Even when [Melissa] gave us articles to read, it was like we were the people in the articles! It wasn't learning [useless facts]—it was *more*. "Oh that's what that's called." "Oh that's what this means." "Ok. This is normal. This is actual psychology. This is what I'm supposed to be feeling."

Another important concept I tried to include throughout Sister Stories was intersectionality. A term originally coined by Crenshaw (1989), intersectionality is the idea that our social identities interact with each other and impact how we experience life with multiple lenses that cross. As we noted in the Introduction, intersectionality is one of the five tenets of critical race theory (Solórzano, 1998). Moreover, it is a focus of critical race feminists who explicate the importance of honoring the complexity of women's lives (Crenshaw, 1989; Wing, 2003). Student learning about intersectionality is covered extensively in the forthcoming chapters. Here, I share why intersectionality is so important.

In my previous job, I was responsible for multicultural programming for celebration months such as Latino/a Heritage Month, Coming Out/ Pride Months, Native Peoples Heritage Month, Black History Month, and Asian Heritage Month. Throughout these celebrations, the speakers and performers told multifaceted stories showing the complexity of their identity due to intersectionality. These were the types of rich and compli-cated counterstories I wanted to include in the course. People are more than their race or their gender. Every individual has a variety of social identities (e.g., race, gender, sexual orientation, social class, ability, relig-ion) that intersect in complicated ways to shape their life experiences and worldviews. By focusing on intersecting social identities, we have the capacity to see people as whole human beings.

Unfortunately, locating engaging course materials that reflected the diversity among women of color, and intersectionality, was not always easy. In compiling the readings, videos, etc., the voices I found most frequently were from Black/African/African American women. I also came across a good number from Latinas. However, I struggled in find-ing enough to balance these voices with Asian, Native, biracial, and multiracial women. Some of these readings thoroughly addressed issues of intersectionality, while others did not. Nonetheless, I regularly emphasized the importance of diversity among women of color and intersectionality through classroom conversations and assignments so that students would be able to put together a holistic picture of the historical and contemporary experiences of women of color in the United States.

VALIDATING AND EMPOWERING STORIES

The course pseudonym, Sister Stories, was selected because of the centrality of counterstories to the course. In the Introduction, we explained how CRT and CRF scholars often use counterstories to center the experiences of people who have historically been marginalized (e.g., women of color) (Darder, Baltodano & Torres, 2003; Wing, 2003). By infusing counterstories into a classroom, students can "become empowered participants, hearing their own stories and the stories of others, listening to how the arguments are framed, and learning to make the arguments themselves" (Solórzano, Ceja & Yosso, 2000, p. 64). Educational scholars, like us, who draw from CRT/CRF perspectives, sometimes refer to their work in terms of critical race praxis or pedagogy. Parker and Stovall (2004) explicated how critical race praxis and pedagogy are built upon the following educational beliefs:

> [The] experiences of racial groups merit intellectual pursuit because of the uniqueness of the cultural, historical, and contemporary experiences of persons of color [and] the historical and contemporary experiences of people of color can prove instructive about human interactions. (p. 174)

Their argument reinforces the importance of centering the lives of women of color through empowering counterstories in higher education classrooms. Counterstories were at the heart of my critical race praxis.

Sister Stories course materials were almost exclusively made up of counterstories by women of color. When developing the course, I scoured anthologies and the Internet looking for first-person narratives from diverse women of color. I specifically looked for counterstories that gave insight about who the author was. I used counterstories written in the early 1900s as well as articles written by twenty-first century girls and women of color. The format of the counterstories ranged from first-person narratives to poetry and spoken word art.

In addition to traditional chapters and articles, I included counterstories via other types of multimedia in order to meet the needs and learning styles of today's media-savvy college students (Barnes, Marateo & Ferris, 2007; McGlynn, 2008). Students appreciated the multi-modal approach to teaching. Mindy explained: "Just mixing it up, it wasn't your typical lecture . . . [or] like let's watch a movie and write a paper. I think it encompassed all different types of learning and teaching styles. That helped everyone." Multimedia counterstories came from blogs, motion pictures, and YouTube videos. Students learned from not only the content, but also the modern format, of these materials. Camilla shared:

> I never knew about spoken word. I never knew that was a way of poetry or anything. But when I would see it, I just felt like there was so much anger between all these people and the things that they . . . go through. It was kind of inspirational to see them talk in that kind of way. It was all *so* real—everything that they were saying. And it made me want to go on YouTube and see some more!

Sister Stories curricular materials conveyed stories of slavery, discrimination, activism, immigration, family dynamics, body image, media portrayals of women of color, interactions with friends and strangers, and leadership. Some counterstories echoed each other while some contradicted one another—highlighting the diversity of experiences and perspectives among women of color. Many challenged the status quo and sometimes even explicitly critiqued men or White people. Other counterstories were about stereotypes and/or unrealistic expectations held by family, friends, or strangers. The counterstories also implicitly or explicitly described the importance of women of color fighting systems of oppression—a foundational tenet of CRT/CRF theories (Solórzano, 1998; Wing, 2003) and a goal of critical race praxis/pedagogy (Parker & Stovall, 2004).

Elsy was deeply moved by stories of struggle and triumph by women of color. Their counterstories prompted her to reflect upon her own life:

> They each said some eye-opening things and made many things clear in my life. . . . They talked about their ups and downs and many struggles they have gone through pursuing their careers. . . . They made it pretty clear that things are not going to be easy in life but just because it wasn't easy it doesn't mean we shouldn't keep pushing and working hard toward what we want to do in life. All of these women went through many obstacles and still seemed to fully enjoy their lives and wouldn't do anything differently. One thing that I really enjoyed that really stood out to me was: things that some people may see as a disadvantage—like being a woman of color or being poor or being a woman—they used these things as an advantage and worked hard to prove people wrong to build a name for themselves.

Counterstories about identity struggles, oppression, and resilience helped Nicole feel better about her identity. Narratives by other women of color also validated her own perspectives. She explained: "I feel like as a woman of color [those stories] made me feel a lot better with who I am. It helped validate some of the things that I was feeling myself." Lacey also spoke of eye-opening and validating experiences prompted by curricular counterstories:

> I enjoyed all the readings, discussions, and movies we watched. This class has opened my eyes. . . . It made me notice how hard women of color have to work to prove people wrong and gain the respect they deserve. It showed me that in order to get a higher position as a woman of color you have to be better than better. It made me appreciate my Blackness and not to be ashamed of being a woman of color.

In chapter 3, we examine the ways the Sister Stories counterspace and curricular materials provided validation and support for students. In chapter 7, we delve more deeply into identity-related topics.

By centering the counterstories of women of color in curriculum, I attempted to create a venue where students could reflect upon those stories, apply them to their lives, and then gain the confidence to share their own counterstories. The first major Sister Stories assignment — originally called the "I Am" paper and later changed to "Your Story" paper — simply asked students to write about themselves. The intent was to have students go beyond merely stating their name, class year, major, and hometown to begin crafting their own counterstory. Students were asked to share the story of who they were and who they hoped to become in the future. At the end of the semester, students returned to this paper and incorporated it into a final project. In that final project, students reflected upon their growth in the class and presented their "updated" personal narrative to classmates and instructors. Ife talked about creating her evolving counterstory:

> We even got to write about ourselves. At the beginning of class, we wrote about ourselves. At the end of class, we did a presentation about ourselves. Not everything we wrote about ourselves in the beginning of class was what we presented at the end of the class. I guess you got to learn a little bit more about yourself.

Throughout *Centering Women of Color in Academic Counterspaces*, we share many student excerpts from these powerful assignments.

REFLECTION ON, AND
APPLICATION OF, COURSE MATERIALS

Curriculum is not a static thing. Nor were course readings intended to focus on abstract concepts to be memorized and then forgotten after a test. Instead, my goal was for students to apply Sister Stories curricular materials to their lives. In my teaching, I applied foundational tenets of critical race pedagogy, inclusive pedagogy, and transformational learning. Writers in these genres emphasize: honoring student experiences; empowering individuals to use learning for social change; encouraging deep reflection on self and course materials; and applying course concepts to one's life experiences (Brookfield, 1995, 2000; Dirkx, 1998; Freire, 1970, 2006; Mezirow, 1991; Parker & Stovall, 2004; Tuitt, 2006). As a leadership educator, I also draw upon the Social Change Model of Leadership Development (Higher Education Research Institute [HERI], 1996), a grounding theory for the LDC. The Social Change Model aligns well with the critical race praxis, inclusive pedagogy, and transformational education principles of encouraging students to apply course materials to their everyday lives and use their new knowledge for positive social change. Fincher (2009) explained the consciousness of self aspect of the Social Change Model:

> Consciousness of Self refers to people's awareness of their own personality traits, values, and strengths, as well as their ability to be self-observers who are mindful of their actions, feelings, and beliefs. It involves not only knowing who they are in general, but also being aware of themselves in their current state—how the environment and other people are affecting them and vice versa." (pp. 300–01)

Through classroom conversations, online discussions, and assignments, I encouraged Sister Stories students to be conscious of self and to wrestle with the ways course materials related to their every lives. Students appreciated and enjoyed this pedagogical approach because it was so different from traditional lectures in other courses. Ife explained:

> [In other classes, I am] always studying for exams. Or I am not even able to talk in class [or] not able to voice my opinions. . . . I enjoyed writing all the papers that I wrote about myself. I enjoyed almost every assignment.

Because of the course focus on reflection and action, students were asked to reflect upon all course materials and apply them to their lives. Through papers and course conversations, students shared their opinions, critiqued curricular materials, and discussed ways they could (or could not) relate to course materials. The *process* of reflection and action was as important as student conclusions. Brian shared his thoughts on the process of reflection in general, and reflection paper assignments, in particular:

> Those were really good. Instead of just learning something and then taking a test on it, you really got me to think about what I am learning and what really matters to me. That stood out to me. And, it really helped facilitate what I was learning. I didn't just read an article and forget about it. Like I had to read an article and think about how it affected me. The reflections I wrote were just giant rant sessions [Laughter]. Like I said, you don't talk about this stuff anywhere else. Like this whole racism or post racial [topics]. But, in this class, we really get to talk about what's bottled up. Cause you don't really get to talk about it anywhere else.

Brian's commentary suggests that Sister Stories was indeed a course where he engaged in transformational learning (e.g., reflection and application) regarding race and racism—a goal of critical race pedagogy (Parker & Stovall, 2004). His quote also suggests he was becoming more conscious of himself (Finscher, 2009) as a man of color in the context of a society and higher education institution where people tended to avoid topics of race and racism.

As mentioned earlier, Sister Stories is offered through the LDC in conjunction with the university's department of human development and family studies. Because the course falls under the auspices of that academic department, human development theories underpin the course. One of the course outcomes is for students to gain an understanding of racial identity models. Racial identity refers to "a sense of group or collective identity based upon one's perception that he or she shares a common racial heritage with a particular racial group" (Helms, 1993, p. 3). Ethnic identity is a similar multidimensional process whereby individuals learn about and adopt an identity rooted in a particular ethnic and cultural heritage. We distinguish between these concepts and explore student learning regarding racial and ethnic identity development in chapter 6. Here, I note my motivations and challenges related to identity.

In Sister Stories, I expect more than mere comprehension of racial identity theories. I want students to consider how these models inform, and are informed by, their everyday lives. It is essential for students to *apply* the models to their lived realities. One of the challenges in teaching racial and ethnic identity is deciding which models to use. In a semester-long undergraduate course, it is impossible to cover everything. Yet, it is important for the curriculum to be inclusive of the array of racial and ethnic identities students bring to the classroom. My intention is for all students to have an opportunity to see themselves reflected in the theories. It is also challenging for me to keep current on new and evolving identity theories since my expertise and appointment is in leadership development, not psychology or human development. Some of the identity development models used by prior instructors had been revised or critiqued. So, I updated the reading list. I used Cross and Fhagen-Smith's Model of Black Identity Development (2001). I also invited students to read Sue and Sue's (2003) Racial and Cultural Identity Development Model, which is a revision of Atkinson, Morten, and Sue's (1979) earlier model. I also added the following models to the syllabus: Rowe, Bennett, and Atkinson's White Racial Consciousness Model (1994), Ferdman and Gallegos's Model of Latino Identity Development (2001), Kim's Asian American Identity Development Model (1981, 2001), Horse's American Indian Identity Development Model (2001), and Wijeyesinghe's Factor Model of Multiracial Identity (2001). I also started teaching Harro's Cycle of Socialization (2013) before introducing racial identity models so students could understand contextual forces that influence identity development. See chapters 6 and 7 for a more comprehensive discussion of identity development and the cycle of socialization.

Before sharing identity development models with students, I always state a disclaimer: these theories are *not* meant to box people in or marginalize them within their racial or ethnic communities. Students may not necessarily see themselves fitting into most of these models. That's okay. Theories are not intended to serve as prescriptions of how life should be experienced by women of color. Instead, identity models offer insight into the possible processes through which individuals become aware of their social identities and figure out what those identities mean to them. Identity development models have the potential to provide context and some explanations about what people experience (DiCaprio, 1974).

A major Sister Stories assignment was the Theory Paper. For this assignment, students were asked to select one of the identity development theories and show how their own identity development mirrored, or contrasted with, their chosen model. Because of the disclaimer mentioned previously, students were also invited to critique their chosen model, particularly if they did not feel like it reflected their lived experiences. Students expressed so much learning about racial identity, that we dedicated an entire chapter (chapter 6) to their identity narratives.

ROLE MODELS, NETWORKS, AND MENTORS

Research suggests mentoring from faculty, staff, peers, and community members is an important aspect of campus leadership programs (Dugan & Komives, 2007). Other literature shows how important social support, networking, and mentoring are for all students, and students of color in particular (Ortiz & Pichardo-Diaz, 2011; Pope, 2002). In fact, Ortiz and Pichardo-Diaz (2011) argued this generation of college students is particularly prone to relying on adults as guides and mentors. Others have noted the crucial role that mentors and role models of color play in the development of social capital, satisfaction, and retention of students of color (Brayboy & Castagano, 2011; Mena & Vaccaro, 2015; Palmer & Maramba, 2015) and biracial and multiracial students (Renn, 2011). Therefore, opportunities for students to develop connections with peers, faculty, and staff of color were infused throughout Sister Stories. In chapter 3, we explicate the many benefits students gleaned from interacting with role models, networks, and mentors. Here, I describe how access to role models, networks, and potential mentors was built into the curriculum.

Sister Stories had a formal relationship with a campus affinity organization for women faculty and staff of color, known as the Women of Color Network (WOCN). As a staff woman of color, I was introduced to that organization within my first month of employment at the university. The WOCN was a small group of faculty and staff committed to building community and mentorship among women of color at the university. As I learned more about the WOCN and the women in it, I thought there was a natural connection to Sister Stories. So, I sought formal involvement from members in various parts of the course. Two specific ways I did this were including students in a women of color dinner program and inviting women of color to speak as panelists during the Sister Stories course.

One course requirement was for students to attend a women of color dinner that included a keynote speaker. Along with Sister Stories students and WOCN members, other faculty, staff, and student leaders from campus were invited—many of whom (but not all) identified as women of color. Keynote speakers addressed the topics of leadership and mentoring among women of color. The talks were always inspirational and motivational in tone. In order to provide visible role models for Sister Stories students, keynote speakers identified as women of color. Goals for the dinner were for Sister Stories students to see a keynote speaker who looked like them and to hear from an influential and successful woman role model. Another goal was for students to network with women of color on campus and find potential campus mentors. Making connections with faculty and staff members can feel awkward or be intimidating for students. Therefore, students were seated at round tables with nine other attendees—allowing for intimate conversation. Dinner conversations were structured so that everyone was included. Members of the WOCN served as "table hosts" for the event. The hosts were charged with making sure everyone at the table was introduced. They were also tasked with engaging their tables in guided conversation about the keynote address. Liza wrote about the significance of the women of color dinner:

> This event was just something to remember. Not often do we get the chance to talk about women of color *or* see women of color. So, this dinner was made to focus on that topic. I was able to see how many people are passionate about these issues. [It is also nice to be among others who acknowledge subtle forms of oppression as] something that is true and it is happening! . . . The whole point of this event was that we can't just brush it under the rug. . . . Truth is, it is a *big* issue and it will continue to get worse if we don't get together and make a difference. It doesn't take one women to do so; it takes many women to come together and help one another. Because, let's face it—how often do you see that? We women tend to not come together.

Liza was empowered by the speaker to "come together" with other women to fight oppression and "make a difference." Liza's realization aligns with decades of writings from critical race feminists and other women writers of color who argued women must come together to fight oppression (Hill Collins, 1991, 2000; Lorde, 1984). I also agree with Parker and Stovall (2004), who explained: "Critical pedagogy calls for educators to be agents working for social change and equity in schools and communities." One way social justice can happen in schools and communities is if students feel empowered to be agents of change. Liza and her peers got the message that "coming together" and networking with other women of color was crucial for fighting oppression.

While the women of color dinner was a great way to introduce students to role models and potential mentors, one evening event was not enough. Sister Stories students deserved to interact with an array of faculty, staff, and students of color in a more intimate setting. Therefore, I scheduled a variety of guest speakers throughout the semester. Often, speakers were asked to participate in a panel conversation with two to three other women of color. As opposed to individual guest lectures, the panel format provided a more intimate space for students to get to know women of color on campus.

The panels afforded students an opportunity to broaden their networks and hopefully identify women of color role models on campus. Ana explained how she was inspired by the panelists and considered them role models:

> The panel was by far my favorite. I felt like the women opened up about some of the issues they have been faced with and how they dealt with those issues. It was very inspiring, and I admire each and every single one of them for reaching the position in which they are at. To me, they are all role models to follow.

Sofia echoed these sentiments. After hearing their stories of success, she was motivated to achieve excellence too:

> The women who sat before us all had odds against them and they sat before us educated—doctorate degrees—and in the place where they want to be. I look up to them and I feel like I, too, can achieve anything I want to—even obtain my bachelors and continue my studies beyond that, as long as I want to achieve excellence.

While networking with faculty and staff was important, it was imperative for women of color to also build connections with peers . During my third year, I added another panel to Sister Stories—this one with students who had previously taken the course. Sister Stories alumni talked at length about how the course impacted their lives. Current students were deeply moved by peers—specifically their post-course application of course materials. Bonnie explained:

> When the panel of students came . . . we got an insight on how they act and feel outside of class, and after the class is done. I saw how much the class actually affects a person—even after the class is over. They are still tracking microaggressions, thinking about their image, and dealing with being the only women of color in their classes. I feel like after this class I would still be using the things I learn in this class. It isn't like some math equations that you forget after a while; these things I learn

helped me grow as a person already. I see things differently, and realize that I don't have to deal with people's ignorant comments; that I should address it.

Since this panel has been part of the class for a number of years now, former students are usually quite excited when they are asked to serve as panelists for a new group of Sister Stories students.

Due to the powerful interactions between current Sister Stories students and alumni during these panel presentations, I was excited to infuse more formal peer mentoring into the course. So, I added a peer mentor position to the teaching team. That position is held by an undergraduate student who previously took the course. Peer mentors receive academic credit for their role and are expected to contribute to class planning, facilitate class activities, and provide some content delivery throughout the semester. Most importantly, the mentor serves as a resource, inside and outside the classroom. In many ways, the student in this position acts as a resident mentor, providing support and guidance to Sister Stories students.

SETTING A TONE OF TRUST AND RESPECT

Creating classroom environments of trust and respect are foundations for inclusive educational practice (Tuitt, 2006; Vaccaro, 2013). It is especially important to build trust and respect among students before asking them to share candidly about emotion-evoking social justice topics like oppression, privilege, microaggressions, and racial identity. As I start the course each semester, I make it clear that Sister Stories is heavily reliant on student engagement and discussion. I note that much of the dialogue revolves around counterstories. While it is not necessary for students to reveal their deepest, darkest secrets, they need to make personal connections with the content in order to get something out of the course. And so, by the second class meeting, I share my own story, as I indicated in the preface. I do this so students can start to get to know me on a deeper level and to "model the way" (Kouzes & Posner, 2012, p. 3). I firmly believe that I cannot expect my students to share personal stories if I am not willing to do so myself. I expect the same from graduate assistants and the peer mentors. By sharing our stories as women of color, I hope to create a classroom environment of trust and respect.

Building trust and respect does not happen quickly. There is always a tension between wanting students to share counterstories early in the semester, and the reality that trust and respect is a requisite for sharing. Trust must develop over time. This dilemma was solved in part by a request from students themselves. Students expressed an interest in getting to know each other more at the beginning of the class. Based on their feedback, I added a class retreat at the beginning of the semester. The half-day retreat was planned for a Friday or Saturday early in the semester. Goals of the retreat included starting to build community and beginning discussions about race, gender, and identity in the United States. Activities of the retreat include name games, icebreakers, and activities that showcased women of color as leaders throughout history. The goals of building trust and respect did not go unnoticed by students. Carolina understood the purpose of the retreat was "to open up to each other more. So we can actually be more comfortable as we get to know each other and to express more in depth what we think." Students consistently reported the retreat as a highlight of Sister Stories. Bonnie explained: "that one day when we had the retreat, that really affected me, because this is really at the beginning when we started to really think about our identity and different things that affect who we are and how we identify ourselves." When prompted for more details, she described one of the most memorable activities:

> It was an eye opener—a conversation starter. It really took us out of the classroom and to a more intimate place where we played games and we did things that were fun, but also there was like a message behind it. We did one activity where [we had to name] women of color that are in powerful positions. And, I realize that I don't know many of them. . . . It was frustrating that we knew certain big names—but these other [women of color] that are just as big or even bigger—we know nothing about.

This activity, and retreat as a whole, served as a venue for trust building as well as a "conversation starter" regarding the Sister Stories goal of exposing students to diverse women of color role models.

In the classroom, I also tried to build trust and respect in other ways. To create a feeling of community, students sat in a circle facing one another, rather than sitting in lecture style. This set-up allowed students to look at each other as they were talking. After feedback from students in year one, I also began distributing blank index cards at the start of each class. I collect them at the end of each period. Students are encouraged to write questions or comments they want to share anonymously with me and/or the class. I start every class period by responding to each comment written in the prior session to show students their opinions and questions were valued. As the level of trust and respect increased over the semester, the need for anonymous comment cards seemed to decrease. Students felt more comfortable stating their opinions, asking questions, and challenging others after a solid foundation of trust and respect had been built. I hand out index cards at every class session through final exams. However, as students begin to feel trust, they often begin to speak their minds freely—often making the anonymous cards unnecessary toward the end of the semester.

THE STUDY

We quickly learned that Sister Stories was *not* a typical class. As such, we decided to collect empirical evidence about the teaching, learning, and classroom dynamics in this unique counterspace. Our hope was that empirical findings could be valuable to students and educators interested in creating counterspaces for women of color. This book was inspired by the results from a five-year holistic multiple case study (Yin, 2014) of the Sister Stories course. Case study methods are ideal for studying unique social phenomena bounded by context and time. In this project, the phenomena included teaching, learning, and interpersonal dynamics in an undergraduate course centered on the historical and contemporary experiences of women of color in the United States.

The holistic multiple case study was bounded by time (five semesters) and the context of a unique course offering at one predominantly White institution (PWI). In a holistic multiple case study, data collection from two or more case studies are analyzed independently and collectively. In this project, we considered the whole case to be the collective cross-sectional results gleaned from all five semesters Sister Stories was offered. Overarching themes from the whole case study served as the organizing frame for the book. In fact, the major topics for each chapter reflect consistent thematic patterns that emerged from the data set as a collective whole.

We also analyzed each semester independently as a case in and of itself. Analyzing each single case within a multiple case study provides an important lens to view data. Yin (2014) explained, "Each individual case study consists of a 'whole' study in which convergent evidence is sought regarding the facts and conclusions for the case" (p. 59). In the following chapters, the uniqueness of each individual case is described within the context of the five-year collective case study project. Even though the curriculum and pedagogical approach remained fairly constant, the students changed. As the demographics of the class changed, so did Sister Stories classroom dynamics. Analyses of these independent cases offered rich detail about the subtle differences that emerged from year to year.

Data Collection

Multiple modes of data collection are used to gather evidence in case study research (Yin, 2014). We obtained rich data from participant observations, interviews, focus groups, and student work. I (Melissa) engaged in participant observations during the course, writing field notes and keeping a journal about my reflections. As the primary researcher, I (Annemarie) visited the class multiple times and kept field notes about those experiences. At the end of the semester, I (Annemarie) conducted individual and group interviews (i.e., focus groups) with students, alumni, graduate teaching assistants, and the undergraduate mentor. Student papers, presentations, and on-line discussion posts offered a wealth of information for the case study. To gain retrospective perspectives on the academic counterspace, we also invited alumni to engage in a focus group.

At the beginning of each semester, Sister Stories students were informed of the case study project. They were assured that they could decline participation in the study without any impact on their grade. A few weeks prior to the end of the term, students were invited to sign up for an optional extra-credit focus group. So that students would not feel pressured to volunteer for a focus group, an alternative extra-credit assignment was offered.

Literature has suggested that White students and students of color often hesitate to be candid in mixed race conversations (Fox, 2009; Watt, 2007). To create a setting where such fears would be minimized, White students and students of color were invited to participate in separate focus groups. In the year when men of color comprised a large portion of the enrollment, they were invited to participate in separate focus groups from women. Following this logic, we also invited White men and White women to conduct individual interviews since they were often the "only one" in the class. With such small numbers (i.e., one or two), focus groups were not possible. The same questions were asked in the focus groups and individual interviews.

A series of semi-structured questions were used to collect reflective feedback from students about their Sister Stories experiences. Probes were used to delve deeply into responses when necessary. Typical probes included: "Tell me a little more about that" and "Can you provide examples?" Interview and focus group questions for students included:

- What was it like being in a class centered on the lives of women of color? How did it make you feel to be in this class?
- What expectations did you have of the class? Were those expectations met?
- Talk to me about the most moving content from this class.
- What was your biggest learning moment?
- How did the class content relate (or not) to your lived experiences?
- Were there ever any classroom discussions that made you uncomfortable? Why? How did you respond?
- Did you ever hold back from talking or self-censor? Why?
- Tell me about the things you appreciated about the teaching styles/methods.
- Please describe your reaction to the instructor and/or TAs sharing personal stories in class.

In focus groups, alumni were asked the following questions:

- Looking back, what was the most moving aspect of the class?
- Now that you've had some space from the class, what was it like being in a course dedicated to women of color? How did it make you feel to be in the class?
- What would you say to students who might be thinking about taking the class?
- If you could go back in time, would you do anything differently as a student in this class?
- Tell me about the things you appreciated about the teaching styles/ methods? How were they different or similar to other classes at this university?

Focus group questions for the instructor, graduate assistants, and under-graduate mentor included:

- What is your philosophy of teaching?
- What strategies (teaching, grading, etc.) do you use to design a safe yet challenging academic counterspace?
- What are your perceptions of the class and students?
- What were the dynamics like in the classroom? How did you navigate them?
- What role do the counterstories of instructors have in the classroom and what impact do you think they had on students?
- How do you navigate your own triggers or powerful emotional responses in the classroom? How about those of students?

Data Analysis

A number of analytic techniques can be used in case study research (Yin, 2014). In this project, we used a "ground up" strategy for working with the data, meaning we used an inductive process to document emergent themes from each embedded case and across the cases (Yin, 2014, p. 136). We coded focus group and interview transcripts, field notes, and student work. We utilized three levels of coding in the analysis. First-level codes were basic concepts which were combined into like categories for second-level coding. Third-level codes were developed by analyzing the interconnections between second-level codes. The chapter topics for *Centering Women of Color in Academic Counterspaces* were informed by third-level codes.

Qualitative research must be trustworthy. Research that is trust-worthy is credible and confirmable (Jones, Torres & Arminio, 2014). Credibility refers to the accurate interpretation of participant perspectives. We used a number of strategies to achieve credibility. First, we engaged in prolonged field work over five years. Second, we developed trust with participants. As described in the prior section, I (Melissa) adopted a variety of pedagogical techniques which foregrounded trust building, risk taking, and personal reflection (Tuitt, 2006). Graduate assistants, the undergraduate mentor, and I (Melissa) modeled inclusivity and risk taking by sharing our counterstories as women of color. Student trust in the research process was also gained from the assurance that student grades would not reflect their focus group comments and Melissa would only read the transcripts after grades were posted. Additionally, we devised a plan to allow me (Annemarie) to build trust with students over the course of the semester. Prior to the focus groups, I (Annemarie) visited the course two or three times—sharing my personal journey as a White woman and presenting findings from my research on racial microaggressions.

In an effort to achieve credibility, we utilized rich description to convey counterstories throughout the book. To ensure trustworthiness, we also triangulated multiple sources of evidence (e.g., observations, field notes, focus groups, interviews, student assignments) (Yin, 2014) and revisited discrepant information throughout the analytic process. One way we accomplished this was through investigator triangulation (Merriam, 2009) where we engaged in independent analysis of the data and then used agreed-upon codes and categories to generate findings. We also used member checking with students and alumni as well as peer validation from colleagues (Jones et al., 2014; Yin, 2014). Key themes presented in *Centering Women of Color in Academic Counterspaces* were presented at regional and national conferences and at a campus diversity event where credibility of study findings and plausibility of the analysis were evaluated by students and peer reviewers from a variety of racial backgrounds.

In qualitative studies, the researcher is the key instrument. Therefore, reflexivity is an essential piece of validity. A scholar's paradigms and social identities can influence the why, what, and how of a research project (Jones et al., 2014; Stewart, 2010). (For details about our social identities and approach to this project, see the preface.) During data analysis, we engaged in deep self-reflection about the impact of our identities (e.g., race, class, gender, sexual orientation) on course delivery, the research process, and our study conclusions. For instance, as a White, middle-class, bisexual, feminist, and cisgender woman, I (Annemarie) constantly wrestled with honoring data from all students while not overshadowing the voices of women of color. I also lamented the lack of attention to sexual orientation and gender identity beyond the man/woman binary. As I (Melissa) mentioned in the preface and this chapter, my experiences heightened my awareness of including the voices of women of color from all racial and ethnic backgrounds. As we analyzed the data, I regularly asked myself: Do I expect women of color to have similar experiences as me? Am I too focused on any particular racial or ethnic group? Both of us were concerned about honoring and validating *all* students while resisting the pressure to center Whiteness and/or maleness. Throughout the collection, analysis, and writing processes, we regularly challenged each other about our assumptions and privileges. We also talked at length about how our CRT and CRF lenses shaped our perspectives on the entire research project, including our emergent themes which serve as the foundations for each chapter of this book.

DEMOGRAPHICS

Centering Women of Color in Academic Counterspaces offers a holistic account of the teaching, learning, and interpersonal dynamics from the perspectives of students, alumni, graduate teaching assistants, instructor, and undergraduate mentors. Demographics of *all* of these individuals, as well as the primary researcher (Annemarie) contributed to Sister Stories dynamics and study outcomes. While student demographics comprise most of this section, we begin with a brief overview of the racial and gender identities of the graduate teaching assistants and undergraduate mentor. We introduced ourselves in the preface, so we do not repeat our demographics here. One graduate assistant, Angel, self-identified as a woman of color, specifically a Cape Verdean woman. Daniella, the other graduate assistant, self-identified as a Cape Verdean/African woman. Vera served as an undergraduate mentor after completing the course as a student. She described herself as first-generation American, Cape Verdean, woman of color, Black, and African.

Every student who enrolled in the course during the five-year time frame was invited to participate in the study. Those who chose to participate completed a short demographic form where they identified their gender (i.e., woman, man, transgender, other) and race. They selected one or more races from a pre-designated list of racial categories including Black, Latino/a, Asian American/Pacific Islander, Native American Indian, White, and other. The demographic form also included a blank line where students were encouraged to use their own words to describe their racial and/or ethnic identity. Students listed their majors and minors and noted a class year (i.e., first, sophomore, junior, senior). In the following sections, participant demographics are summarized by year. We provide total Sister Stories enrollment per semester, as well as the number who volunteered to participate in the study. Student demographics (70–100 percent students of color) contrast with those of the predominantly White university, which had a population of roughly 70 percent White students. See the Appendix for a complete table of participant demographics, including pseudonyms which we use throughout the book.

Enrollment for Sister Stories is kept low to allow for an environment where in-depth dialogue can occur. Over the period of our five-year study, between 11 and 16 students registered for Sister Stories annually. Even though Sister Stories was designed as an academic counterspace for, and about, women of color, enrollment could not be restricted to women of color. Any interested student was required to meet with me (Melissa) in order to learn more about the course and obtain a registration code. During that meeting, all students were informed that the assignments, readings, and discussions would be centered on the historical and contemporary experiences of women of color. Throughout this book, we center the voices of women of color by focusing on their experiences in Sister Stories. Yet, the presence and perspectives of a small number of men of color and White students shaped the dynamics and outcomes of the course. As such, throughout *Centering Women of Color in Academic Counterspaces*, we include selected prose from White students and men of color to provide a comprehensive picture of the Sister Stories counterspace. In sum, we center the voices of women of color, but not at the exclusion of other student voices.

Year 1

Of the thirteen students enrolled, twelve chose to participate in the research project. Participant majors included: human development (n=4); sociology (n=2); communication (n=2); women's studies (n=1); pharmacy (n=1); business (n=1); and nursing (n=1). Three study participants self-identified as a declared leadership studies minor. Students represented all class years with two first-year students, six sophomores, two juniors, one senior, and one who chose not to share his class year.

Two participants identified as cisgender men and ten as cisgender women. From the pre-designated list of racial categories, students identified as White (n=4), Black (n=6), and Latina/o (n=2). When offered the opportunity to use their own words to describe their racial and/or ethnic identity, Black students identified as: African American, Black/African American, Ghanaian/Native American, Nigerian American, Liberian American, and Cape Verdean. Latino students described themselves as Colombian and Puerto Rican. Four students wrote White on the form.

Year 2

Of the twelve students who enrolled, eleven participated in the study. Majors included: political science (n=1); human development (n=3); communication (n=3); communicative disorders (n=1), early childhood education (n=1); nursing (n=1); and criminal justice (n=1). Two participants self-identified as a declared leadership studies minor. Three participants were sophomores, four were juniors, and four were seniors.

Five participants identified as cisgender men and six identified as cisgender women. Racially, they identified as Black (n=6); Latino/a (n=2); bi/multiracial (n=2); and Other (n=2). Black students identified as: Black/African descent, African American, Nigerian, Cape Verdean/African, Cape Verdean & Native American, and African American. Latino/a students identified as: Hispanic American, and Puerto Rican and Domini-can. Bi/multiracial students described themselves as: Indian and Portu-guese as well as African American and Italian American. Finally, two students who selected "Other" described themselves as Nigerian and Nigerian/Brown skinned. One White woman initially enrolled in the course, but withdrew from the university due to personal reasons. Thus, throughout this book, we will refer to year two as having only students of color in the class.

Year 3

Ten of the eleven students enrolled in the course participated in the study. Their majors included: political science (n=2); elementary educa-tion and psychology (n=1); biology (n=1); accounting (n=1); human devel-opment (n=3); health studies (n=1); and communication (n=1). Eight of the ten also self-identified as a declared leadership studies minor. Partici-pants represented all class years with two first-year students, three soph-omores, two juniors, and three seniors.

All ten participants identified as cisgender women. From the list of racial categories, they identified as Black (n=3); Latina (n=3); bi/multira-cial (n=2); and White (n=2). Black students described themselves as: Cape Verdean, African American, and an American-born woman of Cape Ver-dean descent. Latina students self-identified as: Dominican/Hispanic, Hispanic, and Purebred Puerto Rican and American citizen. Bi/multira-cial students described themselves as: Multiracial–Syrian, Italian, and Ja-maican, and Haitian and Cape Verdean American. Lastly, the White stu-dents wrote Caucasian and Caucasian (White) on the form.

Year 4

Of the sixteen students enrolled, thirteen chose to participate in the study. Their majors included: forensic chemistry (n=1); human develop-ment (n=4); accounting (n=1); psychology (n=2); theater (n=1); nursing (n=1); communication (n=1); textiles, fashion merchandising, and design (n=2); business marketing (n=1); and health studies (n=1). One student indicated an undeclared major. Eight students declared a minor in lead-ership studies. Participants represented all class years with six first-year students, five sophomores, one junior, and one senior.

Five of the participants identified as cisgender men and eight as cis-gender women. Racially, they identified as Black (n=7); Latino/a (n=2); Asian American/Pacific Islander (n=2); Native American Indian (n=1); bi/multiracial (n=2); and White (n=1). Black students described themselves as: Cape Verdean and Senegalese, Cape Verdean, West African, Cape Verdean/African American, Cape Verdean, and African. Latino/a stu-dents described themselves as: Latina and Columbian. One Asian

American/Pacific Islander student specified Hmong while the other provided no other self-identifier. One student who selected Bi/multiracial wrote Black, Bi/multiracial, Nigerian/American, while the other noted Cape Verdean/Native American Indian. Finally, the White student described himself as Greek, American, and Western European.

Year 5

All eleven students enrolled in the course participated in the study. Their majors included: kinesiology (n=1); human development (n=3); industrial engineering (n=2); psychology (n=1); political science (n=1); criminal justice (n=2); film (n=1); gender and women's studies (n=1); biology (n=1); and communication (n=1). Six identified as leadership studies minors. Participants represented all class years with two first-year students, two sophomores, five juniors, and two seniors.

Two of the students identified as cisgender men and nine as cisgender women. Racially, they identified as Black (n=5); Latino/a (n=5); bi/multiracial (n=1); and White (n=1). Black students self-identified as: Nigerian-American, African American, biracial, or African American and part Cuban. Latino/a students described themselves as: Guaterican American, biracial, Dominican, and Dominican American/Latina/Hispanic. The student who indicated biracial specified Latina and Black. Finally, one student indicated White on the form.

CONCLUSION

In this chapter, we provided an overview of the Sister Stories course, case study, and student demographics. Sister Stories was unlike most other courses at the predominantly White university. This special counterspace likely resulted from the diverse student body and the CRT and CRF paradigms and pedagogy upon which the course rested. In this chapter, we also discussed five foci that contributed to the unique Sister Stories experience: diversity among women of color and intersectionality; validating and empowering stories; reflection and application of course materials; role models, networks, and mentors; and trust and respect. This chapter detailed the how and why of Sister Stories and provided context for forthcoming chapters. Each of the following chapters contains student narratives that illustrate the impact of Sister Stories.

REFERENCES

Atkinson, D. R., Morten, G., & Sue, D. W. (1979). *Counseling American minorities*. Dubuque, IA: William C. Brown.
Barnes, K., Marateo, R. C., & Ferris, S. P. (2007). Teaching and learning with the net generation. *Innovate: Journal of Online Education, 3*(4), Article 1.

Belenky, M. F., Clinchy, B. M., Goldberger, N. R., & Tarule, J. M. (1986). *Women's ways of knowing: The development of self, voice and mind.* New York: Basic Books.

Brayboy, B. M. J., & Castagano, A. E. (2011). Indigenous millennial students in higher education. In F. A. Bonner II, A. F. Marbley & M. F. Howard-Hamilton (Eds.) *Diverse millennial students in college: Implications for faculty and student affairs* (pp. 137–55). Sterling, VA: Stylus.

Brookfield, S. D. (1995). *Becoming a critically reflective teacher.* San Francisco, CA: Jossey-Bass.

———— (2000). The concept of critically reflective practice. In A. L. Wilson & E. R. Hayes (Eds.), *Handbook of adult and continuing education* (pp. 33–49). Hoboken, NJ: Wiley.

Crenshaw, K. (1989). Demarginalizing the intersection of race and sex: A Black feminist critique of antidiscrimination doctrine, feminist theory and antiracist politics. *University of Chicago Legal Forum,* 139–67.

Cross, W. E., Jr. & Fhagen-Smith, P. (2001). Patterns in African American identity development: A life span perspective. In C. L. Wijeyesinghe & B. W. Jackson, III (Eds.), *New perspectives on racial identity development: A theoretical and practical anthology* (pp. 243–70). New York: New York University Press.

Darder, A., Baltodano, M., & Torres, R. D. (2003). Critical pedagogy: An introduction. In A. Darder, M. Baltodano & R. D. Torres (Eds.), *The critical pedagogy reader* (pp. 1–21). New York: Routledge.

DiCaprio, N. S. (1974). *Personality theories: Guides to living.* Philadelphia, PA: Saunders.

Dirkx, J. M. (1998). Transformative learning theory in the practice of adult education: An overview. *PAACE Journal of Lifelong Learning, 7,* 1–14.

Dugan, J. P., & Komives, S. R. (2007). *Developing leadership capacity in college students: Findings from a national study.* A Report from the Multi-Institutional Study of Leadership. College Park, MD: National Clearinghouse for Leadership Programs.

Ferdman, B. M., & Gallegos, P. I. (2001). Racial identity development and Latinos in the United States. In C. L. Wijeyesinghe & B. W. Jackson, III (Eds.), *New perspectives on racial identity development: A theoretical and practical anthology* (pp. 32–66). New York: New York University Press.

Fincher, J. (2009). Consciousness of self. In S. R. Komives, W. Wagner & Associates (Eds.), *Leadership for a better world: Understanding the social change model of leadership development* (pp. 299–334). San Francisco, CA: Jossey-Bass.

Freire, P. (1970, 2006). *Pedagogy of the oppressed.* New York: Continuum.

Fox, H. (2009). *"When race breaks out": Conversations about race and racism in college classrooms.* New York: Peter Lang.

Harro, B. (2013). The cycle of socialization. In Adams, M., Blumenfeld, W. J., Casteñada, C., Hackman, H. W., Peters, M. L., & Zúñiga, X. (Eds.), *Readings for diversity and social justice* (3rd ed., pp. 45–52). New York: Routledge.

Helms, J. E. (1993). *Black and white racial identity: Theory, research, and practice.* Westport, CT: Praeger.

Higher Education Research Institute (HERI) (1996). *A social change model of leadership development: Guidebook version III.* College Park, MD: National Clearinghouse for Leadership Programs.

Hill Collins, P. (1991, 2000). *Black feminist thought: Knowledge, consciousness, and the politics of empowerment.* New York: Routledge.

Horse, P. G. (2001). Reflections on American Indian identity. In C. L. Wijeyesinghe & B. W. Jackson, III (Eds.), *New perspectives on racial identity development: A theoretical and practical anthology* (pp. 91–107). New York: New York University Press.

Jones, S. R., Torres, V., & Arminio, J. (2014). *Negotiating the complexities of qualitative research in higher education: Fundamental elements and issues* (2nd ed.). New York: Routledge.

Kim, J. (1981). *The process of Asian-American identity development: A study of Japanese American women's perceptions of their struggle to achieve positive identities.* Unpublished doctoral dissertation, University of Massachusetts, Amherst.

———— (2001). Asian American identity development theory. In C. L. Wijeyesinghe & B. W. Jackson, III (Eds.), *New perspectives on racial identity development: A theoretical and practical anthology* (pp. 67–90). New York: New York University Press.

Kouzes, J. M., & Posner, B. Z. (2012). *The leadership challenge: How to make extraordinary things happen in organizations.* (5th ed.). San Francisco, CA: Jossey-Bass.

Lorde, A. (1984). *Sister outsider.* Berkeley, CA: The Crossing Press.

McGlynn, A. P. (2008). Millennials in college: How do we motivate them? *Education Digest: Essential Readings Condensed for Quick Review, 73*(6), 19–22.

Mena, J., & Vaccaro, A. (2014). Role modeling community engagement for college students: Narratives from women faculty and staff of color. In S. V. D. Iverson & J. H. James (Eds.), *Feminist community engagement: Achieving praxis* (pp. 53–74). New York: Palgrave Macmillan.

Merriam, S. B. (2009). *Qualitative research: A guide to design and implementation: Revised and expanded from qualitative research and case study applications in education.* San Francisco, CA: Wiley.

Mezirow, J. (1991). *Transformative dimensions of adult learning.* San Francisco, CA: Jossey-Bass.

Ortiz, A. M., & Pichardo-Diaz, D. (2011). Millennial characteristics and Latino/a students. In F. A. Bonner II, A. F. Marbley & M. F. Howard-Hamilton (Eds.), *Diverse millennial students in college: Implications for faculty and student affairs* (pp. 117–33). Sterling, VA: Stylus.

Palmer, R. T., & Maramba, D. C. (2015). The impact of social capital on the access, adjustment, and success of Southeast Asian American college students. *Journal of College Student Development, 56*(1), 45–60.

Parker, L., & Stovall, D. O. (2004). Actions following words: Critical race theory connects to critical pedagogy. *Educational Philosophy and Theory, 36*(2), 167–82.

Pope, M. L. (2002). Community college mentoring: Minority student perception. *Community College Review, 30*(3), 31–46.

Renn, K. A. (2011). Biracial and multiracial college students. In M. J. Cuyjet, M. F. Howard-Hamilton & D. L. Cooper (Eds.), *Multiculturalism on campus: Theory, models, and practices for understanding diversity and creating inclusion* (pp. 191–212). Sterling, VA: Stylus.

Rowe, W., Bennett, S. K., & Atkinson, D. R. (1994). White racial identity models: A critique and alternative proposal. *Counseling Psychologist, 22,* 129–46.

Solórzano, D. G. (1998). Critical race theory, race and gender microaggressions, and the experience of Chicana and Chicano scholars. *Qualitative Studies in Education, 11*(1), 121–36.

————, Ceja, M., & Yosso, T. J. (2000). Critical race theory, racial microaggressions, and campus racial climate: The experiences of African American college students. *The Journal of Negro Education, 69*(1/2), 60–73.

Stewart, D. L. (2010). Researcher as instrument: Understanding "shifting" findings in constructivist research. *Journal of Student Affairs Research and Practice, 47*(3), 291–306.

Sue, D. W., & Sue, D. (2003). *Counseling the culturally diverse: Theory and practice* (4th ed.). Hoboken, NJ: Wiley.

Tuitt, F. (2006). Afterword: Realizing a more inclusive pedagogy. In A. Howell & F. Tuitt (Eds.), *Race and higher education: Rethinking pedagogy in diverse college classrooms* (pp. 243–369). Cambridge, MA: Harvard Educational Review.

Vaccaro, A. (2013). Building a framework for social justice education: One educator's journey. In L. Landreman (Ed.), *The art of effective facilitation: Reflections from social justice educators* (pp. 23–44). Sterling, VA: Stylus.

Watt, S. K. (2007). Difficult dialogues, privilege and social justice: Uses of the privileged identity exploration (PIE) model in student affairs practice. *College Student Affairs Journal, 26*(2), 114–26.

Wijeyesinghe, C. L. (2001). Racial identity in multiracial people: An alternative paradigm. In C. L. Wijeyesinghe & B. W. Jackson, III (Eds.), *New perspectives on racial identity development: A theoretical and practical anthology* (pp. 129–52). New York: New York University Press.

Wing, A. K. (2003). *Critical race feminism: A reader* (2nd ed.). New York: New York University Press.

Yin, R. W. (2014). *Case study research: Design and methods* (5th ed.). Los Angeles, CA: Sage.

TWO

Microaggressions on Campus

"We still have a long way to go."

In the *Centering Women of Color in Academic Counterspaces* Introduction, we provided a brief overview of contemporary racism, describing racial and gender taxonomies as well as forms of environmental and interpersonal microaggressions. In this chapter, we synthesize highlights from recent microaggression studies conducted in education settings. To center women of color, we also review the smaller, but very relevant body of research highlighting intersections of racial and gender microaggressions experienced by women of color. The overview of literature is followed by student vignettes that reveal five common types of microaggressions experienced by women of color on campus. We titled those common themes: 1) Ignorant, rude, and stereotypical comments and jokes; 2) I'm not a criminal; 3) They expect less from me; 4) I'm not welcome here; and 5) Objectification: I am not food, nor am I nasty. First, however, we begin the chapter by describing the appraisal process, which is the process of determining whether an incident is oppression and deciding if, and how, to respond. The section titled "Did That Just Happen?" speaks to the early stages of the microaggression appraisal process.

Critical race feminist perspectives suggest that gendered racism is not an individual phenomenon perpetrated by narrow-minded individuals. Instead, consistent patterns of microaggressions point to pervasive gendered and racist oppression (Wing, 2003). As we noted in the Introduction, counterstories are often utilized by CRT scholars to expose pervasive and embedded forms of exclusion in systems, policies, and practices. Therefore, we encourage readers to view forthcoming student narratives not as isolated campus incidents, but as evidence of patterned forms of institutional exclusion experienced by women of color on a regular basis.

MICROAGGRESSIONS ON CAMPUS

Collegiate microaggressions experienced by people of color include being excluded and stereotyped by peers or tokenized when topics of diversity, race, or gender are brought up (Domingue, 2015; Minikel-Lacocque, 2012; Yosso, Smith, Ceja & Solórzano, 2009; Vaccaro, 2016). A prominent theme in studies of collegiate racial microaggressions reveals deficit assumptions about the academic capabilities of students of color (Gildersleeve, Croom & Vasquez, 2011; Strayhorn, 2008; Vaccaro, 2016). Findings from these higher education studies have roots in the microaggression whereby people of color are assumed to have low levels of intelligence (Sue, 2010a; Sue et al., 2007). Sue (2010b) refers to this taxonomy category as "ascription of intelligence," which connotes the racist stereotype that "people of color are generally not as intelligent as whites" (p. 32). Even high achieving Black collegians in two different studies felt the need to prove themselves academically to counter pervasive beliefs that students of color were not intelligent enough for college (McGee & Martin, 2011; Strayhorn, 2008). When students of color excel academically, they are sometimes accused of cheating. In other cases, students are ignored by faculty or have their ideas dismissed when they speak up in class (Vaccaro, 2016). As such, students of color often become hypervigilant about disproving stereotypes about academic inferiority, which can be an emotionally taxing endeavor (McGee & Martin, 2011).

Another common theme in collegiate microaggression studies includes being targeted by campus police or university administrators for supposedly doing something wrong (Hwang & Goto, 2009; Solórzano, Ceja & Yosso, 2000; Smith, Allen & Danley, 2007). Such microaggressions relate to the taxonomy category assumption of criminal status (Sue, 2010b; Sue et al., 2007). In a study titled "Assume the Position . . . You Fit the Description," Smith et al. (2007) found Black men attending five selective universities were assumed to be criminals and subjected to regular stops, searches, and harassment by campus and community police. McCabe (2009) also documented how Black men on campus were consistently viewed as threatening.

A subset of microaggression research focuses on the intersecting forms of gender and racial oppression directed at women of color. Gendered racial microaggressions experienced by women of color often do not fit neatly into a single taxonomy category (Capodilupo, Nadal, Corman, Hamit, Lyons & Weinberg, 2010; Sue, 2010b; Sue et al., 2007) (see introduction). In fact, many of the contemporary microaggression studies mirror earlier writings by women scholars of color (Crenshaw, 1989; hooks, 1984, 2000; Hill Collins, 1991, 2000) and reveal overlapping taxonomy themes such as assumptions of inferiority, objectification, traditional gender roles, and sexist language (Capodilupo et al., 2010). As such, we do not attempt to categorize the findings from these higher education studies about women of color into any single taxonomy theme.

In 1991, Hill Collins documented four controlling images of Black women that included women as mammies, matriarchs, welfare recipients, and sexually aggressive jezebels. More than a quarter of a century later, scholars have elucidated similar stereotypical images that oppress contemporary women college students of color (Domingue, 2015; Vaccaro, 2016). For instance, Domingue (2015) found Black graduate and undergraduate women were stereotyped as the "Angry Black Woman," "Jezebel," and "Black Mama." During focus groups with eighteen adult women learners of color attending a predominantly White women's college, Vaccaro (2016) elucidated a host of offensive comments rooted in deficit images about women's cultural groups—including the stereotype that women of color were sexually promiscuous, produced too many babies, and misused government services.

Gender oppression often manifests in a form of objectification (Fredrickson & Roberts, 1997) which includes viewing women through narrow lenses and judging them for their physical appearance. Wolf (1991, 2002) described the beauty myth which relates to an ever-present pressure on women to obtain a male-defined and unrealistic standard of beauty. Judgments about beauty and body emerge as interlocking forms of racial and gender oppression for women of color who are not only subjected to a patriarchal beauty myth, but are also compared to a standard of beauty based upon White women's characteristics. In a recent study of twelve undergraduate and graduate Black women, Domingue (2015) found critiques about their looks were commonplace. In a qualitative secondary analysis of prior microaggression research, scholars found that women of color were consistently exoticized (Nadal et al., 2015). This is a unique form of sexual objectification that has long been documented by women writers of color who explain how women of color are seen as hypersexual, sexually available, and/or exotic (hooks, 1984, 2000; Harris-Perry, 2011; Hill Collins, 1991, 2000; McCabe, 2009; Shah, 1997). Since beauty and body issues are long-standing in the literature, and an aspect of the Sister Stories curriculum, students shared extensive narratives about these topics. A brief discussion of objectification is included in this chapter to highlight its role as one of the five recurring forms of microaggressions experienced by women of color. We also dedicate an entire chapter (chapter 6) to beauty and body image.

Microaggression studies conducted with women of color in higher education suggest they experience contrasting realities of being invisible or hypervisible (Capodilupo, et al., 2010; Domingue, 2015; Vaccaro, 2016). Being silenced is a well-documented form of gendered racism (Domingue, 2015; Hill Collins, 1991, 2000; Lorde, 1984; Wing, 2003). On campus, invisibility can include being ignored during classroom discussions, overlooked for leadership positions and awards, or not considered for membership in campus groups (Vaccaro, 2010, 2016). Hypervisibility refers to experiences where a person's race and/or gender become the sole focus. For instance, twelve Black women in Domingue's study (2015) were hypervisible to White peers and fielded constant questions about their citizenship and heritage. They also had their authority regularly challenged.

THE EFFECTS OF MICROAGGRESSIONS

Despite their often subtle manifestations, microaggressions can have serious repercussions (Pierce, 1974; Sue, 2010a, 2010b). Decades ago Pierce (1974) argued, "In and of itself a microaggression may seem harmless, but the cumulative burden of a lifetime of microaggressions can theoretically contribute to diminished mortality, augmented morbidity and flattened confidence" (p. 516). More recent research shows that microaggressions affect both physical and mental health. Microaggressions engender feelings of frustration, anger, and low self-esteem (Nadal, Wong, Griffin, Davidoff & Sriken, 2014; Sue, Capodilupo & Holder, 2008), helplessness and hopelessness (Smith et al., 2007), stereotype threat (Yosso, Smith, Ceja & Solórzano, 2009), and race-related traumatic stress (Carter, 2007). Microaggressions also contribute to binge drinking (Blume, Lovato, Thyken & Denny, 2012) and other physical health problems (Brondolo, Rieppi, Kelly & Gerin, 2003; Sue 2010a, 2010b). Similarly, objectification has been linked to feelings of shame and anxiety (Fredrickson & Roberts, 1997), eating disorders (Wolf, 1991, 2002), and confrontation-related anxiety (Kaiser & Miller, 2004). Others have noted the combination of racism and sexism results in unique and deep psychological and physical harm (Lewis, Mendenhall, Harwood & Browne Huntt, 2013). The combined effects of interpersonal and environmental microaggressions for women of color can make a campus feel like a hostile place, and engender feelings of self-doubt, alienation, and discouragement—resulting in dire educational consequences (Smith et al., 2007; Solórzano et al., 2000; Yosso et al., 2009). In the following section, student narratives show that microaggressions can indeed take psychological, physical, and educational tolls on students of color.

STUDENT EXPERIENCES WITH MICROAGGRESSIONS

Dealing with microaggressions can be a laborious journey. Psychologists describe a two-part process of responding to any form of stress as primary and secondary attribution (Lazarus & Folkman, 1984). Even though Lazarus and Folkman's (1984) work focused on all types of stressors, their primary and secondary appraisal process is helpful for understanding how individuals respond to microaggressions. Immediately after an incident takes place, people of color expend psychological energy to determine if an event was oppression and whether or not the incident is, or should be, offensive. During primary attribution, an individual attempts to make meaning of an event. Once an incident is deemed to be an ism (e.g., racism, sexism), individuals move into secondary appraisal. During secondary appraisal, people wrestle with how to cope with the offensive incident. Microaggression scholars have built upon the work of Lazarus and Folkman (1984) to coin the term *attributional ambiguity* (Sue, 2010b; Sue et al., 2007) to describe the often ambiguous process of navigating microaggressions. Questions individuals might ask as they wrestle with the ambiguity of making meaning of subtle microaggressions include:

> Did what I think happened, really happen? Was this a deliberate act or an unintentional slight? How should I respond? Sit and stew on it or confront the person? If I bring the topic up, how do I prove it? Is it really worth the effort? Should I just drop the matter? (Sue et al., 2007, p. 279)

Women of color are often in no-win situations, or a catch-22, when they experience a microaggression (Sue 2010b). There could be potentially negative consequences for responding or for doing nothing. Challenging perpetrators can put women of color at risk. When confronted, perpetrators can respond with resistance or violence. Perpetrators who are supervisors, teachers, advisors, or landlords hold the power of a person's job, grades, or home in their hands. Yet, doing nothing can also cause psychological harm. When recipients of microaggressions suppress shock, frustration, or anger, they can experience the negative ramifications of pent up stressors (Sue et al., 2007). In short, microaggressions engender a complex and psychologically taxing process of deciding whether an incident is a microaggression, whether to respond, and how to do so.

Women of color who expend emotional energy on microaggression attribution may have less to devote to educational endeavors. In fact, many women of color enrolled in Sister Stories talked about the time and energy it took to wade through the psychologically taxing and ambiguous attributional processes (Folkman & Lazarus, 1988; Lazarus & Folkman, 1984; Sue et al., 2007). The combination of surprise, disbelief, and hurt made students ask themselves, "Did that really just happen?" In a paper, Lucy described the process as:

> Many times when I have heard derogatory remarks about my own race or other races I have truly been taken back. I become speechless and the thought of "did they just really say that" runs through my mind. It's like an instant moment of denial of what just happened.

Ana described an experience where her supervisor made an offensive comment. She discussed her initial confusion regarding the ambiguity of the incident as well as the resulting psychological energy it took to determine whether or not the incident was racist. "I was just, like 'what did she just say?' You know? Like is she forgetting that I'm Spanish? I feel, sometimes you notice things, but yet it's so uncomfortable, or hard to say something." Lucia wondered if she worried too much about whether or not subtle interactions were microaggressions. She said, "I feel like I think about it too much. I feel like that is a microaggression. The more it happens, the more it hurts. It's little things that keep happening and it makes no sense." Camilla also talked about how subtle forms of exclusion, and the resulting mental process of determining if something was oppression, really did take an emotional toll. To her, microaggressions felt like a subtle "vibe" or rudeness directed at her because she was a woman of color.

> When we use the library study rooms, I just feel like one of the [library staff] in there is like—she was just very rude to us. I was with a group of minority students. She just, ugh I . . . I don't know what it is, but you can just sense it when they are being rude just to be rude. So, I just felt that kind of negative vibe from her like. It's just . . . (hmm) it's just little things.

As Camilla recounted this microaggression incident, she struggled to find the right words to convey her experiences. Such struggles are not uncommon for minoritized people as they try to explain subtle microaggressions to people with privilege who often do not notice or recognize incidents as microaggressions. In fact, microaggression scholars argue that struggling to explain isms to privileged people is "a common, if not a universal, reaction of persons [from minoritized groups]" (Sue et al., 2007, p. 279). Explaining an incident as a microaggression requires women of color to legitimize their perspective that an incident was a form of racial or gender oppression to White people or men who might not see it as such. Defending one's perspective can make an offensive incident and the psychologically taxing attribution process even more emotionally draining. In the rest of the chapter, we summarize the five most common manifestations of microaggressions experienced by women of color in Sister Stories.

IGNORANT, RUDE, AND
STEREOTYPICAL COMMENTS AND JOKES

Women of color talked at length about ignorant, rude, and stereotypical comments made by peers, campus supervisors, and faculty members. While some were not surprised by these forms of oppression, others were taken aback by the sheer volume of ignorance expressed on campus. Diana explained:

I hear some conversations and I'm like, "Oh my god! People talk like this?". . . I've become more aware of my race in college than ever before in my life. Maybe because I expect everyone here to be educated. This is higher learning so you should be aware, but I just feel like there is so much ignorance.

Like many of her peers, Diana did not always use the term *microaggressions* and instead focused on ignorance. We contend, however, the ignorance experienced by Diana and her peers were indeed microaggressions rooted in stereotypes about women of color.

Students described hearing many ignorant and offensive comments about people who shared their racial and ethnic backgrounds. Jocelyn worked in a campus restaurant with a stage that could be reserved by student groups. One evening, a student organization for men of color (MOC) was hosting an open mic night. Jocelyn's story shows that comments evoking stereotypical images of people of color eating watermelon and fried chicken were not the only offensive things she heard in her campus workplace. Jocelyn explained, "I hear a lot of things at [The Campus Eatery]—it's the best place to hear things if you wanna hear people discriminate on other people." She continued:

MOC had an open mic night and they were supposed to be gone at a certain time so we could close. . . . I think they were supposed to be gone at eleven and it was like maybe twelve already and they were still back there. One of the White girls that works with me said, "If I had a slice of watermelon and some fried chicken, I bet you I can get them to leave." . . . At first, I was like, "Should I say something?" It really bothered me that I didn't say it immediately. But eventually, I went over to her and said, "So if there was a whole bunch of White people I could get some pasta and get them to leave." She was like, "I didn't mean it like that." I'm like, "If you didn't mean it like that, you shouldn't be saying stuff like that."

As noted earlier, the internal debate about if, and how, to respond to a microaggression can take a psychological toll. Jocelyn's questioning about "Should I say something?" exemplifies the presence and power of attributional ambiguity (Lazarus & Folkman, 1984; Sue 2010b).

Suzanna was so shocked by comments from White men in her residence hall that she was at a loss about how to respond. Their comments played into the stereotype that all Black people look the same. Refusing to learn or use her real name objectified her and devalued her as a person. Suzanna shared:

There's these boys that live across the hall from me. . . . Since we're Black, every time they come out [of their room] they're like, "Oh hey Rhianna, hey Beyonce." They called me Harriet Tubman one time! I never know what to say back. My roommate's just like, "Okay, Justin

Bieber" or Justin Timberlake or something like that. I don't really say
anything, but it gets on my nerves now—a lot!

Even though she did not use official psychological terms to convey harm,
her exclamation that their behavior "gets on my nerves now—a lot!"
speaks volumes about the grinding and cumulative emotional toll of
microaggressions.

It was not only students who conveyed ignorant, rude, or stereotypical comments. Faculty members did too. Women of color experienced
microaggressions from university employees. Participants in the alumni
focus group had a conversation about a White faculty member who made
offensive comments about Indian people in the process of trying to recruit people to take a class about India. While none of the women in the
conversation identified as Indian or Indian American, they still recognized the incident as a microaggression.

> **Regina**: And she was explaining about India and how it was growing
> as a major third-world country. It was growing and it was gonna be
> this big thing. And so she was like, "You know you can describe to
> [your peers] that if they want a better understanding of the people
> they call when they want their phone fixed or their computer fixed,
> tell them to take this course."

> **Nicole**: No she didn't! [groans]

> **Regina**: I wish I was making this stuff up. And I remember I stood
> there and I was like, "Are you kidding me?" Now, I'm not of Indian
> descent, but like, what? And then she laughed. It was supposed to be
> funny. And I just didn't find it funny. I just felt like it was so ridicu-
> lous. It's just little things like that, like people sometimes [are] ignor-
> ant.

As Regina and Nicole's exchange suggests, interpersonal microaggressions in the form of stereotypical and offensive comments aimed at people from other cultural backgrounds can still hurt.

In the focus group conversation, Regina also noted how the professor
thought she was being funny. Jokes have always been a vehicle to deliver
oppression under the guise of humor. In 1948, Sartre argued that humor
was not only a method for delivering anti-semitism, but an act that
brought pleasure to bigots. Billig (2001) studied how Internet jokes were
used by supporters of the Ku Klux Klan (KKK) to degrade people of
color, convey hate publicly, and encourage violence under the guise of
humor—often posting comments like "It is just a joke" next to horrific
statements. We are not suggesting that this faculty member was (or was
not) an anti-Semite or KKK supporter. We are, however, drawing a connection between a history of hatred conveyed through humor and con-

temporary microaggressions in the form of jokes and comments filled with stereotypes and hurtful messages about women and people of color. In fact, Cullen (2008) includes jokes as some of the *35 Dumb Things Well Intentioned People Say* to cause harm to people of color. She argued it is not the intent of the joke that matters, but the painful impact on people of color that is important. Scholars have also studied the impact of jokes that degrade or stereotype women. Burdsey (2011) documented how Asian members of a sporting team felt forced to downplay painful racist jokes to maintain comradery with teammates. Ryan and Kanjorski (1998) found a correlation between men's enjoyment of sexist jokes with rape-related attitudes and beliefs, self-reported likelihood of forcing sex on women, and actual sexual psychological and physical aggression. More recently, Ford, Woodzicka, Triplett, and Kochersberger (2013) found men who were exposed to sexist jokes expressed viewpoints that aligned with the devaluing of women in society and maintaining of gender inequality. In sum, jokes are a form of oppression that simultaneously cause individual harm and perpetuate systemic inequities.

On campus, students interact with a variety of staff members who oversee programs, advise student groups, manage enrollment and payments, and supervise student employees. There is no research explicating microaggressions from university employees other than faculty. Yet, women of color in Sister Stories experienced microaggressions from a host of university staff members.

Contemporary college students work more hours than ever before. The number of students working more than 30 hours is increasing, while a 10 to 15-hour work week (once considered the norm) is declining (Perna, 2010a). Like many contemporary U.S. college students (Perna, 2010b), many of our participants worked. Often these positions were in campus offices where they were supervised by university employees. Since students spend many hours at work, a campus job environment can be a very influential microclimate (Ackelsberg, Hart, Miller, Queeny & Van Dyne, 2009; Vaccaro, 2012). A microclimate is a sub-environment of a campus that fosters feelings of comfort or exclusion for those who frequent that space (e.g., department, building, area). Microaggressions in a particular microclimate (such as a job site) can impact student psychological well-being, as well as influence perceptions of the overall campus climate (Vaccaro, 2012). For instance, if a student feels unwelcome at her campus job or residence hall—a microclimate where she spends significant time—she might ultimately feel unwelcome at the university itself.

As Jocelyn's earlier story showed, microaggressions can be perpetrated by student co-workers. However, peers are not the only individuals who can make a work environment feel hostile; supervisors can also perpetrate microaggressions. Carmen described:

> I'm Columbian, so they just have like, really bad stereotype jokes, espe-
> cially my boss. You wouldn't think that your boss would make them,
> or be the one who would start up with the jokes—but she always does.
> Because I'm Columbian, I sell crack and stuff like that. She thinks it's
> funny and she constantly now says it. Now it's really bothering me. . . .
> It's a microaggression and it's unconscious to her and she just says it.
> But it's actually uncomfortable because [her comments] make other
> people think that I really do sell crack or something. . . . The customers
> look at me and it's like they [makes a gasping noise].

Of course, if she wanted to keep her job, Carmen felt like she could not
confront her supervisor. She was in what Sue (2010b) called the catch-22
regarding microaggression responses. It was emotionally painful to be
the target of oppressive comments. But, confronting her supervisor could
have resulted in the loss of her job.

Nicole's supervisor also perpetrated a microaggression. In fact, she
described her supervisor to be among the many "ignorant" people she
interacted with on campus.

> There's a lot of ignorant people on this campus. They're every-
> where. . . . [My supervisor] asked me about a meme she saw on Face-
> book about *Ghetto Beauty and the Beast*. She asked me, "What does it
> mean?" She's like, "I don't mean to offend you, but I know you prob-
> ably know what this, know more about this.". . . She's ignorant.

Nicole's supervisor seemed to genuinely want to understand an online
meme about *Ghetto Beauty and the Beast*, but did not consider the negative
impact of assuming Nicole would understand and explain it to her. Her
supervisor, however, may have had an inkling that her inquiry was offensive, since she said, "I don't mean to offend you." She seemed to think
that using a disclaimer like "I don't mean to offend you" somehow made
her behavior acceptable. In this case, like many others, the supervisor
focused on the intent of her comment, while the student had to deal with
the impact. Disclaimers may make a perpetrator feel better about themselves, but it certainly does not lessen the harm to students. In fact, such
disclaimers can make it even harder for women of color to respond to
microaggressions. Many scholars have actually written about the ways
that disclaimers (about not being racist or sexist) offer a vehicle for individuals to perpetrate oppression (Bonilla-Silva, 2006; Harris, Palazzolo &
Savage, 2012; Van Dijk, Ting-Toomey & Smitherman, 1997). When perpetrators say, "I don't mean to sound racist or sexist," it makes it difficult
for women of color to label a comment as offensive. In fact, harm can be
exacerbated by such disclaimers. When disclaimed comments are challenged, women of color are often charged with being overly sensitive
(Cullen, 2008; Sue, 2010a). Such deflections take the onus off the perpetrator and compound harm to individuals dealing with the initial microag-

gression as well as a backlash from confronting a perpetrator who used the disclaimer.

I'M NOT A CRIMINAL

One common theme in microaggression taxonomies is the assumption of criminal status of people of color (Sue et al., 2007; Sue 2010b). Research has shown that this manifestation is especially salient for Black and Latino men (Hwang & Goto, 2009; Solórzano et al., 2000). However, women of color in Sister Stories also described unfair treatment by campus police officers who assumed they were doing something wrong. In one focus group, students had a lengthy discussion about how White sororities and fraternities were treated differently by campus police than organizations for women of color. They also described campus administrators taking no action while Greek organizations had dangerous, raging parties. Sometimes, campus police even escorted drunk White students home as a courtesy. In stark contrast, alcohol-free dances held in the student union by organizations made up of women of color were required to have a security guard on duty for the duration of the event. Those guards and campus police officers did not offer courtesy escorts. Instead, they verbally harassed men and women of color and followed them to make sure they did not damage university property or engage in other disruptive actions as they left the party.

> **Laura**: It's just crazy. Last fall semester they let one of the fraternities have a full-blown house party. Like a crazy party. There are cops at the end to escort people home.

> **Diana**: I've never seen anything like this in my life. Literally, someone could have died.

> **Nicole**: Greek life has a party every single day of the week.

> **Laura**: And our party? We have to end our party at one o'clock with security. We get yelled at [by police and security]. Get the fuck outta here. Like go home. . . . Go to your dorms. Then, they follow us down to our dorms to make sure we aren't breaking windows. They don't realize how racist they are. The fraternity had a full-blown party— there was like 250 people on campus. It was right across from a residence hall. Right on campus! Like, no ID [was required to drink]. No pat down. Students walk right in, walk right out. Back and forth, back and forth, all night long. Weed, liquor, sexual activities.

Women of color understood they were treated by police as potential criminals, even when they were doing nothing wrong. They also recognized White student organizations were never treated like criminals. As such, women of color felt like targets for the police.

When she was alone or in small groups of friends, Jewel felt targeted by campus police. She knew she was doing nothing wrong, but the fear of police surveillance caused her to refrain from acting like her happy, jovial self. During a focus group conversation about campus police, she shared:

> Police officers? Like, you have to put it in context. . . . I'm a Black woman so I'm gonna speak for myself. I already feel uncomfortable stepping onto this campus at times because I'm the only one or one of the few Black women [on campus]. Now, if, let's say I'm with a group of my friends and . . . I'm really happy to see them. I haven't seen in a long time and I'm yelling and talking loud and doing this [waving her hands in the air]. And somebody tells me that they called the cops because I was being too loud. . . . I'm not doing anything wrong, am I? I'm not gonna feel comfortable [on campus], you know?

Assuming criminal status or unsavory intentions of women of color was not reserved solely for campus police. In Jewel's case, the police were called by someone who felt she was doing something wrong simply because her volume and animated body language were considered outside the norm. In microaggression taxonomies, scholars refer to this form of oppression as pathologizing someone's communication style (Sue, 2010a, 2010b; Sue et al., 2007).

Many women of color shared instances where White peers behaved in ways that reflected fear of people of color or assumptions about their criminal intent. Sometimes White students crossed the street to avoid walking near students of color. Elsy was stunned and saddened when her first White campus roommate admitted to harboring fears about women of color.

> I would say the first time I actually experienced a microaggression . . . was the first time I actually came to [campus]. My freshman year roommate, she was quick to judge me by my looks. [After a couple of weeks] she was like "I was so scared of you. I just didn't know what to expect." And, I was just like, "huh, ok."

Assumptions about the criminal nature of people of color pervaded every aspect of academe—even activities that took place off campus. Ana experienced microaggressions at her academic internship. To better understand how things worked, she asked a legitimate technical question. Instead of getting an educational response from her site supervisor, the answer was filled with assumptions of criminality of people of color. Ana explained:

> I'm interning at the prison and they are having a problem with drugs inside the prison. When I asked [my supervisor], "How do they manage to get this in?"—her automatic answer was, "We have all these new

minority staff. They probably went to school with these guys or grew up being their best friends, so that's probably why." I didn't know how to respond, I was just like wait. It left me speechless. I didn't expect that from her. [Then she continued to say] "We had to lower the [hiring] standards, so we can let all these minorities in and that's probably the reason why we are having such a big drug problem." She could have easily just said, "It's probably the staff who have more contact with the inmates," but she had to narrow it down to the minority staff . . . I was just like, [sarcastically] "Whoa. Wow. We're dangerous indeed."

As Ana learned, assumptions of criminality were impossible to escape, even off campus.

THEY EXPECT LESS FROM ME

Students come to a university to learn. Unfortunately, women of color regularly encountered teachers and peers across the educational pipeline, who assumed they were not smart or capable of succeeding. This experience aligns with the microaggression taxonomy category regarding assumptions of inferiority (Capodilupo et al., 2010; Sue, 2010b; Sue et al., 2007). Despite the fact that they were admitted to a selective research institution, a number of students talked about high school teachers and guidance counselors who suggested they enroll in community college. Once they arrived at the research university, women of color found faculty, academic advisors, and classmates harbored low expectations of them.

Students like Kendra explained how White peers and faculty assumed she was in the special bridge program for conditionally admitted students. The assumption was rooted in the stereotype that students of color were not academically capable of being admitted to the research university through traditional admission processes. Kendra explained, "Becoming a student on this campus, I was automatically assumed to be a [bridge program] student because I am from . . . Cape Verdean descent. Don't get me wrong, there is nothing wrong with that [bridge program], but [people's assumptions] never allowed me to portray my own identity." In this case, Kendra explained how the assumptions of academic inferiority kept people from seeing the real her.

Others shared vignettes of classroom microaggressions perpetrated by faculty and peers rooted in assumptions about their intellectual inferiority. Elena explained:

> Some teachers I can tell they're racist. They just treat the White people better. They hold them to a higher standard than minorities. . . . They call like on just White students because they want to hear what they have to say. . . . If I was to raise my hand they wouldn't call on me because [they assume] what I had to say wouldn't be right.

Fola also shared an instance where a professor clearly expected less from her. She explained:

> My writing teacher, she set my standards *so* low. Like my first paper with the class, she said, "Oh, you did really well." I got an 85. I was like, "That's not [a great grade]." She disagreed with me. . . . She always worked with us one-on-one and I would always be the last person. She would always like doubt me and [say comments like] "I don't think you're going to do too well on this assignment." She would *always* doubt me, and I felt like she was just really racist because nobody else in the class [got treated that way]. She would talk so nice to them, but if I did something, she would make an example out of me. She would stop the class and be like "no, no." I just felt like really small in that class. . . . I really felt silenced. It hurt me.

Fola's quote shows the intersections of assumptions of inferiority, a common racial and gender microaggression, (Capodilupo et al., 2010; Sue, 2010b; Sue et al., 2007), with being silenced—a manifestation of second-class citizenship and invisibility for women of color (Capodilupo, et al., 2010; Domingue, 2015; Vaccaro, 2016; Wing, 2003).

In a paper, Lucy also reflected on the hurtful effects of low expectations and offensive comments made by a White math teacher.

> A fairly older, white, male teacher . . . constantly made racial remarks and derogatory comments in class which made all of his students of color feel less than what they were. I would try so hard to learn the formulas and concepts that he taught in class, but my scores on tests and quizzes were not high. One day, he told me that it was ok, that girls like me always seem to struggle. I did not know what he was saying at the time, but I just knew that I didn't like the comment. I started to believe what he said about girls like myself and wouldn't see any improvement in my scores. It wasn't until my mother sat me down one day and told me that if I didn't believe in myself and do whatever it was I had to do to pass this class, I was not going to graduate.

Luckily, Lucy's mother intervened and helped her learn that she was smart. She inspired Lucy to have faith in herself, even if the professor did not. Unfortunately, other women of color in Sister Stories were not so lucky. Quite a few admitted to internalizing the subtle (and not so subtle) messages of inferiority conveyed by peers and professors. Internalizing oppression is a damaging psychological process whereby people from historically marginalized backgrounds begin to believe the dominant ideologies perpetuated by society about people like them (David, 2013). We delve more deeply into internalized oppression in chapters 6 and 7.

When Suzanna compared her educational preparation to that of her White and male classmates, she concluded, "I feel like they have more knowledge than me, and if I say something, everyone's just quiet and it's awkward so I feel like I'm wrong." Camilla concurred and said, "In a class with predominantly White students . . . I feel like what I'll say isn't as smart or like just isn't good. . . . I just feel like they'll disagree with what I have to say cuz I'm different from them." Lucia also harbored feelings of self-doubt which kept her from speaking out in classes. She said:

> I don't like talking in my other classes. I read. I'm up to date with everything, but because it's all like all White students, I feel like I'm not as smart as them. . . . I feel I'm not articulate. I know the material, but I feel like I'm not as smart as the other students.

In addition to engendering internalized feelings of inferiority, microaggressions also took an educational toll. Fola, Lucy, Camilla, and Lucia's narratives suggested that they often felt silenced because they worried their contributions were "not smart enough." On top of the emotional toll of being treated as less capable and smart, Lauren alluded to educational ramifications of disengaging from classroom conversations.

> Well, basically it just secludes people in wanting to engage in conversations. Or, if they have any questions, like it kind of makes people feel degraded. If I were to ask questions, they are obviously going to expect for me . . . not to know anything. And so it just kind of makes you not reach your limit because you just kind of step back and take in an observer [role] rather than like, being more hands-on and involved with those around you.

As Lauren argued, women of color who were degraded and silenced by microaggressions of assumed academic inferiority sometimes missed out on valuable educational opportunities.

I'M NOT WELCOME HERE

Women of color shared many stories of being ignored and excluded in study groups, sororities, the library, student union, and other spaces on campus. While the microaggressions took place in different campus spaces and with different people, the impact was the same—students received the message that they were not welcome at the university.

Bonnie consistently felt excluded from classroom work groups. When students were allowed to self-select into project teams, she was left out by the White students. As the only person of color in the classroom, she could not help but wonder if her exclusion was because of her race. Bonnie shared:

> I also feel that the major I'm in, I am always *the* person of color. I mean *always* unless it's an elective! . . . I just feel sometimes excluded in projects. If I don't create a personal relationship with someone in that class, they won't ask me to be part of their project or help them.

To Bonnie, it felt like a burden to be the one to reach out, develop personal relationships, and combat exclusion. Her alternative, though, was to be left out of working groups. Unfortunately, this type of exclusion is not uncommon for women of color. In fact, Charleston, Adserias, Lang, and Jackson (2014) found women of color were not only excluded by White peers; men of color also did not invite them to partner on laboratory experiments.

Many women of color talked about feeling unwelcome in predominantly White sororities on campus. In order to recruit new members, sororities would set up information tables in high-traffic areas of the student union or campus dining hall. As women walked by, sorority members would say hello, hand out flyers, and invite students to consider rushing their sorority. As they walked by the tables, women of color were treated as if they were invisible—a common form of microaggression for women of color (Capodilupo et al., 2010; Domingue, 2015; Vaccaro, 2016). White students who passed behind or in front of women of color were invited to join. Women of color got the message: you do not belong in predominantly White sororities. Lucy explained:

> They don't stop or even look at the minority kids. I don't know if I'd feel better even if they would just be like, "Well, hi." They don't even look at you—like you don't exist. You walk by as if you're invisible. So, it just makes you feel ten times worse, because you already know that they aren't going to ask you to join. Or if you want to join, to be honest, they'd say no.

As described earlier, primary and secondary appraisal (Lazarus & Folkman, 1984) and attributional ambiguity (Sue, 2010b; Sue et al., 2007) are ever-present psychological challenges for women of color. While most students were confident that being ignored by White sorority sisters was a form of overt exclusion, others were not so sure. Jocelyn and her friend tested out their hunch to make sure it was oppression. Initially Jocelyn did not notice the microaggression. However, her friend, who was interested in joining, did notice. Jocelyn said:

> They had a blue table set up and you know they were trying to get women to sign up for rush week. We literally walked by and [my friend was] looking at the table [because] she wanted to join a sorority. They completely ignored us. She's like, "No they're not ignoring us. She grabbed my hand [and made me] sit down [at a table down the hallway where we could see the sorority table]. She's like, "I want to see if it's just me or are they really just ignoring me cause I'm Spanish." So, we sat down. We see them looking at people of color come by and ignore them. Right behind the group [of women of color] . . . were three White girls. [The sorority sisters said,] "Hi," and told them what sorority they were and the [rush meeting] time. [My friend exclaimed,] "See! I knew it!" She's like, "Because I'm Spanish they didn't ask me to join

and I really wanted to join. I heard good things about them, but I'm not going to join them now. Because I'm Spanish I can't be in their group."

Instances of exclusion in other campus spaces also sent the message that women of color were not welcome. Hanna shared:

> One time in the library, it was me and a group of my African American friends. We wanted to get a seat in the library to study and stuff and [there was] a group of White girls sitting in one place. So, we picked the table [near] where they were sitting. I noticed they just packed their stuff and went somewhere else.

This was not an isolated incident. Many women of color in Sister Stories described similar forms of exclusion. For instance, Julianna resigned herself to being alone and feeling excluded in predominantly White classrooms. She said, "nobody wants to sit next to me. I'll sit in the front in the corner by myself." We delve more deeply into feelings of isolation and discuss the importance of counterspaces in the next chapter.

OBJECTIFICATION: I AM NOT A FOOD, NOR AM I NASTY

Microaggressions aimed at women of color often include objectification—which is the process of dehumanizing people by reducing them to objects. Women of color reported being objectified by white peers and faculty members. Bonnie shared a story about an art professor making a comment that devalued her work, sexualized her, compared her to food, and minimized positive feedback about her art. Bonnie said:

> I was sharing some of my work. One of the [White] students always compliments my work. . . . He goes "I always like your work. You always have something good to show." And the teacher said, "Why is that? Do you like chocolate ice cream too?" And the whole class . . . went really tense. . . . The kid who had said something to me about liking my pictures, he was just really shocked. The teacher kind of just chuckled and went on with the class. I was so angry and shocked. . . . In my head, I was like, "Are you serious?" Being compared to chocolate ice cream? Why? Like I think it would have been less awkward if she even just said, "Oh do you have a crush on her?" You know? Comparing me to a food? She didn't have to say that. He likes my pictures. That's it! It has nothing to do with who I am— it's my creativity and it's the product I show. . . It's just crazy. I've never experienced a teacher or never noticed a teacher saying something *so* like —I don't even know if I would call it racist but ignorant, saying something really ignorant and thinking that it's ok to say.

In this case, the instructor likened Bonnie to food. The professor also turned an academic critique into an uncomfortable sexual situation whereby Bonnie was exoticized as a potential love interest. The professor's comment shows the power of intersecting racial (chocolate ice cream) and gender (sexualizing women) objectification.

Jocelyn was painfully aware of sexually objectifying images of Black women as hypersexual beings (hooks, 1984, 2000; Harris-Perry, 2011; Hill Collins, 1991, 2000). To resist such stereotypes, Jocelyn stopped telling people her major and career interests.

> I want to be a teen advocate. . . . When I tell people . . . sex therapy is my major, I automatically get categorized as this freak. Like [people think or say,] "You just want sex all the time. You're so nasty." I'm like, allow me to get out what I want to get out and tell you what I want to do with it before you guys put me into a little box. . . . Black women are [assumed to be] nasty automatically. That's what I get when I tell people. There was a point when I didn't even tell people that was my major. . . . I didn't even wanna go into detail, because I didn't want to be categorized as this nasty Black girl.

Her experience affirms the contemporary relevance of decades-old writings by Hill Collins (1991), who named "the Jezebel, whore, or sexually aggressive woman" as common stereotypes used to degrade women of color (p. 77).

Carolina named a host of stereotypical portrayals of women of color for what it was: oppression. During a focus group, she lamented the narrow images of women of color she was constantly judged against. She said: "Another thing that bothers me when women of color are [portrayed] . . . as overly sexual, meaning that women of color are more sexually active than other women." These quotes show that controlling images of women of color continue to shape the realities of contemporary college students of color (Hill Collins, 1991, 2000). In sum, women of color experienced microaggressions that reduced them to food and portrayed them as hypersexual beings—an all too common manifestation of oppression for women of color (hooks, 1984, 2000; Harris-Perry, 2011; Hill Collins, 1991, 2000).

CONCLUSION

In this chapter, we provided a brief overview of the microaggression literature, paying special attention to the attribution process and studies conducted on college campuses. Then, we explicated the complex attribution process of microaggression appraisal. Student narratives showed how common it was for them to engage in the psychologically taxing process of wondering: "Did that just happen?" and then deciding if, and how, to respond. The heart of the chapter included student narratives regarding five types of subtle (and not so subtle) microaggressions in classrooms, residence halls, student union, Greek life, campus jobs, and internships. The cumulative impact of microaggressions in these campus microclimates sent the message that women of color were not welcome at the university. Such a finding aligns with a lengthy history of scholarship about hostile campus climates and environmental microaggressions experienced by women and students of color (Davis, 2004; Feagin, Vera & Imani, 1996; Fleming, 1983; Hall & Sandler, 1984; Harper, 2008; Howard-Hamilton, Morelon-Quainoo, Johnson, Winkle-Wagner & Santiague, 2009; Hurtado, 2002; Vaccaro, 2010, 2012, 2014; Watson, Terrell & Wright, 2002).

Sister Stories students were overtly and covertly excluded from study groups and extra-curricular activities, treated like criminals, and subjected to ignorant, rude, and stereotypical comments and jokes. Students sometimes disengaged from educational endeavors because they did not want to reinforce stereotypes about assumed academic inferiority or hypersexuality. As Lauren so eloquently conveyed, lack of engagement "makes you not reach your limit." Every student deserves the opportunity to learn in supportive environments where they can reach their full potential. Student narratives affirmed that the psychologically and educationally harmful effects of microaggressions can be hurdles for students trying to "reach their limit." Drawing upon our CRT and CRF theoretical foundations, we contend women of color received an unequal educational experience because of these microaggressions. Moreover, the narratives shared in this chapter highlight the pervasiveness of oppression within a system of higher education and the corresponding need for counterspaces where students could feel safe, valued, and affirmed.

REFERENCES

Ackelsberg, M., Hart, J., Miller, N. J., Queeny, K., & Van Dyne, S. (2009). Faculty microclimate change at Smith College. In W. Brown-Glaude (Ed.), *Doing diversity in higher education: Faculty leaders share challenges and strategies* (pp. 83–102). New Brunswick, NJ: Rutgers University Press.

Billig, M. (2001). Humor and hatred: The racist jokes of the Ku Klux Klan. *Discourse & Society, 12*(3), 267–89.

Blume, A. W., Lovato, L. V., Thyken, B. N., & Denny, N. (2012). The relationship of microaggressions with alcohol use and anxiety among ethnic minority college students in a historically White institution. *Cultural Diversity and Ethnic Minority Psychology, 18*(1), 45.

Bonilla-Silva E. (2006). *Racism without racists: Color-blind racism and the persistence of racial inequality in the United States*. Lanham, MD: Rowman & Littlefield.

Brondolo, E., Rieppi, R., Kelly, K. P., & Gerin, K. W. (2003). Perceived racism and blood pressure: A review of the literature and conceptual methodological critique. *Annals of Behavioral Medicine, 25*, 55–65.

Burdsey, D. (2011). That joke isn't funny anymore: Racial microaggressions, color-blind ideology and the mitigation of racism in English men's first-class cricket. *Sociology of Sport Journal, 28*(3), 261–83.

Capodilupo, C. M., Nadal, K. L., Corman, L., Hamit, S., Lyons, O. B., & Weinberg, A. (2010). The manifestation of gender microaggressions. In D. W. Sue (Ed.), *Microaggressions and marginality: Manifestation, dynamics, and impact* (pp. 193–216). Hoboken, NJ: Wiley.

Carter, R. T. (2007). Racism and psychological and emotional injury: Recognizing and assessing race-based traumatic stress. *The Counseling Psychologist, 35*(1), 13–105.

Charleston, L., Adserias, R., Lang, N., & Jackson, J. (2014). Intersectionality and STEM: The role of race and gender in the academic pursuits of African American women in STEM. *Journal of Progressive Policy & Practice, 2*(3), 273–93.

Crenshaw, K. (1989). Demarginalizing the intersection of race and sex: A Black feminist critique of antidiscrimination doctrine, feminist theory and antiracist politics. *University of Chicago Legal Forum,* 139–67.

Cullen, M. (2008). *35 dumb things well-intended people say: Surprising things we say that widen the diversity gap.* Garden City, NJ: Morgan James.

David, E. J. R. (2013). *Internalized oppression: The psychology of marginalized groups.* New York: Springer.

Domingue, A. D. (2015). "Our leaders are just we ourself": Black women college student leaders' experiences with oppression and sources of nourishment on a predominantly white college campus. *Equity & Excellence in Education, 48*(3), 454–72.

Feagin, J. R., Vera, H., & Imani, N. (1996). *The agony of education: Black students at white colleges and universities.* New York: Routledge.

Fleming, J. (1983). Black women in Black and White college environments: The making of a matriarch. *Journal of Social Issues, 39*(3), 41–54.

Folkman, S., & Lazarus, R. S. (1988). Coping as a mediator of emotion. *Journal of Personality and Social Psychology, 54,* 466–75.

Ford, T., Woodzicka, J. A., Triplett, S. R., & Kochersberger, A. O. (2013). Sexist humor and beliefs that justify societal sexism. *Current Research Social Psychology,* 64–81.

Fredrickson, B. L., & Roberts, T. A. (1997). Objectification theory. *Psychology of Women Quarterly, 21*(2), 173–206.

Gildersleeve, R. E., Croom, N. N., & Vasquez, P. L. (2011). "Am I going crazy?!": A critical race analysis of doctoral education. *Equity & Excellence in Education, 44*(1), 93–114.

Hall, R. M., & Sandler, B. R. (1984). *Out of the classroom: A chilly climate for women?* Washington, DC: Association of American Colleges, Project on the Status and Education of Women.

Harper, S. R. (Ed.) (2008). *Creating inclusive campus environments for cross-cultural learning and student engagement.* Washington, DC: NASPA.

Harris, K. L., Palazzolo, K. E., & Savage, M. W. (2012). "I'm not sexist, but . . .": How ideological dilemmas reinforce sexism in talk about intimate partner violence. *Discourse & Society, 23*(6), 643–56.

Harris-Perry, M. V. (2011). *Sister citizen: Shame, stereotypes, and Black women in America.* New Haven, CT: Yale University Press.

Hill Collins, P. (1991, 2000). *Black feminist thought: Knowledge, consciousness, and the politics of empowerment.* New York: Routledge.

hooks, b. (1981). *Ain't I a woman: Black women and feminism.* Cambridge MA: South End.

——— (1984, 2000). *Feminist theory: From margin to center.* Cambridge MA: South End.

Howard-Hamilton, M. L., Morelon-Quainoo, C. L., Johnson, S. D., Winkle-Wagner, R., & Santiague, L. (Eds.) (2009). *Standing on the outside looking in: Underrepresented students' experiences in advanced degree programs.* Sterling, VA: Stylus.

Hurtado, S. (2002). Creating a climate of inclusion: Understanding Latina/o college students. In W. A. Smith, P. G. Altback & K. Lomotey (Eds.), *The racial crisis in American higher education: Continuing challenges for the twenty-first century* (rev. ed., pp.121–36). New York: State University of New York Press.

Hwang, W. C., & Goto, S. (2009). The impact of perceived racial discrimination on the mental health of Asian American and Latino college students. *Asian American Journal of Psychology, S*(1), 15–28.

Kaiser, C. R., & Miller, C. T. (2004). A stress and coping perspective on confronting sexism. *Psychology of Women Quarterly, 28*(2), 168–78.

Lazarus, R. S., & Folkman, S. (1984). *Stress, appraisal, and coping.* New York: Springer.

Lewis, J. A., Mendenhall, R., Harwood, S. A., & Browne Huntt, M. (2013). Coping with gendered racial microaggressions among Black women college students. *Journal of African American Studies, 17*(1), 51–73.

Lorde, A. (1984). *Sister outsider*. Trumansberg, NY: The Crossing Press.

McCabe, J. (2009). Racial and gender microaggressions on a predominantly White campus: Experiences of Black, Latina/o and White undergraduates. *Race, Gender and Class, 16*, 133–51.

McGee, E. O., & Martin, D. B. (2011). "You would not believe what I have to go through to prove my intellectual value!" Stereotype management among academically successful Black mathematics and engineering students. *American Educational Research Journal, 48*(6), 1347–89.

Minikel-Lacocque, J. (2012). Racism, college, and the power of words: Racial microaggressions reconsidered. *American Educational Research Journal, 50*(3), 432–65.

Nadal, K. L., Davidoff, K. C., Davis, L. S., Wong, Y., Marshall, D., & McKenzie, V. (2015). A qualitative approach to intersectional microaggressions: Understanding influences of race, ethnicity, gender, sexuality, and religion. *Qualitative Psychology, 2*(2), 147.

Nadal, K. L., Wong, Y., Griffin, K. E., Davidoff, K., & Sriken, J. (2014). The adverse impact of racial microaggressions on college students' self-esteem. *Journal of College Student Development, 55*(5), 461–74.

Perna, L. W. (2010a). Understanding the working college student. *Academe, 96*(4), 30–33.

——— (2010b). *Understanding the working college student: New research and its implications for policy and practice*. Herndon, VA: Stylus.

Pierce, C. (1974). Psychiatric problems of the Black minority. In S. Arieti (Ed.), *American Handbook of Psychiatry* (pp. 512–23). New York: Basic Books.

Rankin, S., & Reason, R. (2008). Transformational tapestry model: A comprehensive approach to transforming campus climate. *Journal of Diversity in Higher Education, 1*(4), 262–74.

Ryan, K. M., & Kanjorski, J. (1998). The enjoyment of sexist humor, rape attitudes, and relationship aggression in college students. *Sex Roles, 38*(9–10), 743–56.

Sartre, J. P. (1948). *Portrait of the anti-Semite*. London, England: Secker & Warburg.

Shah, S. (Ed.) (1997). *Dragon ladies: Asian American feminists breathe fire*. Boston, MA: South End.

Smith, W. A., Allen, W. R., & Danley, L. L. (2007). Assume the position . . .You fit the description: Psychological experiences and racial battle fatigue among African American male college students. *American Behavioral Scientist, 51*(4), 551–78.

Solórzano , D. J., Ceja, M., & Yosso, T. J. (2000). Critical race theory, racial microaggressions, and campus racial climate: The experiences of African American college students . *The Journal of Negro Education, 69*(1/2), 60–73.

Strayhorn, T. L. (2008). The burden of proof: A quantitative study of high-achieving Black collegians. *Journal of African American Studies, 13*(4), 375–87.

Suarez-Orozco, C., Casanova, S., Martin, M., Katsiaficas, D., Cuellar, V., Smith, N., & Dias, S. (2015). Toxic rain in class: Classroom interpersonal microaggressions. *Educational Researcher, 44*(3), 151–60.

Sue, D. W. (Ed.) (2010a). *Microaggressions and marginality: Manifestations, dynamics and impact*. Hoboken, NJ: Wiley.

——— (2010b). *Microaggressions in everyday life: Race, gender and sexual orientation*. Hoboken, NJ: Wiley.

———, Capodilupo, C. M., & Holder, A. M. B. (2008). Racial microaggressions in the life experience of Black Americans. *Professional Psychology: Research and Practice, 39*(3), 329–36.

———, Capodilupo, C. M., Torino, G. C., Bucceri, J. M., Holder, A. M. B., Nadal, K. L., & Esquilin, M. (2007). Racial microaggressions in everyday life: Implications for clinical practice. *American Psychologist, 62*, 271–86.

Vaccaro, A. (in press). *"Trying to act like racism is not there":* Women of color at a predominantly White women's college challenging dominant ideologies by exposing racial microaggressions. *The Journal About Women in Higher Education.*

—— (2010). What lies beneath seemingly positive campus climate results: Institutional sexism, symbolic racism, and male hostility toward equity initiatives. *Equity and Excellence in Education, 43*(2), 202–15.

—— (2012). Campus microclimates for LGBT faculty, staff, and students: An exploration of the intersections of social identity and campus roles. *Journal of Student Affairs Research and Practice, 44*(4), 429–46.

—— (2014). Campus climate for diversity: Current realities and suggestions for the future. *Texas Education Review, 2*(1), 129–37.

Van Dijk, T. A., Ting-Toomey, S., & Smitherman G. (1997). Discourse, ethnicity, culture and racism. In T. A. Van Dijk (Ed.), *Discourse as Social Interaction* (pp. 144–80). London, England: Sage.

Watson, L., Terrell, M. C., Wright, D., & Associates (2002). *How minority students experience college: Implications for planning and policy.* Sterling, VA: Stylus.

Wing, A. K. (2003). *Critical race feminism: A reader* (2nd ed.). New York: New York University Press.

Wolf, N. (1991, 2002). *The beauty myth: How images of beauty are used against women.* New York: Harper Collins.

Yosso, T., Smith, W., Ceja, M., & Solórzano, D. (2009). Critical race theory, racial microaggressions, and campus climate for Latina/o undergraduates. *Harvard Educational Review, 79*(4), 659–69.

THREE

What Are Counterspaces and Why Do We Need Them?

"It's a refuge on campus."

While critiques of U.S. educational systems abound, they often focus on topics such as standardized testing, the nutritional content of school lunches, or safety. With the exception of writings by critical race theory (CRT) and critical race feminist (CRF) scholars (Bergerson, 2003; Gildersleeve, Croom & Vasquez, 2011; Love, 2004; Pérez Huber, 2010; Smith, Yosso & Solórzano, 2007; Solórzano, 1998; Solórzano, Ceja & Yosso, 2000; Yosso, Smith, Ceja & Solórzano, 2009), rarely do we question the privileges upon which American educational systems are founded. Women of color in our study, however, did just that. In this chapter, we convey student perceptions of exclusion in their collegiate environment. We then discuss the concept of counterspaces and use student voices to exemplify the benefits associated with these unique spaces such as: a reprieve from exclusionary educational environments, space to network and build social capital, and environments where validation is fostered.

EXCLUSIONARY EDUCATIONAL SPACES: PRIVILEGE, NORMALCY, DOMINANT IDEOLOGIES

As described in the Introduction, privilege is a set of unearned benefits and advantages afforded to individuals because of a social identity such as race, gender, or social class. Privilege confers dominance, offering some social identity groups (e.g., men, White people) control over the life experiences of those from minoritized social identity groups (e.g., women of color) (Johnson, 2006; McIntosh, 1988). Conferred dominance is embedded in society as systemic advantages that can be gleaned without individuals doing anything intentional.

Privilege is also a vehicle through which people with unearned assets and benefits create and perpetuate dominant ideologies. In fact, the word *dominant* in the phrase dominant ideology refers to the fact that those in powerful positions in society construct and perpetuate messages that become taken for granted realities. Karl Marx and Fredrick Engels described this process as:

> The ideas of the ruling class are in every epoch the ruling ideas, i.e. the class which is the ruling material force of society, is at the same time its ruling intellectual force. The class which has the means of material production at its disposal, has control at the same time over the means of mental production, so that thereby, generally speaking, the ideas of those who lack the means of mental production are subject to it. (Marx & Engels, 1846–1847, as cited in Arthur, 1974, p. 64)

Even though Marx and Engels were referring to oppressive social class ideologies from over a century ago, their emphasis on the ruling class (e.g., those with privilege) controlling mental production is quite similar to contemporary CRT and CRF critiques of dominant ideologies perpetuated by those with privilege (e.g., men, White people). CRT and CRF scholars attempt to debunk and expose dominant ideologies such as colorblindness, meritocracy, and equal opportunity (Bergerson, 2003; Harper, Patton & Wooden, 2009; Pérez Huber, 2010; Solórzano, 1997). Such myths lead people to believe that the educational system is not racist or sexist; failure for women and people of color occurs because students of color and women simply do not work hard enough. As such, the blame for failure is not placed upon systemic inequalities, but individuals who are oppressed by them.

Dominant ideologies about racial and gender equality in U.S. society, and in our educational systems, are hegemonic. Bell (2007) argued: "Through hegemony, a dominant group can so successfully project its particular way of seeing social reality that its view is accepted as common sense, as part of the natural order" (p. 10). Many individuals want to believe dominant ideologies because the alternative—societal inequality—is not something privileged people want to acknowledge. Wise and Case (2013) explained how belief in these myths is a

> psychological necessity for the privileged. After all, to believe that one is the master of one's own destiny allows the perception of control and hope for a better future. To let go of such faith can be difficult, especially for White Americans confronted with evidence of unearned advantages. (p. 21)

One of the characteristics of privilege is normalcy.

The dominant group [e.g., men, Whites] becomes the point of reference against which other groups are judged. It becomes "normal." This standard of normalcy is also used to define what is good and right. . . . Schools are one place where this is evident. (Goodman, 2011, pp. 12–13)

The under-representation of women of color in collegiate environments is an environmental microaggression which contributes to feelings of outsiderness for women of color and a sense of normalcy for White and male students. Anderson (2015) described White spaces as those inhabited or frequented by a majority of White people. In White spaces, people of color are considered out of place. The severe under-representation of people of color enrolled in higher education institutions perpetuates the idea that people of color do not belong. In fact, over the last 20 years the gap between Black and Latino people and Whites attaining a college degree widened (NCES, 2015). In many educational reports, scholars note that Native American people are too few in number to include in statistical comparisons. Thus, they become invisible, which is a common manifestation of systemic racism, especially salient for women of color (Domingue, 2015; Hill Collins, 1991, 2000; Wing, 2003). Moreover, a 2015 report by the College Campaign for College Opportunity debunked the myth (perpetuated in national reports that use race categories) that all Asian American/Pacific Islander (AAPI) students are enrolling and succeeding in higher education. Using data from California, the state with the largest growing AAPI population, *The State of Higher Education in California* (2015) report showed gross disparities among different AAPI ethnic groups in terms of access, academic preparation, and college completion. For instance, Chinese, Indian, Vietnamese, and Japanese students completed college at two to three times the rate of their Laotian, Samoan, and Native Hawaiian peers.

As we have argued throughout *Centering Women of Color in Academic Counterspaces*, intersectionality matters. Looking through the lens of race only tells part of the educational story for women of color. White, Black, and Latina women outnumber men in terms of enrollment on college campuses (NCES, 2015a). Yet, these numbers are misleading. Women of color are under-represented in fields associated with status and high paying occupations such as business (Phelps, 2015) and science, technology, engineering, and math (STEM) (Charleston, Adserias, Lang & Jackson, 2014; NSF, 2014). A recent National Science Foundation report showed differences in STEM majors among men and women, with women opting into softer majors in social sciences, psychology, and biology, while men select majors that often lead to higher paying jobs like engineering, computer sciences, and physics (NSF, 2014). The precise reasons for these disparities are hard to pinpoint. Yet, researchers have documented chilly and hostile campus climates for women of color in higher education settings (Charleston et al., 2014; Phelps, 2015; Vaccaro, 2010). Women of color may leave a post-secondary institution or a major if they regularly experience hostility in their classes.

While Anderson (2015) explained the notion of White space, other scholars have documented a masculine discourse of organizations which is a social framework of hegemonic masculine ideologies, gendered work practices, routines, and norms that privilege the life situations and interests of men (Billing, 2011; Crawford & Mills, 2011; Phelps, 2015; Meyerson & Kolb, 2000). As they navigate the often invisible masculine discourse, women experience chilly climates (Hall & Sandler, 1984, 1991; Vaccaro, 2010), limited access to good advising and research collaboration with faculty (Sadker & Sadker, 1994), and patriarchy in the dissertation process (Wolgemuth & Harbour, 2008). Phelps (2015) found that masculine discourse in an undergraduate business school served as an invisible, but powerful form of oppression diverting women from particular business majors and creating environments rife with subtle forms of hostility and outright sexual harassment. In a qualitative study with Black women in STEM fields, Charleston et al. (2014) found women of color felt excluded by both White students and Black men—highlighting the unique experience of isolation stemming from intersecting oppressions. In sum, campuses are White spaces, replete with masculine discourses that can be exclusionary, hostile, and isolating for women of color.

One way women of color in Sister Stories felt excluded and isolated was by the lack of teachers and role models on campus who shared their social identities. Lucy lamented how infrequently she had the opportunity to learn from women of color:

> I never get to take any classes with Black professors. . . . It would be nice—I mean reassuring, helpful, comforting to know that there are actually women of color in authoritative positions or teacher or whatever positions they hold here. . . . I would love to take classes from them.

Mayra also discussed the absence of faculty of color and the impact it had on her:

> I think that this is also a crucial time in which we are taught race especially when in school. Black people for the most part, myself included, were taught by White people in academics, sports, hospitals, etc. It was hard viewing myself as any of the people I was supposed to look up to because I could not relate to any of them.

Lucy and Mayra certainly learned about race in school—but this education was by and about White people. They could not see themselves in the curriculum, nor could they envision themselves as leaders in education. Critical race feminists have long argued women of color are often treated as if they are invisible (hooks, 1981; Collins, 1998; Vaccaro &

Mena, in press; Wing, 2003). Students like Lucy and Myra recognized the lack of visibility of women of color in higher education and described the impact this form of exclusion had on them as learners.

Students of color in Sister Stories described feeling out of place in most educational settings. Often the only woman of color, Diana felt pressure to adapt to masculine discourses and White standards. Moreover, she felt the added burden of putting White people around her at ease. Diana explained:

> When I step into a college classroom I realize that every time I walk in, I am a woman of color. . . . We have to live our lives according to White standards. . . . It's so aggravating always having to be the adapter. It's just annoying. Why do I always have to make sure that all the White people around me are comfortable when they don't have to see through the same lens that I have to see through; it's that dual perspective.

Diana ended her quote with a reference to a dual perspective. In 1903, W.E.B. DuBois wrote about the concept of double consciousness. Double consciousness is a strategy used by people of color to reconcile living in two cultures. Women of color had to adopt a double consciousness to navigate White educational spaces while maintaining a sense of their cultural identity. Such a process is never easy. Lena experienced the tension when "trying to maintain [my] cultural identity in a White society. It is not easy to integrate the two."

White students do not need to adopt a double consciousness because they are the "norm" in predominantly White environments. They have the privilege of seeing their lives and perspectives reflected in the curriculum and the people (e.g., peers, faculty, staff) in the educational space. Moreover, Whites can be unaware of their own privilege or the ways normalcy affects women of color. In fact, only when they find themselves in a setting where they are the numerical minority do some men and White students begin to think about how their worldview and interactions are shaped by privilege and normalcy. Emily was one of two White women in her Sister Stories course. She admitted:

> I never really recognized it until I took this class. . . . Wow—there are really no people of color in [my other classes]. I never recognized that before. . . . When I first walked into this class . . . I only saw the other obviously Caucasian girl. . . . I'm not use to being a minority.

Andrew had a similar experience as the only White man to enroll in Sister Stories. He admitted, "it was really my first time being the only White person in a classroom setting. . . . It was kind of a culture shock . . . like really scary." In all other educational spaces, Andrew had the privilege of seeing himself represented in the curriculum, teachers, and educational leaders. He was so used to White normalcy (Goodman, 2011) and the masculine discourse (Billing, 2011; Crawford & Mills, 2011; Phelps, 2015;

Meyerson & Kolb, 2000) that it required "being a minority" and "culture shock" for him to realize inequities embedded in educational environments. The bottom line: White students have the privilege of being the "norm" until they take a course like Sister Stories where they become the "only one." They also had the privilege to return to the comfort and "normalness" of White educational spaces after the hour and forty-five-minute Sister Stories class session ended. On the contrary, students of color were forced to navigate White spaces all the time. That is why the Sister Stories counterspace was such a valuable place for women of color.

MY COUNTERSPACE: MY GETAWAY

One of the ways students of color maintain their cultural identities in exclusionary educational spaces is by finding support, affirmation, and similar others in campus counterspaces. To combat isolation created by feeling like the "only one," women of color often seek the refuge of counterspaces (Pérez Huber & Cueva, 2012; Solórzano et al., 2000; Yosso et al., 2009). In counterspaces, people from similar marginalized social identity backgrounds (e.g., race, gender) are the majority. Counterspaces offer students from minoritized backgrounds venues where they can be themselves in the presence of peers who share one or more of their socially marginalized identities. They are unique settings where students from similar social identities can "vent frustrations and cultivate friendships with people who share many of their experiences" (Yosso et al., 2009, p. 677). Harper and Hurtado (2007) described them as "ethnic enclaves that offer shelter from the psycho-emotional harms of racial microaggressions" (p. 14).

The 1954 *Brown v. Board of Education* U.S. Supreme Court decision determined that separate schools for Whites and people of color were not constitutional. As schools (i.e., elementary, secondary, university) began to integrate, they were faced with the reality that students of color experienced prejudice and discrimination from White peers, educators, and administrators. In the early 1960s, multicultural student services offices began to appear on college campuses. Some initial impetuses for those first multicultural centers were to help students of color adjust to predominantly White campuses in the wake of hostility and overt racism, and to address resulting attrition issues (Shuford, 2011; Stewart & Bridges, 2011). In the past three decades, the purpose of multicultural centers has expanded to include supporting students of color, educating the campus community about issues of diversity, and leading university-wide inclusion efforts (Shuford, 2011).

While CRT and CRF scholars focus on racial counterspaces, they can be created for members of any minoritized social identity group. Historically, women's, ethnic, queer, and other identity-based classes have been sites of social justice resistance, identity exploration, empowerment, and healing for members of minoritized social identity groups (Butler & Walter, 1991; Nuñez, 2011; Yosso et al., 2009). As such, they can be considered academic counterspaces. Literature read by students in women's, queer, and ethnic studies classes highlights the untold history of women, LGBTQ people, and people of color. Such courses offer counterstories that expose the fallacies of dominant ideologies. In counterspaces like Sister Stories, first-person accounts of resiliency and resistance by women of color were affirming for students—especially given the pervasiveness of White normalcy and the masculine discourse in higher education. Academic counterspaces, like Sister Stories, can engender feelings of belonging, empowerment, and resiliency (Pérez Huber & Cueva, 2012). Smith (2009) argued that it is often in academic counterspaces like "ethnic and women's studies where students feel that they matter" (p. 219). Sister Stories was intended to be a validating academic counterspace for women of color. Student narratives suggest they found the classroom to be so.

Sister Stories was described as a refuge by many women of color. It was a place to find connection after experiencing the "culture shock" of coming to a predominantly White co-educational campus—especially for students who attended racially diverse high schools. Mindy explained:

> They get here and they're like, "Oh this is definitely a culture shock." This one course (Sister Stories) [is] one little zone for them to kind of feel comfortable. It's kind of sad to see that it's only one course . . . for women of color. . . . It's a step in the right direction, but I think there's a lot more that can be done.

Mindy's quote suggests she was thankful for Sister Stories. It was an academic counterspace where women of color could feel comfortable. While the counterspace was appreciated, she wished there were more counterspaces on campus instead of merely "one little [Sister Stories] zone."

Women of color perceived Sister Stories to be a very different learning environment than all of their other educational experiences. Ana contrasted the Sister Stories counterspace with the rest of the university.

> In my four years here . . . this has been the first class where I have been surrounded by so many students from different ethnicities. It had become the norm for me to step in a classroom in which I was the only woman of color.

Because Sister Stories was a unique counterspace unshrouded by White normalcy and the masculine discourse, women of color expressed excitement about coming to class. While Bonnie was tempted to skip her other classes, she never wanted to miss Sister Stories. The counterspace was such a valuable educational experience, even with the hefty workload, she would rather walk in late than miss the class altogether. Bonnie shared:

> I didn't feel outside in this classroom. This is my favorite class—even though the work load was a lot .. . . I tried not to miss any class even though I would come late sometimes. I was comfortable in this class.

Camilla described Sister Stories as her "getaway" from White normalcy and the discomfort other classes caused her.

> I felt comfortable being in this class because it's like so many minorities in here that you don't really see in a regular class. . . . It was kind of my getaway [from] all my other classes that are predominantly White.

When women of color compared Sister Stories to other courses, they juxtaposed feelings of isolation with comfort. Elena was much more comfortable speaking up in the counterspace than other courses.

> When I'm in a class full of predominantly White students, I won't talk at all just because I don't feel comfortable. Because I feel like if I would say something I would be judged. Or, like you know what I mean? Not up to their standards. Or, they have different views as me. And when I'm in this classroom . . . I just felt a lot more comfortable.

Elena's feeling of being judged alludes to White and male standards possibly rooted in microaggressions of assumed inferiority (Sue, 2010a, 2010b; Sue et al., 2007). It also aligns with critical literature suggesting a common experience for women of color is being silenced (Domingue, 2015; Hill Collins, 1991, 2000; Wing, 2003). To Becca, and many of her peers, the Sister Stories counterspace offered reprieve from microaggressions of assumed inferiority:

> Being the only minority in [other] classes . . . I always have to prove myself. . . . I just like how comfortable this class really made me feel. It was kind of like a stress relief because I didn't have to play that role. I didn't have to go out of my way to make sure [I was seen as competent].

When Becca talked about playing a role, she was referring to the pressure to adapt and assimilate to White and male normalcy. For decades, scholars have shown how assimilation by people of color can lead to negative outcomes such as higher risks of delinquency and substance abuse (Greenman & Xie, 2008; Nagasawa, Qian & Wong, 2001; Zhou & Bankston, 1998). By contrast, attachments to one's country of origin and cultural group can promote positive well-being (Schwartz, Waterman, Umaña-Taylor, Lee, Kim, Vazsonyi & Zamboanga, 2013). Sister Stories was a place where students were encouraged to honor, explore, and share their cultural backgrounds. As such, Becca felt less pressure to assimilate and prove herself in Sister Stories. Carolina did too. She said:

> My other classes were overwhelming because I feel like if you say something as a minority, they're looking at you like: "Is she really speaking? She's not going to say anything intelligent or she's not going to say the right answer." In this class it's like relaxed because you can actually be yourself and you can speak your mind more easily.

Carolina's quote shows the emotional taxation students feel in White educational spaces compared to the comfort of an academic counterspace like Sister Stories.

When White and male privilege is taken for granted, diversity topics like race, gender, and sexual orientation become special or unique issues instead of an unquestioned aspect of the standard curriculum. As such, many professors include diversity as a topic for a single class session instead of infusing diversity into every aspect of a course (Vaccaro, 2016). When conversations about diversity topics (i.e., race, gender, sexual orientation) do happen, students who hold those social identities are often tokenized. Kanter (1977a, 1977b) explained how women, who are underrepresented in male-dominated work settings, often experience heightened visibility and greater scrutiny. Their limited presence can be viewed as a token or perfunctory gesture toward inclusion.

One of the byproducts of tokenization is that women and people of color experience heightened visibility. They are also subject to the assumption that all members of minoritized social identity groups (i.e., gender, race) are alike. As a result, they are often tokenized by being asked to represent, or speak for, everyone who shares their social identity. For instance, women are sometimes asked to give a women's point of view. People of color are asked to give a Black, Latino, Asian, or Native American perspective on a topic. Because people in a counterspace typically share at least one minoritized identity, students can find a reprieve from tokenism. Sister Stories was one of the few educational spaces where women of color were not expected to speak on behalf of their race or gender. Nicole explained how she was not tokenized as a woman of color in Sister Stories, but she was in most other classes:

> Often, for my major, when diversity comes up, everyone looks at me and asks me: "What do you have to say?" . . . I have to speak for my race. . . . It was nice that in this course when we spoke about diversity—it's all we spoke about. I wasn't expected to speak for my race. It was my favorite class.

Nicole was passionate about topics of diversity. However, she dreaded diversity discussions in White educational spaces where she was tokenized. Jewel concurred and said "it gets tiring" to always have to speak for her race. Men of color enrolled in Sister Stories also agreed the course was a safe counterspace where they felt a reprieve from racial tokenism. Brian explained:

> Usually I hate talking about anything that has to do with Black history or culture in my classes because the students are predominantly White and I'm the token Black person. That's not the case in this class. The diversity makes me feel more comfortable to open up and share.

In the Sister Stories counterspace, women (and men) of color got a break from the pervasive forms of racial tokenization prevalent in most White educational spaces. However, as we will describe in chapter 4, women sometimes experienced gendered racism, in the form of tokenization and objectification, when men of color were present in the counterspace. Most often, however, women of color described the Sister Stories counterspace positively—as a getaway and space to build networks.

COUNTERSPACE VALIDATION AND BELONGING

One of the benefits of counterspaces is that students are surrounded by like others. Compared to feeling like the "only one" in predominantly White and male spaces, women of color felt at home in the Sister Stories counterspace. Learning in the presence of students who share a marginalized identity can be empowering and validating (Rendón, 1994, 1995; Rendón Linares & Muñoz, 2011). Rendón defined validation as "an enabling, confirming, and supportive process initiated by in-class and outside of class agents that fosters academic and personal development" (1994, p. 44). Validation is a process that can be fostered by faculty, family, and peers and can reduce feelings of alienation, outsiderness, or lack of belonging, which are common feelings for minoritized students in exclusionary educational spaces.

Belonging is the "degree to which an individual feels respected, valued, accepted, and needed by a defined group" (Strayhorn, 2012, p. 87). Hurtado and Carter (1997) described belonging as a phenomenon that "captures the individual's view of whether he or she feels included in the college community" (p. 327). Unfortunately, decades of research suggests that feeling comfortable or developing a sense of belonging in higher education institutions may be especially challenging for women and students of color (Hall & Sandler, 1984, 1991; Hurtado & Carter, 1997; Johnson et al., 2007; Locks, Hurtado, Bowman & Oseguera, 2008; Nuñez, 2011; Phelps, 2015; Strayhorn, 2012; Vaccaro, 2010).

Students who experience a sense of belonging, comfort, and validation are more likely to achieve valuable educational outcomes such as academic success (Freeman, Anderman & Jensen, 2007; Strayhorn, 2012), persistence (Hausmann, Schofield & Woods, 2007; Hoffman, Richmond, Marrow & Salomone, 2002/2003), and psychological adjustment (Pittman & Richmond, 2008). In fact, Strayhorn (2012) even referred to belonging as a "basic human need and fundamental motivation that drives student behaviors, and facilitates educational success" (p. 87). When students feel belonging and validation, they feel more confident, capable, and proud. In turn, they achieve greater academic success (Rendón, 1994, 1995; Rendón Linares & Muñoz, 2011). Women of color often found belonging and validation in the Sister Stories counterspace. Diana explained: "the thing that makes it so magical is that we can validate each other's feelings."

Nicole appreciated how the counterspace allowed her to have candid conversations with peers and faculty who validated her lived realities with oppression.

> We got to talk about things that you don't regularly get to talk about as a student of color. . . . I feel like as a woman of color it made me feel a lot better with who I am. It helped validate some of the things that I was feeling that maybe I wouldn't be able to talk about with [White] people. It just let me know that I wasn't crazy and I am not the only one talking about these things.

Her quote suggests that Sister Stories validated Nicole's identity and experiences as a women of color. Nicole's relief that she was not "crazy" is a common response from students of color who constantly navigate exclusion in educational environments. In fact, CRT scholars like Gildersleeve et al. (2011) have written about the oppressive and dehumanizing conditions in predominantly White educational environments, aptly titling their article: "Am I Going Crazy?!" This title mirrors Nicole's sentiments about the psychological toll that insidious forms of subtle racism and White normalcy take on people of color in educational settings.

In counterspaces, people with similar life experiences can share, learn, and affirm one another. As such, counterspaces often serve as safe places where women of color can speak candidly about their experiences with microaggressions. Conversations about shared realities can reduce the loneliness associated with navigating exclusionary educational spaces. Bonnie explained:

> I was able to speak about things that I experienced in other classes and I was able to understand more about myself and others. . . . Being around people that are going through the same things that I'm going through . . . makes me feel like I'm not alone. When I say something and people agree—"Yeah, I've been through something like that"—I don't feel like an outsider.

It was not only peer-to-peer connections that were gained from the Sister Stories counterspace. I (Melissa) and teaching assistants identified as women of color. In fact, Sister Stories was often the only place on campus where women of color could see themselves reflected in campus leaders. As we described in the Introduction, a common environmental microaggression (Sue, 2010b) is a lack of people of color (especially women of color) in leadership positions on campus. Sister Stories was a welcome reprieve from such environmental microaggressions. Sofia was far less excited to attend courses taught by White teachers, especially when the content was not inclusive of diverse perspectives. She compared those exclusionary educational environments to Sister Stories.

> For the first time in my college career, I was excited to be sitting in this course. Finally, a course where everyone in the room looked similar to me, including the instructors! It was definitely a different classroom environment from any other course I have taken. . . . In my four years at [college], this is the first time I've ever had instructors who are women of color. . . . We might not have had the same experiences, [but] I feel like [they are] more relatable and more approachable.

It was not just being surrounded by women leaders of color that made the counterspace an exciting place to be. Educators of color affiliated with Sister Stories understood and validated students' lived realities. Diana explained:

> It was almost an out-of-body experience because it's not anything like any other classroom that I've been in. . . . The entire class was people of color, including the professor, which is even stranger! The fact that the professor could really relate to everything we were saying [was amazing].

Camilla felt "more connected because we all [shared] our own stories." She went on to explain how listening to women of color (faculty and students) share their experiences made her feel like "I belong in this class." In sum, counterspaces like Sister Stories can provide students a sense of validation and belonging in otherwise isolating and emotionally taxing exclusionary educational spaces.

BUILDING A NETWORK

Counterspaces can be important places to build social capital. Social capital refers to the actual or potential resources gained from interpersonal networks built upon a sense of trust and collectively agreed upon norms (Bourdieu, 1986; Putnam, 1995). It is a form of interpersonal currency fostered by networks of people. McIntosh's (1988) definition of privilege references social capital by including unearned access to resources, assets, and relationships that men and White people draw upon, often without realizing it. As people with privilege network with one another, these resources and assets transform into mutual benefits. When women of color talked about feeling alone or like the "only one," they were alluding to a lack of opportunity to obtain social capital. It is hard to make connections and build social capital when you are the only one. Social capital is inherently *social* as it is fostered through interpersonal connections. Anderson (2015) explained the connections between White space and the difficulty for people of color to develop social capital.

Anderson's prose, which specifically references Black people, also applies to other people of color and women:

> White space is where many social rewards originate, including an elegant night on the town, or cultural capital itself—education, employment, privilege, prestige, money, and the promise of acceptance. To obtain these rewards, Blacks must venture into the White space and explore its possibilities, engaging it to the extent that they can while hoping to benefit as much as possible. To be at all successful, they must manage themselves within this space. But the promise of acceptance is too often only that, a promise. All too frequently, prejudiced actors pervade the White space and are singly or collectively able and interested in marginalizing the Black person, actively reminding him of his outsider status to put him in his place. (p. 16)

Recent research with women also suggests they have less access to valuable forms of social capital in higher education settings. For instance, women are excluded by peers in classroom working groups (Charleston et al., 2014) and receive less access to effective advising and research opportunities with faculty (Sadker & Sadker, 1994) or support from faculty during the dissertation processes (Wolgemuth & Harbour, 2008). These studies show that social capital comes from interpersonal relationships with faculty and peers—capital that women of color are often barred from obtaining.

Even when women of color develop friendships with students from privileged backgrounds (e.g., Whites, men), the lack of perspective taking on behalf of those friends can prohibit women of color from gaining social capital. If a person with privilege does not comprehend their struggles and perspectives, they cannot be very supportive. Carmen explained, "I have a lot of Caucasian friends. I can talk to them sometimes about [racism]. Like, they'll feel bad, but they can't like, relate."

Despite lack of access to systemic forms of privilege and power associated with certain kinds of social capital, women of color had an opportunity to develop other forms of social capital in the Sister Stories counterspace. These forms of social capital may not always have been rich with access and power, but they did offer invaluable psychological and interpersonal benefits. Yosso et al. (2009) explained counterspaces as sites where students can "cultivate friendships with people who share many of their experiences" (p. 677). In Sister Stories, Bonnie "created relationships with other students of color." Nicole developed lasting connections in the course. She said, "we were a really close-knit class. I think some of us even were friends after [the class ended]." Vera felt the structure of the course encouraged dialogue, which helped her develop meaningful social relationships. She said:

> That's what the class is based off . . . the readings are the basis of the class and also talking to other people . . . in the class time, but even

afterwards if you see them. Some people I knew of when I took the class. [Others] I didn't know them all [but] then afterwards we built a connection. I feel like I built my network. Definitely. I had that class freshman year, so I think it was a good start as a freshman.

Even as a first-year student, Vera realized how important it was to build her network and make connections with other women of color on campus.

Sister Stories was a place where women of color could share life experiences without fear of oppressive assumptions or reactions. This safe setting helped foster interpersonal relationships and social capital. A classmate said to Bonnie, "I didn't know you until this year and now I feel like I can tell you my life." Lena lamented the end of the course and the loss of the weekly access to her newly developed social network of women of color.

> Now that the class is over, I am both sad that I will no longer be able to meet with a group of amazing people twice a week, and shocked at how much this class affected me. I got so much more out of taking Sister Stories than I ever imagined I would. Not only did I learn about my identity as a woman of color, but I got the opportunity to bond with new people and hear their incredible stories and perspectives.

Social networks developed in Sister Stories were invaluable forms of social capital that Mindy could draw upon when she experienced microaggressions. She noted how social networks can help individuals achieve their goals (e.g., graduation) despite obstacles like microaggressions. Mindy explained:

> There are people here to help you achieve those goals. So, like, you have a purpose, whatever that may be, you can do it if you put your mind to it, and utilize those resources on the way. Like, if you're missing a block, you know, find someone who can help you build that block, to help you cross the bridge. So, you're not alone.

Indeed, Sister Stories was a counterspace where women of color could locate some missing blocks of social capital.

As described in chapter 1, successful women of color (i.e., faculty, staff) were invited to guest speak in Sister Stories. Time was allotted for discussion and informal networking between students and presenters. During focus groups, and in course writings, students described the development of social capital with campus leaders who visited Sister Stories. To Suzanna, guest speakers were valuable social networks that she could draw upon in the future. Suzanna explained:

> After that panel . . . when I saw these women of color on campus, they would say hi to me and I felt comfort. Yeah, I feel more comfortable on campus a little bit. And, I feel like I . . . if I ever need a recommendation in the future they will know me personally and stuff.

Sister Stories afforded Suzanna and other women of color invaluable social networks that could be tapped for important academic credentials such as letters of recommendation and personal references. Suzanna's quote also suggests that merely knowing women of color on campus provided another valuable benefit: comfort and a sense of belonging in an otherwise isolating campus environment.

The Sister Stories counterspace included a required women of color dinner where women faculty and staff from a variety of racial and ethnic backgrounds networked with students. Carla reflected on the process of making authentic connections at the dinner and building social capital with mentors and role models of color on campus. She contrasted the value of building social capital through support as opposed to seeing other women on campus as competition:

> I was able to sit at a table where I did not really know anyone and I was forced to interact with people who, to my surprise, were not so different from me. During this time, I was able to interact with faculty and staff who were interested in knowing who I was as a student and as a person. . . . When you find the correct person, he or she can impact your life in so many different ways that you would have never imagined. There are a lot of bad people in this world, but I believe we should recognize more those who positively impact our lives. . . . Nowadays, everything has become about competition and being better than the women next to you. We do not realize that we need each other and if we do it together we could be successful instead of trying to fight with each other, to become better than one another.

We concur with Carla. Building a network of supportive, inspiring, and validating people is an invaluable asset to students, especially women of color who have often been excluded from access, privilege, and social capital throughout the educational pipeline.

Kendra was simultaneously enrolled in Sister Stories and another course where university leaders were asked to guest speak and network with students. After the panel presentation in the other course, students were invited to lunch with the presenters—one of whom was a man of color. Kendra was deeply hurt by the actions of that leader of color who chose to sit with White Greek students rather than the students of color. In her mind, White students always got the attention (and corresponding resources). They had White privilege and did not need social capital. Kendra felt this administrator should have made an effort to connect with students of color instead of Whites, because students of color had less access to social capital. Kendra shared:

> It gets me aggravated when I don't see the support they give [to White students]. I'm just gonna give an example: Dr. X is very high up there [in the university administration]. . . . He was on one of our panels [in a different class]. I know part of his work is with the Greek system. . . . We were supposed [to network and] to eat [together]. He automatically

went to the table of all the Greeks and it bothered me. . . . I understand that's your field of work, but then again, you see them every day and you just had this panel talking about diversity and like it would be nice to have you at my table.

It was frustrating and painful for Kendra to see a man of color walk past her and offer social capital to White students. Even though students like Kendra did not use the terms *social capital* or *privilege*, their quotes suggest they were well aware of the disparities in access to social capital (e.g., support, resources) between themselves and their privileged peers.

Professional leaders of color were few and far between on campus. Kendra knew only one woman of color in her academic department. Unfortunately, this dean was in such high demand, Kendra never had an opportunity to interact with her. She said, "it's nice to know that there's a woman of higher authority in my own department. [But] her office is all the way in the [back] corner . . . and there's a waiting list like to see her." As a result of their severe under-representation, women faculty and staff of color can experience an added cultural tax, whereby they are expected to serve on diversity committees, advise students of color, and teach about issues of race in addition to their typical job responsibilities (Ford, 2011; Harley, 2008). Harley (2008) argued that African American women are the "maids of academe" who are expected to exceed the traditional duties associated with their roles by serving as "the advocates for black issues, translators of black culture, navigators of a patriarchal and racial minefield, and serve as community liaison and conduits for others' problems" (pp. 20–24). Students of color also expect them to become mentors, advisors, and supporters. In short, women employees of color can be stretched thin. Unfortunately, students like Kendra do not necessarily see this cultural taxation. As such, students can become disappointed by the perceived inaccessibility of women of color role models and corresponding missed opportunities to build social capital.

CONCLUSION

All classrooms should be welcoming spaces where students feel like they belong. However, decades of scholarship suggests that this is often not the case for women of color. White privilege, White normalcy, masculine discourses, and microaggressions pervade higher education settings, creating chilly climates and exclusionary environments for women of color. Women of color described Sister Stories as an invaluable counterspace and a getaway where they experienced validation from peers and instructors who "got it." They also developed important social networks with students and university leaders of color. Until oppression is a vestige of the past, students from minoritized backgrounds need counterspaces, like Sister Stories, where they can gain validation, comfort, and social capital. However, as we show in the next two chapters, academic counterspaces like Sister Stories are not a panacea.

REFERENCES

Anderson, E. (2015). The white space. *Sociology of Race and Ethnicity, 1*(1), 10–21.

Arthur, C. J. (Ed.) (1974). *The German ideology: Part one.* New York: International Publishers.

Bell, L. A. (2007). Theoretical foundations for social justice education. In M. Adams, L. A. Bell & P. Griffin (Eds.) *Teaching for diversity and social justice: A sourcebook.* New York: Routledge.

Bergerson, A. A. (2003). Critical race theory and White racism: Is there room for White scholars in fighting racism in education? *Qualitative Studies in Education, 16*(1), 51–63.

Billing, Y. D. (2011). Are women in management victims of the phantom of the male norm? *Gender, Work & Organization, 18*(3), 298–317.

Bourdieu, P. (1986) The forms of capital. In J. Richardson (Ed.), *Handbook of theory and research for the sociology of education* (pp. 241–58). New York: Greenwood.

Butler, J. E., & Walter, J. C. (1991). *Transforming the curriculum: Ethnic studies and women's studies.* Albany, NY: State University of New York Press.

Campaign for College Opportunity (2015). *The state of higher education in California.* Retrieved from: http://collegecampaign.org/wp-content/uploads/2015/09/2015-State-of-Higher-Education_AANHPI2.pdf.

Charleston, L., Adserias, R., Lang, N., & Jackson, J. (2014). Intersectionality and STEM: The role of race and gender in the academic pursuits of African American women in STEM. *Journal of Progressive Policy & Practice, 2*(3), 273–93.

Crawford, J. B., & Mills, A. J. (2011). The formative context of organizational hierarchies and discourse: Implications for organizational change and gender relations. *Gender, Work & Organization, 18*(S1), 88–109.

Domingue, A. D. (2015). "Our leaders are just we ourself": Black women college student leaders' experiences with oppression and sources of nourishment on a predominantly white college campus. *Equity & Excellence in Education, 48*(3), 454–72.

DuBois, W. E. B. (1903). *The souls of the black folk.* New York: W. W. Norton & Company.

Ford, K. A. (2011). Race, gender, and bodily (mis) recognitions: Women of color faculty experiences with White students in the college classroom. *The Journal of Higher Education, 82*(4), 444–78.

Freeman, T. M., Anderman, L. H., & Jensen, J. M. (2007). Sense of belonging in college freshmen at the classroom and campus levels. *The Journal of Experimental Education, 75*(3), 203–20.

Gildersleeve, R. E., Croom, N. N., & Vasquez, P. L. (2011). "Am I going crazy?!": A critical race analysis of doctoral education. *Equity & Excellence in Education, 44*(1), 93–114.

Goodman, D. J. (2011). *Promoting diversity and social justice: Educating people from privileged groups.* New York: Routledge.

Greenman, E., & Xie, Y. (2008). Is assimilation theory dead? The effect of assimilation on adolescent well-being. *Social Science Research, 37*(1), 109–37.

Hall, R. M., & Sandler, B. R. (1984). *Out of the classroom: A chilly climate for women?* Washington, DC: Association of American Colleges, Project on the Status and Education of Women.

Hall, R. M., & Sandler, B. R. (1991). *The campus climate revisited: Chilly for women faculty, administrators, and graduate students.* Washington, DC: American Association of Colleges.

Harley, D. A. (2008). Maids of academe: African American women faculty at predominately White institutions. *Journal of African American Studies, 12,* 19–36.

Harper, S. R., & Hurtado, S. (2007). Nine themes in campus racial climates and implications for institutional transformation. In S. Harper & L. D. Patton (Eds.) Responding to the realities of race on campus. *New Directions for Student Services* (120), pp. 7–24. San Francisco, CA: Wiley.

Harper, S. R., Patton, L. D., & Wooden, O. S. (2009). Access and equity for African American students in higher education: A critical race historical analysis of policy efforts. *The Journal of Higher Education, 80*(4), 389–414.

Hausmann, L. R. M., Schofield, J. W., & Woods, R. L. (2007). Sense of belonging as a predictor of intentions to persist among African American and White first-year college students. *Research in Higher Education, 48*(7), 803–39.

Hill Collins, P. (1991, 2000). *Black feminist thought: Knowledge, consciousness, and the politics of empowerment.* New York: Routledge.

Hoffman, M., Richmond, J., Morrow, J., & Salomone, K. (2002/2003). Investigating "sense of belonging" in first-year college students. *Journal of College Student Retention, 4*(3), 227–56.

hooks, b. (1981). *Feminist theory: From margin to center* (2nd ed.). Cambridge, MA: South End Press.

Hurtado, S., & Carter, D. F. (1997). Effects of college transition and perceptions of the campus racial climate on Latino students' sense of belonging. *Sociology of Education, 70,* 324–45.

Johnson, A. G. (2006). *Privilege, power and difference* (2nd ed.). Boston, MA: McGraw Hill.

Johnson, D. R., Soldner, M., Leonard, J. B., Alvarez, P., Inkelas, K. K., Rowan-Kenyon, H. T., & Longerbeam, S. D. (2007). Examining sense of belonging among first-year undergraduates from different racial/ethnic groups. *Journal of College Student Development, 48*(5), 525–42.

Kanter, R. M. (1977a). *Men and women of the corporation.* New York: Basic Books.

——— (1977b). Some effects of proportions on group life: Skewed sex ratios and responses to token women. *American Journal of Sociology, 82* (5), 965–90.

Locks, A. M., Hurtado, S., Bowman, N. A., & Oseguera, L. (2008). Extending notions of campus climate and diversity to students' transition to college. *Review of Higher Education, 31*(3), 257–85.

Love, B. J. (2004). Brown plus 50 counter storytelling: A critical race theory analysis of the "majoritarian achievement gap" story. *Equality and Excellence, 37,* 227–46.

Marx, K., & Engels, F. (1846–1847). The German ideology. In C. J. Arthur (Ed.). *The German ideology: Part one.* New York: International Publishers.

McIntosh, P. (1988). *White privilege and male privilege: A personal account of coming to see correspondences through work in women's studies. Working Paper No. 189.* Wellesley, MA: Wellesley Centers for Women.

Meyerson, D. E., & Kolb, D. M. (2000). Moving out of the 'armchair': Developing a framework to bridge the gap between feminist theory and practice. *Organization, 7*(4), 553–71.

Nagasawa, R., Qian, Z., & Wong, P. (2001). Theory of segmented assimilation and the adoption of marijuana use and delinquent behavior by Asian Pacific youth. *The Sociological Quarterly, 42*(3), 351–72.

National Center for Education Statistics (NCES) (2015). *The Condition of Education 2015.* Figure 3. "Percentage of 25- to 29-year-olds who completed at least a high school diploma or its equivalent, by race/ ethnicity: Selected years, 1990–2014." Retrieved from: http://nces.ed.gov/programs/coe/pdf/coe_caa.pdf.

——— (2015a). *The Digest of Education Statistics.* Table 302.60. "Percentage of 18- to 24-year-olds enrolled in degree-granting institutions, by level of institution and sex and race/ethnicity of student: 1967 through 2012." Retrieved from: http://nces.ed.gov/programs/digest/d13/tables/dt13_302.60.asp.

National Science Foundation (NSF) (2014). *Science and Engineering Indicators 2014.* Chapter 2. Higher education in science and engineering. Retrieved from: http://www.nsf.gov/statistics/seind14/index.cfm/chapter-2#s2.

Nuñez, A. M. (2011). Counterspaces and connections in college transitions: First-generation Latino students' perspectives on Chicano studies. *Journal of College Student Development, 52*(6), 639–55.

Pérez Huber, L. (2010). Using Latina/o critical race theory (LatCrit) and racist nativism to explore intersectionality in the educational experiences of undocumented Chicana college students. *Educational Foundations, 24,* 77–96.

———, & Cueva, B. M. (2012). Chicana/Latina testimonios on effects and responses to microaggressions. *Equity and Excellence in Education,* 45(3), 392–410.

Phelps, A. D. (2015). *Reflections of undergraduate business education alumnae: Shifting perspectives on gender and work.* Unpublished doctoral dissertation. University of Rhode Island, Kingston, RI.

Pittman, L. D., & Richmond, A. (2008). University belonging, friendship quality, and psychological adjustment during the transition to college. *Journal of Experimental Education, 76,* 343–61.

Putnam, R. D. (1995). Bowling alone: America's declining social capital. *Journal of Democracy, 6*(1), 65–78.

Rendón, L. (1994). Validating culturally diverse students: Toward a new model of learning and student development. *Innovative Higher Education, 19* (1), 33–51.

——— (1995). *Facilitating retention and transfer for first generation students in community colleges.* University Park, PA: National Center on Postsecondary Teaching, Learning, and Assessment. (ERIC Document Reproduction Service no. ED383369)

Rendón Linares, L. I., & Muñoz, S. M. (2011). Revisiting validation theory: Theoretical foundations, applications, and extensions. *Enrollment Management Journal, 2*(1), 12–33.

Sadker, M., & Sadker, D. (1994). *Failing at fairness: How America's schools cheat girls.* New York: Macmillian.

Schwartz, S. J., Waterman, A. S., Umaña-Taylor, A. J., Lee, R. M., Kim, S. Y., Vazsonyi, A. T., & Zamboanga, B. L. (2013). Acculturation and well-being among college students from immigrant families. *Journal of Clinical Psychology, 69*(4), 298–318.

Shuford, B. C. (2011). Historical and philosophical development of multicultural student services. In D. L. Stewart (Ed.), *Multicultural student services on campus: Building bridges, re-visioning community* (pp. 29–37). Sterling, VA: Stylus.

Smith, D. G. (2009). *Diversity's promise for higher education: Making it work.* Baltimore, MD: Johns Hopkins University Press.

Smith, W. A., Yosso, T. J., & Solórzano, D. G. (2007). Racial primes and black misandry on historically White campuses: Toward critical race accountability in educational administration. *Educational Administration Quarterly, 43*(5), 559–585.

Solórzano, D. G. (1997). Images and words that wound: Critical race theory, racial stereotyping, and teacher education. *Teacher Education Quarterly, 24*(3), 5–20.

——— (1998). Critical race theory, race and gender microaggressions, and the experience of Chicana and Chicano scholars. *Qualitative Studies in Education, 11*(1), 121–36.

———, Ceja, M., & Yosso, T. J. (2000). Critical race theory, racial microaggressions, and campus racial climate: The experiences of African American college students. *The Journal of Negro Education, 69*(1/2), 60–73.

Stewart, D. L., & Bridges, B. (2011). A demographic profile of multicultural student services. In D. L. Stewart (Ed.), *Multicultural student services on campus: Building bridges, re-visioning community* (pp. 38–62). Sterling, VA: Stylus.

Strayhorn, T. L. (2012). *College students' sense of belonging: A key to educational success for all students.* New York: Routledge.

Sue, D. W. (Ed.) (2010a). *Microaggressions and marginality: Manifestations, dynamics and impact.* Hoboken, NJ: Wiley.

——— (2010b). *Microaggressions in everyday life: Race, gender and sexual orientation.* Hoboken, NJ: Wiley.

———, Capodilupo, C. M., Torino, G. C., Bucceri, J. M., Holder, A. M. B., Nadal, K. L., & Esquilin, M. (2007). Racial microaggressions in everyday life: Implications for clinical practice. *American Psychologist, 62,* 271–86.

Vaccaro, A. (2010). Still chilly in 2010: The climate experiences of women from diverse backgrounds. In *On campus with women.* Washington, DC: American Association of Colleges and Universities.

——— (2016). Strategies for teaching multicultural psychology: Who, what, and how. In K. Quina & J. Mena (Eds.), *Teaching a multiculturally-informed psychology of people.* Washington, DC: American Psychological Association.

———, & Mena, J. (in press). "I've struggled, I've battled": Invisibility microaggressions experienced by women of color at a predominately White institution. *The Journal about Women in Higher Education.*

Wing, A. K. (2003). *Critical race feminism: A reader* (2nd ed.). New York: New York University Press.

Wise, T., & Case, K. A. (2013). Pedagogy for the privileged: Addressing inequality and injustice without shame or blame. In K. A. Case (Ed.), *Deconstructing privilege: Teaching and learning as allies in the classroom* (pp. 17–33). New York: Routledge.

Wolgemuth, J. R., & Harbour, C. P. (2008). A man's academy? The dissertation process as feminist resistance. *Journal about Women in Higher Education, 1,*181–201.

Yosso, T., Smith, W., Ceja, M., & Solórzano, D. (2009). Critical race theory, racial microaggressions, and campus climate for Latina/o undergraduates. *Harvard Educational Review, 79*(4) 659–69.

Zhou, M., & Bankston, C. L. (1998). *Growing up American: The adaptation of Vietnamese adolescents in the United States.* New York: Russell Sage Foundation.

FOUR

Student Interactions in a Counterspace

"It's complicated."

Despite the many benefits of counterspaces described in chapter 3, they are not a panacea. This chapter highlights the ways intersecting social identities, as well as unique personalities and divergent communication styles, created tensions in the Sister Stories counterspace. Using rich student narratives, we provide readers insight into the less-than-ideal dynamics that happened in the Sister Stories counterspace. It's complicated.

DIVERSITY *WITHIN* COUNTERSPACES

Women of color often sought refuge in the Sister Stories counterspaces to combat the isolation of feeling like the only woman of color on campus (Pérez Huber & Cueva, 2012; Solórzano, Ceja & Yosso, 2000; Yosso, Smith, Ceja & Solórzano, 2009). Counterspaces have been described as safe, validating spaces where students can vent frustrations, cultivate friendships, engage in activism, explore identities, and heal alongside people who share similar identities and experiences (Butler & Walter, 1991; Nuñez, 2011; Yosso et al., 2009). Yet, it is problematic to assume all people in a counterspace will think, feel, or behave similarly. While taxonomies (Capodilupo et al., 2010; Sue, 2010b; Sue, Bucceri, Lin, Nadal & Torino, 2007) explicate some common patterns of microaggression manifestations, there are also distinctions between different forms of oppression, like racism and sexism. Moreover, research has shown that people of color from different ethnic backgrounds are more likely to experience certain manifestations of racial microaggressions. For instance, Blacks and Latinos are more likely to experience microaggressions related to assumptions of criminality, while Asians are treated as if they are invisible or have their citizenship questioned (Sue et al., 2009; Wong, Derthick, David, Saw, Torino & Okazaki, 2013).

As we have noted throughout this book, women of color experience gendered racism (Essed, 1991), which manifests in qualitatively different ways than racism experienced by men of color and sexism by White women. As CRT and CRF scholars have long argued, intersectionality matters (Crenshaw, 1989; Hill Collins, 1991, 2000; Solórzano, 1997; Wing, 2003). While there are a host of definitions of intersectionality, "a consistent thread across definitions is that social identities which serve as organizing features of social relations, mutually constitute, reinforce, and naturalize one another" (Shields, 2008, p. 302). Early thinking about intersectionality is sometimes associated with a group of Black feminists who described how it was difficult "to separate race from class from sex oppression because in our lives they are most often experienced simultaneously" (Combahee River Collective, 1995, p. 234). Intersectional scholars argue against an additive approach that suggests women of color experience racism plus sexism for a double form of oppression. Such additive perspectives fail to recognize the qualitatively different life experiences that result from interlocking manifestations of oppression such as sexism and racism.

Many initial writings about intersectionality tended to focus on the personal, educational, and social realities of those living at the intersections of multiple minoritized identities (Crenshaw, 1989; Combahee River Collective, 1995; Hill Collins, 1991, 2000; hooks, 2000; Moraga & Anzaldúa, 1981, 2002; Wing, 2003). Yet, many people, including women of color, can live at the intersection of privileged and minoritized identities. In fact, recent scholars have argued against focusing only on the intersections of marginalized identities; such narrow perspectives disregard the complex realities of individuals who experience a combination of privilege and oppression (Choo & Ferree, 2010; Museus & Griffin, 2011). In this chapter, we show how intersecting privileged and marginalized identities among students sometimes caused rifts in the Sister Stories counterspace.

COMPLICATED SISTER STORIES DYNAMICS

Student narratives suggest that the intersections of minoritized and privileged identities influenced not only students' lives, but also the dynamics of the counterspace. First, intersectionality shaped how women of color from different ethnicities, classes, and sexual orientations interacted with each other in the counterspace. Second, interlocking systems of racial and gender oppression also played a role in the deep divisions between men and women of color, especially during year two of the study. We also talk about the dynamics of having White students in the Sister Stories counterspace. In sum, student narratives show that camaraderie, support, and validation can be tough to come by in a counterspace when participants self-identify with a variety of races, ethnicities, social classes, and sexual orientations, and when they have divergent personalities, communication styles, and political perspectives.

WOMEN GOING AGAINST OTHER WOMEN

As described in chapter 3, one of the benefits of a counterspace is that women of color find refuge from oppression and glean support from people "like me." However, women of color in Sister Stories sometimes felt like the counterspace presented a whole new set of pressures to connect. For instance, some felt an unspoken pressure to develop camaraderie and express similar worldviews as other women of color. As Zinn and Dill (1996) argued, there is no singular experience for women of color. They hold a variety of perspectives, passions, and interests, and live unique lives shaped by racial, ethnic, and other intersecting social identities. Moreover, hooks (2000) has critiqued claims that there is a singular women's experience or perspective:

> A central tenet of modern feminist thought has been the assertion that "all women are oppressed." This assertion implies that women share a common lot, that factors like class, race, religion, sexual preference, etc. do not create a diversity of experience that determines the extent to which sexism will be an oppressive force in the lives of individual women. (p. 5)

Indeed, women of color in the Sister Stories counterspace realized that they did not always share a common lot. These differences sometimes caused tensions.

Women of color sought counterspaces, like Sister Stories, to locate peers who shared similar experiences. While most found rich interpersonal connections in Sister Stories (see chapter 3), that was not always the case. Some women of color were disappointed to learn classmates from different (or the same) racial and ethnic backgrounds might not understand their reality or have the capacity to provide the kind of support they desired. Jocelyn explained:

> I haven't been able to find someone who has completely been through the things I been through or can understand—they just don't. I know some people really *want* to understand and they just don't. . . . Because you're Black, you have been through the same things I've been through? It's completely *not* like that. I feel like that's when you become women going against other women because you want someone to identify the same way as you. When you don't, you feel like you're

attacked. . . . That day, I felt like I was not getting attacked, but at the same time people were completely disagreeing and kind of telling me how I *should* feel . . . and that's how you get that strain between women of color.

Jocelyn's quote references the pressure to fit in by feeling or thinking a certain way as a woman of color. Others talked more directly about tensions and in-fighting among women of color. Both Jocelyn and Pamela even used the word "attack" to describe how women of color sometimes treated each other. Pamela said:

I just feel like people attack each other. Honestly . . . full Puerto Ricans they attack Dominicans or they'll attack Colombians or whoever else— Really just attack your own, I'd say culture . . . I think we just need to stop fighting among ourselves.

Pamela described in-fighting among women of color from different racial and ethnic groups. She also alluded to the fact that women from the *same* racial background but different ethnicity (e.g., Puerto Rican, Colombian) can also fight among themselves. Because of these tensions, finding genuine support in the Sister Stores counterspace was sometimes difficult.

Women of color were not immune to stereotypes. At times, they perpetuated stereotypes about women of color from their own, or other, racial and ethnic backgrounds. Even though students of color were frustrated and offended when White people expressed stereotypes about people of color, women of color sometimes did it too. Kendra explained how people of color could harbor stereotypes just as easily as White people:

A Spanish person said about Black people being loud all the time. . . . You're upset that those are the stereotypes [held by White people]? But, you're still talking [about those same stereotypes]. You're not making them any better. You're proving them yourself. I think a lot of people of color feel since they are a person of color that they have the right to say the N word, but no it's wrong. I don't understand what makes it different for you to say it or for someone else to say it—even if you are African American.

Kendra's quote also alludes to the fact that certain terms, jokes, and sayings are offensive—no matter who says them.

Troubling interactions in the counterspace also emerged from differences between monoracial and bi/multiracial women as well as between women with different phenotypes (i.e., skin tones). Biracial and multiracial women did not always feel welcome in extra-curricular counterspaces designed for women of color; nor did they feel completely accepted in co-educational student organizations like the Black Student Group or Latino/a Alliance. A number of scholars have documented how biracial and multiracial students often face questions about racial authenticity in monoracial environments such as student organizations designed for specific racial or ethnic groups (Renn, 2004, 2011; Museus, Yee & Lambee, 2011). For instance, Museus et al. (2011) explained how mixed-race students could be considered not loyal, or not legitimately a member of monoracial communities. As a result, mixed-race students can feel excluded and judged in campus counterspaces—even when those spaces are specifically designed to welcome, support, and affirm students of color.

Another layer of difference that emerged between women of color was skin color. While we delve more deeply into issues of phenotype and beauty in chapter 7, we share selected quotes here to explicate the ways skin tone, as well as other aesthetic standards, caused divisions among women of color in the Sister Stories counterspace. Hunter (2005) described a phenomena called *colorism*, which is "the process of discrimination that privileges light-skinned people of color over their dark-skinned counterparts" (p. 237). In her work, Hunter (2005, 2007) explicated decades of research about the benefits lighter-skinned people of color reap over people of color with darker skin, such as higher pay and higher educational attainment. Monoracial individuals with darker skin are also often viewed as more ethnically legitimate or authentic than monoracial individuals with lighter skin (Hunter, 2007).

In Sister Stories, student counterstories revealed what critical race feminists have long noted: dominant ideologies of Whiteness (and lightness) as normative and beautiful are ever-present forms of oppression that shape the way women of color are viewed in society and how they view themselves (Bankhead & Johnson, 2014; Johnson & Bankhead, 2014; Patton, 2006; Rockquemore, 2002). Her biracial background paired with her skin tone made Jocelyn feel like an outsider in an extracurricular campus counterspace for women of color. She explained:

> Women of color don't get it sometimes . . . there have been times I felt like I don't even belong. It's a women of color thing I think because I have the most issues when it comes to my skin color and I haven't really met anyone who's the same skin color as me who understands like how it feels to wake up every day and not really know you're so different. . . . Sometimes you do want someone who has been through the same things you've been through.

As an immigrant from Nigeria, Juba experienced not only exclusion because of her skin color, but also her ethnic heritage. While she hoped for support and acceptance from other women of color, she was instead treated like "a whole different species altogether." She was not in the United States very long before she was subjected to oppressive dominant ideologies about race and skin color. Juba quickly understood that lighter skin was more acceptable than darker skin in the United States.

> When I first came to this country, I didn't even realize that I would be something that you would consider a minority. Growing up in Nigeria,

everyone is brown. They look like me. Coming to this country and seeing other Black people, you're thinking, "Oh, ok so we look like each other, we're gonna be accepted fine." Then it's like: Ok I'm experiencing oppression between identifying as African and having to identify with other African Americans and struggling with them because they don't consider me—not that they don't consider you Black enough—but they consider you a whole different species altogether. When you have people like Native Americans and Asians, growing up I thought that it was more acceptable to the White community. To me, things like light skin was—as cliché as it sounds—more acceptable in society.

Jocelyn and Juba longed for support from other women of color who understood their lived realities. Yet, their quotes show such counterspace benefits were not always reaped by women of color.

Other social identities such as social class, gender identity, and sexual orientation also proved to be hurdles to camaraderie and connection among women of color. For instance, differences in sexual orientation caused rifts in the counterspace. A combination of skin tone and sexual orientation served as a unique type of exclusion for Pamela as she struggled to find a welcoming counterspace among White lesbian, gay, and bisexual (LGB) students and heterosexual Puerto Rican communities on campus. Unfortunately, her intersectional reality as a lesbian *and* woman of color made her feel like an outcast in each of these single-identity counterspaces.

My Spanish friends would be like, "Oh, you're so White." My White friends, "Oh you're so Spanish." So it was never like I could really satisfy anybody. Growing up . . . a lot of people thought I was White. [Another] thing I had trouble with is my sexual orientation [and] once they find out I'm Puerto Rican too, it's like a double whammy. It's just like constant [pressure] . . . to prove myself.

The intersection of race and social class also caused tensions in the counterspace. Kendra often felt out of place in Sister Stories because she was an upper-middle-class Black woman. She perceived her classmates of color to be from middle or working classes. As Kendra noted, her social class privilege kept her from feeling like she belonged in the class. At times, she even felt obligated to prove her legitimacy as a woman of color because of her social class. Kendra explained:

It doesn't help where I live is a wealthy area . . . I like feel like I almost had to like prove myself all the time. And it's like, why should I feel guilty that my mom works her ass off to put me where I am? It's not like we're inheriting this money. It's not just growing on trees.

Kendra's quote reflects the power of intersectionality in shaping the feel of a counterspace. It also shows how layers of privilege complicate counterspaces. Kendra was hesitant to claim her social class privilege. In fact, she drew upon some of the dominant ideologies that critical race theorists seek to debunk like meritocracy and equal opportunity (Bergerson, 2003; Harper, Patton & Wooden, 2009; Solórzano, 1997; Solórzano & Yosso, 2001). Kendra referenced her mother's hard work (i.e., merit) and refuted the notion that her family's wealth was inherited or grew on trees. The underlying message, rooted in an oppressive ideology, is that her family (as well as other families of color) had an equal opportunity to earn wealth. As such, her lack of connection to peers in Sister Stories may have been a result of not merely her social class, but also her resistance to recognizing her economic privilege and her perpetuation of dominant ideologies of merit and equal opportunity during classroom discussions.

Sister Stories was a course about the historical and contemporary experiences of women of color in the United States. Despite their shared identity as women, students sometimes expressed their gender in different ways, which caused tensions. Gender expression is a term that describes the manner in which people convey their gender identity. It can include behavior, dress, hairstyle, voice, and other forms of expression. Two examples show how differences in gender expression prompted feelings of exclusion by women of color in the Sister Stories counterspace. Lauren's gender expression as a "tomboy" made her feel different and disconnected from other women of color. Despite the fact that she shared the same sex (i.e., female), she was unable to relate to her Sister Stories peers who seemed to care a lot about looks and appearance. Her unique gender expression proved to be a hurdle to reaping the supposed counterspace benefit of finding support from others who truly understood her. Lauren explained:

> In that class I feel like I was the only [one sometimes]. . . . Obviously I'm a female, but I . . . I was raised more like a tomboy. So I just couldn't relate to some of the girls in the class sometimes. And like I feel like they wouldn't understand where I came from either.

In another Sister Stories class year, issues of gender expression emerged during conversations about parenting. Sofia was the mother of a young boy. During classroom discussions, she talked about supporting her child's explorations with gender expression (e.g., wearing pink, playing with gendered toys like dolls). In response, she was criticized by classmates of color for encouraging "abnormal" behavior. Her peers believed oppressive ideologies about gender expression. They also expressed their cisgender privilege by suggesting Sofia adopt more gender-restrictive child-rearing practices. Instead of a counterspace where she could find validation and support for allowing her child to engage in gender explorations, Sofia felt attacked and judged during this classroom conversation.

Differences in social identity (e.g., race, ethnicity, class, sexuality) and gender expression were not the only reasons Sister Stories students felt less supported by, or connected to, each other. Zinn and Dill (1996) explained how women of color hold a variety of political and intellectual positions. Therefore, they might not always get along. Women of color in Sister Stories had a range of personalities, perspectives, and communication styles. As is the reality in *any* classroom or counterspace, there were some students who did not get along with one another because of personality and political differences. For instance, Lucia was quite opinionated about politics and very talkative during class sessions. It was apparent from observing her in the classroom, that her talkative nature and tendency to interrupt her peers annoyed many of her classmates. In one heated discussion about people of color in politics, one of her peers called Lucia "ignorant." This hurt Lucia's feelings.

> She called me ignorant . . . I'm just like whaaaat? . . . I'm just going to take it as you're being mean. . . . Because I feel this way about this certain aspect of this topic that we're talking about and it's different from what you think, doesn't mean I'm being ignorant. It just means that my opinion is different from yours. And it's not fair for you to say that. It hurt my feelings.

This incident was one of many where personalities, political perspectives, and communication styles prohibited women from connecting and supporting each other in the Sister Stories counterspace. It is unreasonable to assume all women of color will get along—even those who share similar social identities. Fola explained this reality when she said:

> I feel like we challenged each other so much because we all had different lenses. Although we might be African American or Latinas, we still have different stories that some of us can't relate to. . . . I just think we are going to disagree because we have different experiences.

In sum, intersecting social identities, combined with unique personalities, communication styles, and political perspectives, played a role in the (dis)connections among women of color in Sister Stories counterspace.

MEN AND WOMEN WILL NEVER
FULLY UNDERSTAND EACH OTHER

Interpersonal conflicts were not limited to women in the counterspace. Men and women of color were looking for, but did not always find, cross-gender support in the Sister Stories counterspace. Men of color enrolled in three different Sister Stories class years. During the second year of our study, tensions between men and women caused significant counterspace conflicts. In chapter 3, we noted how students of color share common challenges of navigating White normalcy in educational spaces. However, as critical race feminists have pointed out, such commonalities do not prohibit men of color from directing sexism at women of color

(Wing, 2003). Sister Stories was intended to teach about historical and contemporary experiences of women of color. However, in year two, when almost half the class was men of color, oppression was not merely something students talked about—it happened in the classroom. Men expressed a variety of perspectives rooted in gendered racism (Essed, 1991; Lewis, Mendenhall, Harwood & Huntt, 2013). In this section, we share selected oppressive comments made by men of color about women's appearance, sex appeal, and domineering personalities. We also provide some of the women's responses to these gendered racial microaggressions.

Men of color in Sister Stories alluded to feelings of resentment toward women of color. Diego conveyed a sentiment shared by quite a few men in the class—women of color had it easier than men of color, largely because they could "get away" with things because of their looks or sex appeal. Diego explained:

> There are situations where females have it easier than a male. You could tell a female that and they would be like, "no, no, no, no, no, no, no." But, it's true. There are issues that us males just can't get away with because we're males and females get . . . it easier. It's a double standard just working the other way around in many situations.

Diego's frustration was apparent in his comment about women having it easier. During the post-course focus group, men of color talked at length about women of color supposedly reaping benefits based upon good looks and sex appeal. Brandon explained:

> Yeah that's a fact . . . I just wish more women would realize that they do get advantages. As much as women don't want to admit it, or want to believe it, they do get advantages. If you believe that this is a male-dominated world or a male-dominated field or whatever you're in, men are [still] attracted to women . . . [so] they get advantages.

It is interesting that Brandon used the language "male-dominated world" in the same sentence where be perpetrated a gendered racist (and heterosexist) microaggression. He may have learned the terminology of male dominance in class, but had no idea that his comments about women getting advantages because of sexual attraction were, in and of themselves, forms of exclusion rooted in objectification (Fredrickson & Roberts, 1987). Objectification is the dehumanizing process of reducing people to objects. In fact, Fredrickson and Roberts (1987) explained how "the most subtle and deniable way sexualized evaluation is enacted—and arguably the most ubiquitous—is through gaze, or visual inspection of the body" (p. 175).

In one class session, students had a conversation about gender and racial inequality at work. It quickly turned into a heated debate after a few men expressed that they would want a secretary to be a woman, precisely because they would enjoy looking at her all day. In the post-course focus groups, men and women reflected on this topic. Diego explained, "All the males agreed on the specific question, I think the question was, 'If you had a secretary, would the secretary be a male or a female?' Every male agreed it would be a female." During the focus group, a number of men of color also discussed how they felt it was okay to wear and reproduce sexually objectifying images of women. For instance, Eddie said, "I personally didn't feel like it was wrong to have a naked girl on the cover of your shirt. . . . I don't see anything wrong with it. That's my own personal opinion." He seemed to have no sense that the T-shirt and his perspectives on gender were objectifying and oppressive to women.

Most men of color in Sister Stories seemed to be unaware of how offensive their objectifying comments and behavior were to women of color. Women, however, had a lot to say about the gendered racism exuded by their classmates. Nicole expressed her frustration with their behavior:

> They talked a lot about how being a woman is easier because of our bodies and we have advantages because of that. For example, they said that they would hire her for a secretary because she's pretty and has a nice body instead of a man—just because they'd rather see her in the office everyday. Like, you're stupid! That's nuts! . . . You're from a mother, you can't think like that about women. You'll have daughters, little girls. It's just pretty crazy.

Victoria also wondered how men could objectify women of color, especially since they had relatives who were girls and women. Her frustration seemed to be intensified by her underlying hope that as people of color, men would not think in oppressive ways about women of color:

> One of the guys in class was like, "If a girl was attractive that she would get the job over the guy." . . . I feel like, you're not a woman; you don't understand what we go through. You don't understand . . . I don't know, I just feel like a lot of the stuff was said and I was like, "how can you think that way?"

Gendered racial microaggressions went well beyond hypothetical classroom conversations about the world of work. As men described their actual dating behavior, it was obvious their views on romantic relationships were also shaped by stereotypes about women of color and White women. For instance, Ruben explained how women of color were too domineering, so he preferred to date White women.

> I'm going to a frat party, right? I see all the White girls and I'll talk to them. It's like so it's easy to talk to them. . . . As soon as you come talk to a woman of color it's like you say the wrong thing once they are going to come at you. They have such a barrier—such like a defensive. I can't just talk to them . . . I'll approach a White girl and talk to her

everything will go good. We will be friends and this and that. But a Black girl, it's so much harder and they're so hardheaded some-times . . . If I approach a White girl . . . they are more open. . . . Women of color? Think about what you are going to say before you say it, because you don't want the wrong outcome to possibly come out.

Along a similar vein, Diego lamented that women of color "gotta complain forever." Ruben and Diego's comments reflect the stereotypical images described in literature by CRF and other women writers of color (Domingue, 2015; Hill Collins, 1991, 2000; Lewis et al., 2013). These controlling images about women of color contrast with men's stereotypical notions of White women as ladylike, proper, submissive, less domineering, and easier to talk to than women of color. Victoria recognized this reality when she said:

That's the point that really bothers me because I've had numerous conversations with men and they'll be like, "I like White girls because they do everything for me, they make me feel like I'm the king" . . . I feel like that's what really bothers me because I feel like they especial-ly—at this age—I don't feel like they go for White women because they truly love White women. I feel like they go for them because they treat them better. They don't want to deal with the: all up in your face and if you get me mad I'm gonna cuss you out [from women of color]. They don't want to deal with that.

Victoria wholeheartedly believed that men of color dated White women because they were more subservient and less likely to "get up in their face" when they disagreed.

Gendered racial microaggressions perpetrated by men of color took a toll on woman of color who hoped Sister Stories would serve as a welcoming and validating counterspace. Unfortunately, women of color did not always find what they were looking for. Instead, they were disappointed by men who only saw women through oppressive and objectifying lenses of appearance and sex. Lauren explained, "And I feel like they just think that women act the way they act . . . just to want to satisfy guys. Like that's their main objective. . . . To just generalize every woman in that category, it was just kind of extreme." Ife described the toll that gendered racial microaggressions took on her:

Some of the boys . . . they would say in class when they see females all they see is breasts and butt . . . I grew up around boys. . . . [But] I just didn't think that they would be . . . saying the things that they said [out loud]. It's [the twenty-first century;] why does it matter if I have light skin [or] if I have big boobs for me to get the job? Not only does it upset people, it might make people feel insecure.

Ife's quote alludes to the emotional toll of gendered racial microaggressions perpetrated by men of color. She was frustrated by being objectified when men talked about appearance and sex appeal as requisites for a job.

Like Ife, many women talked about their strategies for dealing with gendered racial microaggressions in the classroom. Quite a few women of color adapted their behavior to avoid reinforcing men's stereotypes. For instance, one of the messages women got from men of color was that they were too emotional. As such, women of color like Diana and Victoria held their emotions inside. Counterspaces are supposed to be safe places where individuals can be themselves, show emotions, and be supported for doing so. Unfortunately, this was not the counterspace reality for women of color in year two. Victoria shared:

> When they talk about certain things like women act this way or that way, I'm a little conscious not to act that way so I don't have that stereotype up against me—that you're really emotional because you're a woman. I try to not be so emotional anymore.

Diana concurred. Even though she described herself as a naturally passionate person, she refrained from being assertive, loud, or too passionate in class to avoid being viewed negatively by men of color.

> I don't think I was as assertive [in class]. . . . [I thought] maybe I need to formulate my ideas before I get passionate. That's how [the men] made me feel. If I just show my raw emotions, then I just may feed into their stereotype that women are emotional. I can't have a conversation [where I am] being passionate, especially being a women of color, because I'm not supposed to be loud or make facial expressions when I'm speaking.

Women of color responded to gendered racial microaggressions by not being themselves. This is in stark contrast to narratives shared in chapter 3 about the benefits of counterspaces as refuges or getaways where individuals could simply be themselves.

In some cases, men of color perceived the counterspace dynamics to be so contentious that they likened them to war. Brandon felt like women in the class actually started to hate the men after the conversations about unequal pay and dating. He believed, "That's how it was for them. 'We hate you guys because you get more money than us.'" What Zuberi initially thought were healthy disagreements among men and women of color eventually turned into an ugly war in the classroom.

> At times it really did feel like there were two armies and we (men) had to stick up for each other because they would always . . . take it too far and try to push, push it, push the limit. We would be like: "No, it's not that serious."

Harry agreed. What he initially believed to be hypothetical discussions about race and gender became, in his opinion, unnecessary points of conflict. He could not understand why women got so upset and took the conversations so seriously. When he tried to lighten the mood, it only got worse. He explained, "When you tell them it's not that serious, they would take that the wrong way too!" As noted in chapter 1, one of the hallmarks of microaggressions is that they are often perpetrated with unconscious awareness (Sue, 2010a, 2010b; Sue et al., 2007). Typically, perpetrators are not aware they have caused harm. When confronted, a common claim is that the microaggression was not a big deal. Clearly, men in year two were unaware of the pain that their behavior caused, nor did they want to acknowledge the impact gendered racial microaggressions had on women of color. Moreover, by claiming their comments, perspectives, and behaviors were "no big deal," men caused secondary harm by blaming women for being too sensitive (Sue, 2010a, 2010b).

Scholars like hooks (2000) and Hill Collins (1991, 2000) document the ways Black women and Black men are united in the struggle for racial equality and often share a special bond in the fight against racial oppression. This literature suggested men and women of color would likely find solidarity, empowerment, and support in a racial counterspace like Sister Stories. However, a critical race feminist (Wing, 2003) analysis of Sister Stories narratives explicated some of the ways male privilege detracted from notions of solidarity and support between men and women of color.

WE GO THROUGH ISSUES TOO!

As we have shown, men's gendered microaggressions caused emotional harm for women who were hoping for support. As scholars who subscribe to critical race tenets of centering race and racism (Solórzano, 1997) we would be remiss if we did not also acknowledge men of color experienced pervasive forms of racism on and off campus. They wanted a space where they could share their experiences, obtain a sense of belonging, and be validated by other people of color who "got it." Such hopes often went unfulfilled in Sister Stories.

Women's overt and covert resistance to men's oppressive comments about work, dating, and beauty ultimately prompted men to disengage from some class topics. The arguments were not "worth it" as one man said. Arguments were not worth their effort or the potential of seriously harming relationships with women of color outside of the classroom. As such, men of color gave up. In chapter 5, we delve deeply into classroom silence. Here, we want to acknowledge that men of color hoped for a safe counterspace to discuss racism. However, during year two, men of color got the message that their experiences with racism were not appropriate topics for conversation in a counterspace by, and for, women of color. Correspondingly, men of color felt their experiences and perspectives were invalidated by women of color who wanted men to "feel the same way" about oppression. Diego explained:

> No matter how much I try to defend myself, my opinion . . . wasn't
> going to get through to the females because they were just going to

disagree. So, I just bothered not saying it. I just kept my opinions to myself. My opinion didn't change because I didn't say it. . . . They want us to feel the same way but it's like we don't go through the issues so we're not going to feel it the same way. You can tell us all you want, but it's not going to mean anything to us.

Through papers, classroom conversations, and focus groups, we came to see that men's frustration with the counterspace was not just about verbal battles about work and dating. Even though men of color enrolled willingly in a course regarding women of color, the omission of conversations about men became a point of contention in year two. Men expressed frustration about having their experiences with racism left out of Sister Stories conversations. One of the benefits of a counterspace is to have experiences validated by similar others. However, in year two, men felt like their lived realities with racism were taboo subjects for the Sister Stories counterspace. Brandon explained:

I would have liked to see more topics on men of color also. Women of color, honestly they go through a lot of things, but men do also. I feel like, obviously, this class is focused on women of color, but I would have liked to see at least two classes—maybe one—on just men of color. We go through issues too!

Diego concurred, "That doesn't mean because we're [men] of color we have it easier just because we're male. We have to do the same things they do because of our skin color. Females try so hard not to believe this." Men seemed to struggle because their lived realities were invalidated by women of color. As such, they were unable to glean the benefits of collective understanding, validation, and support in the Sister Stories counterspace.

WHITES IN THE COUNTERSPACE

Sister Stories was offered at a public higher education institution. It would have been unethical and illegal to prohibit White students from registering. However, as noted in chapter 1, I (Melissa) met individually with every prospective student to be sure they understood the class content and focus were about the historical and contemporary experiences of women of color in the United States. With the exception of year two, a small number (1–4) of White students enrolled in Sister Stories each semester. Their presence added an interesting layer to counterspace dynamics.

Students of color had an array of opinions about whether or not White people should enroll in Sister Stories, and what role they should play. In every end-of-semester focus group, we asked students of color their opinions about having White students in Sister Stories. Overwhelmingly, students of color believed there was a place for White students—largely because it was important for them to learn about race and racism through the counterstories of students of color. Jewel explained how White people could learn more realistic perspectives on race and racism through counterspace conversations:

> I think that they [White students] should take this class because they learn new perspectives. They learn the stories . . . it's real life examples. [They] could . . . watch a movie or look on the media, but that's not. . . . It's not the same as us being in a room talking about the same issue.

As a man of color, Abe learned a lot about women of color in Sister Stories. He also felt it was important for White students to unlearn stereotypes about women of color:

> I feel like we [people of color] need to hear about women of color and their struggles. . . . There's people out there who need to know it more than we do . . . I feel like coming to a predominantly White campus there should be a lot more White kids in here. I'm learning about the issue [of] stereotypes of women of color . . . there should be a lot more White kids in the class . . . it would just increase their learning [too].

Students of color were often the "only one" in predominantly White campus spaces. As such, they empathized with White students who enrolled in Sister Stories. Pamela explained how choosing to take the Sister Stories course reflected their openness to learning about race and racism and, in turn, made the presence of White students a positive one:

> I feel like I respected them because they didn't like object with ignorance. I feel like they understood and really, you know, added on to their knowledge. . . . [Usually I am] the only woman of color in the class. They were the minorities here and they really got to feel what these women felt. So, I respect them for putting themselves in that situation.

A number of students of color felt like White people's perspectives on race topics could be beneficial. Diego was enrolled during the semester when Sister Stories was comprised only of students of color. He said:

> I think that the fact there was all people of color in this class kind of hurt the class at times. There were discussions where maybe a White person's opinion would help. . . . We don't know how they think; we just know how a couple of them act.

At first, Zuberi agreed with Diego's interest in White student opinions, but then expressed second thoughts. He was not sure his White friends would have learned anything from the course. If they had enrolled, and then perpetuated microaggressions rooted in racist stereotypes, it could have destroyed his cross-race relationships. Zuberi explained:

> I completely agree. I sort of wished that some of my friends from home
> could have taken this class with me because I know they just would
> have said how they felt. Do you know what I mean? Actually, I don't
> know. Now that I'm saying it and thinking it, I don't know if they
> would.

Zuberi's hesitation speaks volumes about the potential emotional toll
(Sue, 2010) microaggressions can take on people of color—especially
when perpetrated by friends and loved ones. Zuberi was not ready to
have White friends resist learning about racism or make racist comments
which would certainly have damaged his relationships. Zuberi's hesitation stemmed from fear of harming interpersonal relationships with
White peers.

Our concern about including White perspectives in Sister Stories
stems from our CRT and CRF perspectives that Whiteness is always centered in the United States. Moreover, the inclusion of White perspectives
would be in stark contrast to the goals of the Sister Stories counterspace
as well as critical race counter storytelling. White and male perspectives
always dominate social discourse. Suggesting the need for White and
male opinions in Sister Stories was another way to privilege and center
those perspectives while marginalizing the counterstories of women of
color. Doing so would have conflicted with the purpose of Sister Stories.

Certainly, there is much literature that decries the importance of
White allies in the struggle for racial justice (Broido & Reason, 2005;
Tatum, 1994; Taylor, Gillborne & Ladson-Billings, 2009). We agree that
there is a need for White allies. However, critical race theorists sometimes
question the motivations, readiness, and ability of Whites to successfully
engage in the struggle (Bergerson, 2003; Solórzano, 1997). Becoming an
ally requires increased awareness, knowledge, and skill building—all of
which take time to develop. White students in Sister Stories were at various levels of self-awareness and readiness to challenge oppression. Nonetheless, students of color seemed to think the good intentions of White
classmates justified their participation in Sister Stories. Because White
students enrolled in Sister Stories appeared open to learning, Regina was
glad for their presence. However, her comment suggests that the climate
of the counterspace could have been far less positive if White students
were less open-minded or had ulterior motives.

> The [White] people who took our class were very open and not judg-
> mental or taking offense. . . . They just seemed interested, which made
> it better. You know? Because you don't want to talk to someone who
> doesn't seem interested in what you want to talk about.

During a focus group conversation, Nicole also described how resistant
White students could have turned the Sister Stories counterspace into an
unsafe place. When asked what Sister Stories would have been like with
resistant White students, Regina replied their presence would have:

Ruined it. [silence] Completely ruined it. . . . It would have definitely changed the outcome of my class experience. There definitely would have been censorship because I'm not going to express the way I feel and what I've been through if I feel like it's not going to be received. So, it would have changed my class experience. [I'm not sure if] everyone should take the class, because, like I said, there's some people who can't be helped, and who won't understand, and who don't want to understand—people who are stuck.

Some White students comprehended how their presence could be detrimental to the sanctity of a counterspace. John, a White man, understood Sister Stories was supposed to be a place where people of color could be candid about their experiences and glean support from others who "got it." The presence of White students, especially those who did not believe racism existed, could severely detract from the counterspace benefits. John said:

Not everyone can take this class. It would kind of destroy the nature of what it is. . . . Like, if everyone did take this class, there would be a lot more time [spent] convincing [White] people that racism does exist . . . and that there is White privilege. You know what I mean? . . . You kind of have to know that going into the class. You have to know that racism is still very alive in our society and that White people hold the power and that minorities don't. So, you have to know that, for the class to kind of move a lot more forward. . . . There'd be a lot less room for discussion. You wouldn't really get deeper . . . if you had to take time to basically tell people [racism does exist].

In alignment with the CRT tenet of centering race and racism, Bryan, Wilson, Lewis, and Wilson (2012) explained how classroom conversations about race in mixed-race classrooms must focus on both interpersonal and systemic forms of racism. John's quote suggests he recognized how important it was for White students to understand systemic forms of privilege, power, and oppression. When White students do not comprehend, or resist conversations about, systems of oppression and privilege, the classroom environment can become toxic for students of color. In such spaces, students of color sometimes bear the burden of educating Whites about racism as opposed to gleaning the validation and comfort that should come with being in a counterspace with people who "get it." As we will show in chapter 5, it can be an emotional burden for people of color to speak for their race and educate their peers (Kelly & Gayles, 2010; Martínez Alemán, 2000). In sum, while the presence of White students in Sister Stories did not seem to "ruin" the sanctity of the counterspace dynamics or cause emotional distress for women of color, it certainly could have.

CONCLUSION

Counterspaces, while incredibly beneficial, are not a panacea. In this chapter, student narratives offered insight into the complicated nature of counterspace dynamics. First, we noted how differences among women of color sometimes prohibited them from finding unconditional support from women peers. Next, we described deep divisions between men and women of color that emerged in the counterspace. Finally, we talked about the potential for racial counterspace dynamics to be altered by the inclusion of White students. In the next chapter, we detail more counterspace challenges by exploring silence during classroom discussions.

REFERENCES

Bankhead, T., & Johnson. T. (2014). Self-esteem, hair-esteem and Black women with natural hair. *International Journal of Education and Social Science, 1*(4), 92–102.

Bergerson, A. A. (2003). Critical race theory and White racism: Is there room for White scholars in fighting racism in education? *Qualitative Studies in Education, 16*(1), 51–63.

Broido, E. M., & Reason, R. D. (2005, Summer). The development of social justice attitudes and actions: An overview of current understandings. In R. D. Reason, E. M. Broido, T. L. Davis & N. J. Evans (Eds.), Developing Social Justice Allies. *New Directions for Student Services* (110) (pp. 17–28). San Francisco, CA: Jossey-Bass.

Bryan, M. L., Wilson, B. S., Lewis, A. A., & Wills, L. E. (2012). Exploring the impact of "race talk" in the education classroom: Doctoral student reflections. *Journal of Diversity in Higher Education, 5*(3), 123.

Butler, J. E., & Walter, J. C. (1991). *Transforming the curriculum: Ethnic studies and women's studies.* Albany, NY: State University of New York Press.

Capodilupo, C. M., Nadal, K. L., Corman, L., Hamit, S., Lyons, O. B., & Weinberg, A. (2010). The manifestation of gender microaggressions. In D. W. Sue (Ed.), *Microaggressions and marginality: Manifestation, dynamics, and impact* (pp. 193–216). Hoboken, NJ: Wiley.

Choo, H. Y., & Ferree, M. M. (2010). Practicing intersectionality in sociological research: A critical analysis of inclusions, interactions, and institutions in the study of inequalities. *Sociological Theory, 28*(2), 129–49.

Combahee River Collective (1995). Combahee River Collective statement. In B. Guy-Sheftall (Ed.), *Words of fire: An anthology of African American feminist thought* (pp. 232–40). New York: New Press. (Original work published 1977)

Crenshaw, K. (1989). Demarginalizing the intersection of race and sex: A black feminist critique of antidiscrimination doctrine, feminist theory and antiracist politics. *University of Chicago Legal Forum*, 139.

Domingue, A. D. (2015). "Our leaders are just we ourself": Black women college student leaders' experiences with oppression and sources of nourishment on a predominantly white college campus. *Equity and Excellence in Education, 48*(3), 454–72.

Essed, P. (1991). *Understanding everyday racism: An interdisciplinary theory.* Thousand Oaks, CA: Sage.

Fredrickson, B. L., & Roberts, T. A. (1997). Objectification theory. *Psychology of Women Quarterly, 21*(2), 173–206.

Harper, S. R., Patton, L. D., & Wooden, O. S. (2009). Access and equity for African American students in higher education: A critical race historical analysis of policy efforts. *The Journal of Higher Education, 80*(4), 389–414.

Hill Collins, P. (1991, 2000). *Black feminist thought: Knowledge, consciousness, and the politics of empowerment.* New York: Routledge.

hooks, b. (2000). *Feminist theory: From margin to center* (2nd ed.). Cambridge, MA: South End.

Hunter, M. (2005). *Race, gender, and the politics of skin tone.* New York: Routledge.

——— (2007). The persistent problem of colorism: Skin tone, status, and inequality. *Sociology Compass, 1*(1), 237–54.

Johnson, T. A., & Bankhead, T. (2014). Hair it is: Examining the experiences of black women with natural hair. *Open Journal of Social Sciences, 2,* 86–100.

Kelly, B. T., & Gayles, J. G. (2010). Resistance to racial/ethnic dialog in graduate preparation programs: Implications for developing multicultural competence. *College Student Affairs Journal, 29*(1), 75–85.

Lewis, J. A., Mendenhall, R., Harwood, S. A., & Browne Huntt, M. (2013). Coping with gendered racial microaggressions among Black women college students. *Journal of African American Studies, 17,* 51–73.

Martínez Alemán, A. M. (2000). Race talks: Undergraduate women of color and female friendships. *The Review of Higher Education, 23*(2), 133–52.

Moraga, C., & Anzaldúa, G. (Eds.) (1981, 2002) *This bridge called my back* (3rd ed.). Berkeley, CA: Third Women's Press.

Museus, S. D., & Griffin, K. A. (2011). Mapping the margins in higher education: On the promise of intersectionality frameworks in research and discourse. In K. A. Griffin & S. D. Museus (Eds.), Using mixed-methods approaches to study intersectionality in higher education. *New Directions for Institutional Research* (151), 5–13.

Museus, S. D., Yee, A. L., & Lambe, S. A. (2011). Multiracial in a monoracial world— Student stories of racial dissolution on the colorblind campus. *About Campus,* 20–25.

Nuñez, A. M. (2011). Counterspaces and connections in college transitions: First-generation Latino students' perspectives on Chicano studies. *Journal of College Student Development, 52*(6), 639–55.

Patton, T. O. (2006). Hey girl, am I more than my hair?: African American women and their struggles with beauty, body image, and hair. *NWSA Journal, 18*(2), 24–51.

Pérez Huber, L., & Cueva, B. M. (2012). Chicana/Latina testimonios on effects and responses to microaggressions. *Equity and Excellence in Education, 45*(3), 392–410.

Renn, K. A. (2004). *Mixed race students in college: The ecology of race, identity, and community on campus.* Albany, NY: SUNY Press.

——— (2011). Mixed race millennials in college. In F. A Bonner III, A. F. Marbley & M. H. Hamliton (Eds.), *Diverse millennial students in college: Implications for faculty and student affairs* (pp. 227–42). Sterling, VA: Stylus.

Rockquemore, K. A. (2002). Negotiating the color line: The gendered process of racial identity construction among Black/White biracial women. *Gender & Society, 16*(4), 485–503.

Shields, S. A. (2008). Gender: An intersectionality perspective. *Sex Roles, 59,* 301–11.

Solórzano, D. G. (1997). Images and words that wound: Critical race theory, racial stereotyping, and teacher education. *Teacher Education Quarterly,* 5–19.

———, Ceja, M., & Yosso, T. J. (2000). Critical race theory, racial microaggressions, and campus racial climate: The experiences of African American college students. *The Journal of Negro Education, 69*(1/2), 60–73.

———, & Yosso, T. J. (2001). Critical race and LatCrit theory and method: Counterstorytelling. *International Journal of Qualitative Studies in Education, 14*(4), 471–95.

Sue, D. W. (Ed.) (2010a). *Microaggressions and marginality: Manifestations, dynamics and impact.* Hoboken, NJ: Wiley.

——— (2010b). *Microaggressions in everyday life: Race, gender and sexual orientation.* Hoboken, NJ: Wiley.

———, Bucceri, J., Lin, A. I., Nadal, K. L., & Torino, G. C. (2009). Racial microaggressions and the Asian American experience. *Asian American Journal of Psychology, S*(1), 88–101.

Tatum, B. (1994). Teaching White students about racism: The search for White allies and the restoration of hope. *The Teachers College Record, 95*(4), 462–76.

Taylor, E., Gillborn, D., & Ladson-Billings, G. (2009). *Foundations of critical race theory in education.* New York: Routledge.

Wing, A. K. (2003). *Critical race feminism: A reader* (2nd ed.). New York: New York University Press.

Wong, G., Derthick, A. O., David, E. J. R., Saw, A., & Okazaki, S. (2013). The *what*, the *why*, and the *how*: A review of racial microaggressions research in psychology. *Race and Social Problems, 6*(2), 181–200.

Yosso, T., Smith, W., Ceja, M., & Solórzano, D. (2009). Critical race theory, racial microaggressions, and campus climate for Latina/o undergraduates. *Harvard Educational Review, 79*(4) 659–69.

Zinn, M. B., & Dill, B. T. (1996). Theorizing difference from multiracial feminism. *Feminist studies, 22*(2), 321–31.

FIVE

Silence and Self-Censoring

"Telling my story . . . or not."

Critical race theorists use counterstories to "make central the voices and experiences of those who have historically existed within the margins of mainstream institutions" (Darder, Baltodano & Torres, 2003, p. 14). Counterstories allow people of color to speak their truths while simultaneously challenging racist assumptions and myths. These often include tales of marginalization, exclusion, pain, and resilience. Throughout *Centering Women of Color in Academic Counterspaces*, student narratives suggest reading and listening to counterstories from contemporary and historical women of color was a transformational educational experience.

As noted in chapter 1, centering the counterstories of women of color was a main focus of the Sister Stories course. In order to elicit counterstories from students, discussions were frequently used as a pedagogical tool. During each class session, time was allotted for students to dialogue about topics that touched the lives of women of color and to share their own counterstories. Most students described these conversations as the most enjoyable aspect of the course. Yet, as we describe in the forthcoming pages, some students admitted to self-censoring or not sharing their counterstories at all. The seven most commonly cited reasons for student silence are discussed in this chapter.

DIALOGUES ABOUT AND ACROSS DIFFERENCE

The Benefits

As our world and higher education institutions become more diverse (NCES, 2012), the need for conversations among diverse students, and about diverse topics, is growing. There is a wealth of literature documenting the benefits of student engagement in conversations about difference. Specifically, research points to the benefits of both classroom diversity and interactional diversity (Gurin, 1999; Hu & Kuh, 2003; Strayhorn, 2010). Classroom diversity refers to the inclusion of diverse perspectives and representation of diverse groups in the curriculum, whereas interactional diversity references the interpersonal interactions between students from diverse backgrounds.

What are the specific benefits of diverse students interacting in a classroom? As students from diverse racial backgrounds interact with each other, they have the potential to learn about different cultures and perspectives. As we noted in chapter 4, even when Sister Stories was comprised solely of students of color, there was a vast diversity of races, ethnicities, social classes, and perspectives among students. Educational and social science literature shows that cross-racial interactions have been associated with important educational outcomes such as increased critical thinking, heightened problem-solving skills, negotiation skills, intellectual and social self-confidence, and the ability to communicate across difference (Chang, Denson, Saenz & Misa, 2006; Laird, Engberg & Hurtado, 2005). The growing body of intergroup relations literature documents similar benefits of cross-identity interactions (Maxwell, Nagada & Thompson, 2011; Nagada & Zúñiga, 2003; Zúñiga, Nagada, Chesler & Cytron-Walker, 2007; Zúñiga, Williams & Berger, 2005). Intergroup relations is an educational approach that brings together a small group of people from different social identity groups to discuss their experiences and perspectives. Individuals who participate in intergroup dialogues show a host of positive educational gains (Nagada & Zúñiga, 2003; Zúñiga et al., 2007) such as increased self-awareness, understanding of identity, and respect for difference. One study showed that "cross group interaction [was among] the strongest sources of influence on both motivation to reduce one's own prejudice and taking outward actions to promote inclusion and social justice" (Zúñiga et al., 2005, p. 674). In short, there are a host of educational benefits for students who participate in dialogues across, and about, difference.

The Challenges

Despite the educational benefits of engaging diverse students in diversity dialogues, conversations across and about difference can pose challenges for students and educators. The process of talking about self and others is not always easy or comfortable. In fact, feelings of shame, guilt, anger, embarrassment, and rage can sometimes emerge during classroom conversations about difference (Fox, 2009; hooks, 2003; Watt, 2007). Such strong emotional reactions can stifle conversation. Deep and negative emotions can also evoke feelings of mistrust or cause psychological harm to students.

Two ways students can respond to emotional challenges during diversity dialogues is to either remain completely silent or self-censor their comments. Literature suggests specific reasons why students self-censor or remain silent differ among White students and students of color. White students may self-censor or remain silent because they are afraid of being perceived as prejudiced (Fox, 2009; Richeson & Shelton, 2007). In some cases, feelings of guilt and shame related to privilege can lead White students to resist or avoid diversity conversations altogether (Fox, 2009; Goodman, 2011; Jones, 2008; Watt, 2007).

Higher education scholars suggest the reasons for silence and resistance are quite different for students of color. It can be an emotional burden for people of color to "speak for their race" and educate their peers (Kelly & Gayles, 2010; Martínez Alemán, 2000). This burden can feel even more difficult in classrooms where students of color feel offended, stereotyped, or tokenized by peers or faculty. In these instances, students of color may decide to stop talking and sharing. A number of CRF and other women writers of color have documented how women of color can use silence as a means of self-protection during painful or emotionally exhausting dialogues about difference (Johnson-Bailey & Cervero, 1996; Martínez Alemán, 2000). Women of color in Sister Stories sometimes used this self-protective strategy. They also remained silent during classroom conversations for many other reasons.

SILENCE IN SISTER STORIES

In the following pages, student narratives offer insight into the nature of self-censorship in Sister Stories. First, we share student perspectives on class discussions—which we found to be overwhelmingly positive. Then we detail seven reasons students gave for their silence. We wondered how comprehensively the literature on dialogue and self-censorship explained student silence in the Sister Stories counterspace. Is the only reason White students remained silent a fear of sounding racist? Did women of color only remain quiet because they were tired of educating Whites or engaging in self-protection? Based upon five years of observations, we believed the reasons for student silence were more complex than the literature suggested. So, we invited students to talk about self-censorship and silence. Through focus groups and interviews, we came to learn that students self-censored their counterstories, or remained completely silent, for a variety of reasons. Reasons for silence depended on the topic, the perceived level of trust, classroom dynamics, peer relationships, and the student's personality. While some of these reasons align with the aforementioned literature, others are new.

DISCUSSIONS ARE GREAT, BUT
WE DON'T ALWAYS PARTICIPATE

Over the course of our five-year study, students consistently reported classroom discussions as a favorite aspect of Sister Stories. Mindy said "Having to hear other students' opinions . . . was an eye-opener so I enjoyed the way the class was set up." Regina concurred. She said, "I agree. . . . Because of the way it was set up, it made me less likely to not want to show up because it was like, well you never know what we're going to do today. Like we could be . . . talking about something that was interesting."

When probed about their participation in classroom discussions, however, consistent themes of self-censorship and silence emerged. Despite the fact that the course was structured around sharing counterstories through dialogue, some students admitted Sister Stories discussions did not always get below the surface. Dominic stated, "I feel for the most part everybody tried to like avoid [difficult] situations . . . being politically correct and everything." Malcolm perceived that his peers rarely delved deeply into their own stories or feelings. He wanted to hear more from them, saying, "I would like to hear them get deeper with how they felt." Sia described how the classroom would often get silent when the topic became heavy or the dialogue got too intense. Instead of talking about *why* the class was silent, the topic was quickly changed. Jackie said, "Part of that awkward silence is what we *should* have talked more about—like what we expressed inside instead of just having the awkward silence and then start off on another topic." In essence, some students admitted to self-censoring their verbal contributions. Of course, students *talked* during the class period. They had opinions, jokes, and comments to share. However, such surface-level contributions rarely contained deeply personal counterstories or challenging life narratives.

We wanted to know why some students self-censored and/or decided to remain silent—especially since the class was designed as a counter-space *and* students reported enjoying class discussions. During interviews and focus groups, we asked students whether or not they ever self-censored, and why. Students offered a host of reasons why they refrained from sharing counterstories. Those reasons are explored in the remainder of the chapter.

I DON'T TRUST YOU

As noted in chapter 1, I (Melissa) focused on trust building and development of respect in the Sister Stories counterspace. Some years I was more successful than others. Trust played a large role in student decisions to share personal stories or remain silent. Trust is not always easy to foster, but it is necessary for all meaningful interpersonal relationships. This is especially the case in mixed-race classrooms. Scholars have documented how the presence of racial microaggressions in everyday life leads to racial mistrust for both perpetrators and targets (Sue et al., 2006; Sue, 2010). Such mistrust does not engender learning spaces where students want to divulge personal stories.

Mindy explained how she rarely shared her counterstory in the classroom. Even though Sister Stories was intended to be a trusting and respectful counterspace, Mindy did not feel safe discussing personal information. She explained:

> Why would I share a personal story with someone that I don't even know? Um, and I understand like, yes, it's an open and safe environment and it's a small class. But, even then, you don't know what they're gonna go [say outside] these walls. It could turn back on you [and you would] kind of regret the fact that you did share a personal story.

Becca needed time to decide if her counterstory would be respected by her peers. Her fears slowly began to subside as classmates took risks and shared their personal stories. Their willingness to divulge allowed her to feel more comfortable sharing personal information. It was not hard for her to write her personal story in the "I Am" assignment, but she needed a whole other level of trust to discuss personal narratives with her peers. She explained:

> I was nervous. Writing the paper wasn't the problem, presenting it was *so* nerve-racking. . . . But then, the more I heard everyone else's story I felt comfortable. You know? Everyone [talked] before me, so I was like, "Alright now I can do it."

Brian also talked about his decision to tell only surface level bits of information about himself until he trusted his peers. By watching others take risks and share personal stories, Brian began to feel more comfortable divulging his story:

> At first you're like, "Ok, nobody knows me in this class. I'm not going to share my story with them. I'm just going to [share] this little thing." . . . [But] you build experiences with this class. You become more comfortable sharing your opinion and then you're able to open up and share your story with everyone . . . because you feel comfortable with this class and they are doing the same thing as you, whereas in the beginning you didn't know them at all.

In short, we learned that trust was paramount to students' decisions to share their counterstories. Students needed classmates to *earn* their trust. Building this level of trust took time. Student disclosure often came at the end of the semester after a solid foundation of trust had been built. For others, trust in peers never materialized. Scholars of inclusive and critical pedagogy argue that faculty must build trust before asking students to engage in tough conversations about race, gender, or other diversity topics (Tuitt, 2006; Vaccaro, 2013). As we described in chapter 1, a half-day trust-building retreat was implemented in Sister Stories after students expressed concerns about trust.

YOU WOULDN'T UNDERSTAND

While some students talked generally about their hesitation to entrust classmates with their personal stories, others talked more deeply about the root of their hesitations. Sometimes students did not share their life experiences during discussions because they felt it would be impossible for classmates to truly understand their complicated lives. They did not believe their peers would "get it" or respect their counter narratives. Such fears align with CRT perspectives that dominant ideologies, or normative worldviews, are often accepted and unquestioned, especially by those with privilege (Darder et al., 2003; Delgado, 1989; Delgado & Stefancic, 2000; Solórzano & Yosso, 2002). When the lived realities of women and people of color do not align with dominant ideologies, they are misunderstood and viewed as suspect. In response, people of color can sometimes approach interactions with Whites and interactions with Whites and people of color from other racial and ethnic backgrounds with hypervigilance and skepticism (Sue, 2010).

Women of color viewed counter storytelling in mixed-race and gender classrooms with some apprehension. Their hesitation to share counterstories resulted in a missed opportunity to debunk deficit notions about people of color. For instance, Fola's counterstory may have "challenge[d] dominant deficit perspectives of immigrant[s]" if she had shared it with the class (Pérez-Huber & Cueva, 2012, p. 404). However, Fola decided not to discuss her family situation because of her fear that classmates would not comprehend her lived reality as a child of immigrants. Fola said:

> It's tough. It's really a touchy situation. Like I feel like my parents' immigration status controls everything in my life, whether it be their jobs, what I can do. . . . It controls everything and I feel like if you're not in that situation you can't really understand it. It just hurts 'cause a lot of people don't understand how you live with immigrant parents—the things that they can actually do, what they are limited to, and their actual struggles. So, I just choose to keep that to myself.

During a conversation about family dynamics, Lauren also chose not to disclose her counterstories about kin. She said, "I found myself hesitating. I feel like my story was a little too crazy to be able to explain to the class." One man of color, Paul, shared how he often did not contribute his counterstories because conveying them authentically in a few short moments felt impossible. He said, "the most difficult part of the class for me was having to . . . capture the essence of who I am without writing an entire autobiography." Since he did not feel capable of conveying his authentic self in short sound bites, he kept his counterstory to himself.

Lucy explained how she often held back stories because she felt her White classmates (Kristen and Emily) would not get it. She said:

> If you haven't gone through it—or the saying "You haven't walked in my shoes you can't really completely understand." [That's] what I'm feeling a lot of times. I felt that Kristen and Emily were in that situation. They didn't . . . really understand what was going on and it sometimes made me feel bad because sometimes this was a place for me to just let it all out—just go for it. . . . But then it made me feel kind of bad because I know these two girls were trying to understand as best they can. But they may never really understand until someone treats them . . . the way I've been treated.

Even though Lucy felt like her White peers were *trying* to understand, they could not possibly comprehend her experiences as a Black woman. Her comment also suggested that she saw the classroom as a counter-space where she was supposed to be able to "let it all out." CRT scholars describe counterspaces as places where students of color can "vent frustrations and cultivate friendships with people who share many of their experiences" (Yosso et al., 2009, p. 677). Yet, Lucy did not always find the classroom to be a place where she could comfortably "let it all out." In fact, she self-censored or felt "bad" about divulging her experiences to White peers who could not possibly understand her life.

During one alumni focus group, three women of color had an intense discussion about the appropriateness of talking about certain topics with White students. Jewel, Regina, and Nicole agreed that there were some topics that White people would not understand, and by bringing them up, women of color were placed in uncomfortable positions. As part of the conversation, Regina shared that she was "a little upset" that the documentary *Good Hair* was shown in class. Nicole and Jewel agreed. They rarely had an opportunity to have frank conversations about hair and beauty with other people of color. By including what they perceived to be a hot topic in the mixed-race and gender counterspace, women of color felt they (and their hair) were put under a microscope. We delve much more deeply into issues of beauty and body image in chapter 7. Here, women's quotes show how aesthetic topics, like hair, were difficult to talk about and engendered silence from some women of color. Jewel explained why she remained quiet during the conversation about the documentary:

> We haven't, as a [Black community,] even had a real conversation. When you start to bring in White people who might not understand the idea of weaves and relaxers, then they try to understand and they think they could just touch your hair. You censor yourself because there are

certain things that [White people] just don't understand because they're not within the culture.

Regina and Nicole also admitted to remaining quiet during the conversation—hoping their silence would speed up the conclusion of the discussion about Black women's hair. They knew that whether or not they actually talked during the post-film discussion, they would still be objectified by peers. The focus group touched upon the connection between self-censorship and objectification:

Jewel: When they played *Good Hair*, I was like, ugh, now they're [White people and men] gonna think all of us wear weaves. They're gonna know our struggles. We're trying to blend in already. Jeez, now all our secrets are out! [laughter]

Nicole: Have them looking at your scalp a different way.

Jewel: Yeah, looking for like, closures and stuff.

Nicole: Does she have it? Is that gross? [laughter]

Jewel made another case for limiting the topics discussed in inter-racial dialogues, saying:

That's what I mean by censored. Like there's certain conversations . . . like the n-word for instance. It's a conversation that's tough in the Black community. When you start to bring in people from other races it's like—"I know you want to be part of this conversation, but it's one of those conversations [you should not be a part of]." It's like a family conversation . . . you need to have it at home at the dinner table.

Nicole concurred. She believed that tough racial topics should be restricted to same-race groups—like a family or "a club."

Women of color also described *how* they responded to sensitive or emotional topics in the mixed-race and gender classroom could potentially reinforce racial stereotypes. Lucy self-censored her comments so she would not sound like the "crazy" woman of color, especially to her White peers. She said:

I feel like even in normal conversations you still sugar coat 'cause you . . . don't want to be looked at as you know the crazy Black girl or the crazy Hispanic girl always talking about racial issues [and who] can't get along with anybody else. You don't want to be looked at like that.

Fola also worried that by delving deeply into her counterstory, she might reinforce deficit-based stereotypes of Black women. She said, "I don't want people to think I'm a charity case . . . or that I'm weaker than you. That's why [I] don't really dig deep in public."

The fear of reinforcing stereotypes was not merely about White peers. Laura worried about reinforcing stereotypes with men of color in the classroom. During a heated discussion, she decided to remain silent. She feared that if the men "saw my raw emotions, then I may just feed into their stereotype that women are too emotional." For more about complicated classroom dynamics between men and women of color, see chapter 4.

Student narratives speak to complex dialogic realities in counterspaces. Their references to "in-group" or "family" conversations among people of color align with the literature on ideal counterspace communities that engender feelings of validation, belonging, and empowerment among an in-group of people (Grier-Reed, 2010; Pérez Huber & Cueva, 2012; Solórzano, Ceja & Yosso, 2000; Solórzano & Villalpando, 1998; Yosso, 2006; Yosso, Smith, Ceja & Solórzano, 2009). Yet, as we discussed in chapter 4, the dynamics of a counterspace are complicated by the intersections of race, ethnicity, national origin, gender, sexual orientation, and social class. Instead of being a safe counterspace where women of color could talk candidly about tough topics, the presence of a few White students and/or men of color prompted their silence and self-censorship. Their comments also exemplify the use of hypervigilance (Sue, 2010), which is a common strategy people of color use to disassociate themselves from deficit assumptions in mixed-race settings. Women of color were hypervigilant about not sharing in-group information that could be used by men and White people to reinforce damaging stereotypes about women of color.

I'M NOT GONNA WASTE MY BREATH

Related to the topic of peers not being able to comprehend their stories, some students talked about how they self-censored or remained silent because they perceived closed-mindedness from classmates. Many women of color (and a few men of color) felt it was a waste of time and energy to try to educate resistant peers. This theme relates to literature about how emotionally taxing it can be for people of color to constantly educate their peers (Kelly & Gayles, 2010; Martínez Alemán, 2000). Narratives from our students add richness to this growing body of literature.

Kendra explained how she took the time to share her counterstory only after determining her peers were willing to listen and learn. If they were not open-minded, she remained silent. She shared:

> I think it depends more on the person. If I know they're willing to listen to what I have to say, then I'm gonna take my time. But if you're just gonna act [or think] the same anyways, then I'm not gonna waste my breath.

Brandon also felt it was a "waste" to share his story if people would question his reality. He shared, "Yeah, because they didn't want to believe it. So why am I going to keep telling you? Why am I going to keep forcing this on to you? . . . So, I'm not going to waste my time." Nicole also self-censored when she felt that her peers would not bother to understand her perspective. She said:

> There definitely [was] censorship because I'm not going to express the way I feel and what I've been through if I feel like it's not going to be well received. . . . There's some people who can't be helped and who won't understand and who don't *want* to understand—people who are stuck.

People who were stuck were not worth her breath.

While Kendra, Nicole, and Brandon referenced general close-mindedness and resistance from peers, some women of color remained silent in response to defiant men of color. Critical race feminists lament how women of color can be marginalized not only by Whites, but also by men of color (hooks, 2000; Wing, 2003). Findings described here build upon those shared in chapter 4 where we discussed the complicated intersectional dynamics in the counterspace.

Laura explained how she and many of her peers of color began to self-censor after a man of color made a sexist comment. In this particular cohort, there was a critical mass of men of color and no White students. One woman of color heard a man of color make a comment "under his breath" and news spread fast among the class. Laura decided his closed-mindedness made her uncomfortable and she stopped sharing her stories. Laura described how:

> [He] said something crazy. [We] were talking about how the media sexualizes women of color . . . and someone made a comment like: "Black girls give it up, but White girls basically have training and Black girls don't" but it was under his breath. The girl next to him heard it. He wasn't going to say that out loud. We knew in the end that he said it. After those comments, I wasn't uncomfortable.

After Laura described how she was uncomfortable sharing, Diana chimed into the conversation and explained that she also self-censored because she felt like men "wouldn't see where we were coming from. They were just stuck in the way they saw [things]." Nicole concurred saying, "I feel like the men were set in their ways . . . like really stubborn." Women in the class picked up on the silence of their women peers. Laura noticed how Regina stopped talking and that prompted her own ruminations on self-censorship. Laura said, "I feel like Regina was at that point where she wouldn't say anything because as soon as she would say something, the [men] would be like, 'Well, no!'"

The experiences of women in this particular class align with critical race feminist literature detailing how women of color can "become, literally and figuratively, voiceless and invisible" when their lived realities of intersecting racism and sexism go unaddressed or when men of color engage in sexist behavior (Wing, 2003, p. 2). As we described in chapter 4, the classroom was designed to be an affirming counterspace. Yet, there were times when it was not validating or safe for women of color.

I DON'T WANT TO SOUND IGNORANT OR RACIST

Research suggests that White students self-censor out of fear of sounding racist (Fox, 2009; Goodman, 2001; Jones, 2008; Watt, 2007). In this study, we found that the fear of sounding ignorant or racist transcended race. Women of color feared sounding ignorant or "racist" about people of color from their own or other racial and ethnic backgrounds. Critical race theorists argue that racism permeates U.S. culture and social structures. Dominant ideologies that reinforce stereotypes about people of color are learned by *everyone* in society through socialization (Bell, 2007). As such, people of color can internalize negative messages and stereotypes about other people of color. The psychology literature offers a nuanced view of the interpersonal racism that can result. Clark (2004) explained:

> A member of a given ethnic group may hold prejudiced attitudes and exhibit discriminatory behaviors toward members of a different ethnic group (intergroup racism) or toward members of the same ethnic group (intragroup racism). As such, Blacks as well as members of other ethnic groups can be racist. (p. 507)

All students admitted to self-censoring out fear of revealing ignorance or engaging in intergroup or intragroup racism.

Maria understood how students of color could "feel a little ignorant" in a class where people from so many different ethnicities were present. In Sister Stories, she learned a lot of information about women of color from other ethnic backgrounds. Maria said, "I understand a little bit why other people might feel ignorant at times 'cuz I was." Regina learned about vast differences among women from different and the same racial background. She explained by comparing herself to two other Black women in the room. She said, "I'm a person who is of African American or Black background and she's Cape Verdean, and she's Nigerian. So, even though we all are minorities, we still have cultural differences." In a reflection paper, Brandon connected these cultural differences to the notion of ignorance when he wrote: "I'm not exactly sure how the Latino, Asian, and White cultures differentiate among themselves but I know within the Black community saying the experiences of Black people are all the same would be ignorant."

Mindy talked about her fears of saying something that would be considered racist toward people of color from other racial and ethnic backgrounds. She admitted having personal experiences with White students and other people of color who assumed that since her family was from Columbia that they were drug dealers. She said, "I have experienced it. . . . Everyone's like, 'Your family's the drug dealers.'" Because Maria knew how it felt to be offended by other people of color, she carefully chose her words so she would not do the same. Hanna admitted that she had questions about the experiences of women of color from other racial and ethnic backgrounds. But, she did not ask them out of fear of sounding ignorant. She explained:

> I felt like I didn't know *how* to ask a question. So, that's why I didn't even bother to ask. I didn't know how to word it or speak it. I would have felt dumb or stupid. So, I was like, "Let me not even say anything."

Jocelyn, a self-identified Haitian and Cape Verdean American, also self-censored herself during discussions about Latinas. She worried that her assumptions about Latina classmates might be rooted in deficit stereotypes and misinformation. She said:

> I think it was one of the stereotypes where we talked about Spanish women always having babies . . . I self-censored because I had facts based on something I had learned in a different class about Spanish women having babies. So, I felt like I needed to learn more and I had a little ignorance to the topic. So I felt like it wasn't my place to speak about it. So I kind of self-censored and did not said anything at that time because I didn't want to offend anyone.

Many students of color had never heard the term *women of color* before the first day of class. Or, they admitted to a lack of understanding about the term. For instance, Bonnie explained how she thought only Black women could be considered women of color. She said, "To me, women of color meant like just like Black women because that's all I heard. The only people I ever saw calling themselves women of color [were Black women]." During a focus group, a number of Black and Latina students also admitted that they had assumed Asian Americans and Pacific Islanders were White, and thus not included in the category of people of color. They were embarrassed by their ignorance and remained silent so that they would not sound ignorant to their peers, instructor, or teaching assistants.

Sia summarized her fears when she explained how all students harbor stereotypes about people from other racial and ethnic backgrounds. Fear of perpetuating interracial or intraracial microaggressions shaped her classroom behavior. Sia said:

> After learning about all different types of stereotypes and how it offends people, you kind of try to avoid having those stereotypes. One of the things that came up in [a] presentation [about racial microaggres-

sions] . . . [was how] you do it unconsciously. I think we were all just
trying to avoid that.

To Maria, the fear of sounding racist and offending other women of color
was always on her mind. She stated:

> I kind of think over what I'm going to say to somebody just so that they
> won't get hurt. Like I used to be the person who would say anything
> that came out and that was bad. . . . But now I just think to myself and
> ask, "Does this sound racist? Like how does that sound? Are you label-
> ing somebody by saying that?"

One of the men of color in class also talked about not wanting to offend
students of color from other ethnic groups. Dominic found it difficult to
avoid being offensive in a class full of people from a variety of racial and
ethnic backgrounds. He shared:

> It's hard to get away from that, no matter what. When you got different
> groups of different ethnicities, it's just bound to happen. And you just
> try your hardest not to get an opinion or viewed as a racist so you just
> make sure you say everything correctly and don't offend nobody.

In line with the higher education literature, White students in this
counterspace feared being perceived as ignorant about racial and ethnic
issues (Fox, 2009; Goodman, 2011; Watt, 2007). Jenna explained, "You
don't want to come off as being ignorant." Katie expanded on that idea.
Some of the topics she felt ignorant about were the distinctions between
races and ethnicities and the proper terminology to use to refer to people
of color. Katie shared:

> To be honest, this is going to sound really dumb, but before I came
> here, like I didn't know anything like Cape Verdean . . . I never heard,
> it's just always been like, "Oh, those are like African Americans." Like
> you know what I mean? . . . I didn't know, or didn't realize. Actually
> that is a lot what I learned in this class. Sometimes . . . Black people
> aren't African American.

Even though Katie learned important information about terminology and
race/ethnic distinctions, she still felt the need to qualify her statement by
saying "this is going to sound dumb." Her qualification may indicate
how deep the fear of sounding ignorant ran.

In addition to being perceived as generally ignorant, White students
were especially fearful of seeming racist. As early as the first day of class,
White students were terrified of saying or doing something that would
be seen as racist. Allie said, "I definitely didn't want to be like that White
girl who said something racist the first day." So that they would not come
across as racist, White students mulled over what they wanted to say
before speaking in class. When they did speak, they chose their words
carefully to "make sure" classmates did not think they were racist. For
instance, Allie always couched her comments "in a politically correct

form." Katie described an experience where she talked longer than planned because she was trying not to "sound racist." She explained:

> I've never even thought about like, "Oh maybe these things are offensive." And so then I like really had to think about what I was saying before it came out of my mouth. Sometimes that was like frustrating to me . . . I didn't want to be that [racist] person. So then I would like second-guess myself. [When I presented] I just felt like I was talking longer, because I was trying to be like "I'm really not trying to be racist."

Katie admitted, "I would call my mom and be like 'I just don't know if I can handle this class because I just want to say something but that I'm scared I'm going to sound racist.'" In sum, student narratives in this section push the bounds of higher education literature that suggests only White students are fearful of sounding ignorant or racist. Sister Stories students from a range of racial and ethnic backgrounds expressed similar fears of sounding ignorant or racist.

FEAR OF HARMING RELATIONSHIPS

Classrooms are not merely places to receive new knowledge. They are important social spaces, where students navigate new relationships and build upon previously existing ones with peers and instructors (Johnson & Bhatt, 2003; Tuitt, 2006). In chapter 3, we discussed how the development of social capital is a benefit of counterspaces like Sister Stories. Each year, there were students who knew each other as acquaintances or close friends prior to the start of the semester. There were other students, however, who knew no one on the first day of class. Despite these differences, all students worried about saying something that would harm relationships with classmates.

Katie, a White woman, was friends with a number of women of color in the class. She wondered if they might no longer want to be friends with her if she said something offensive. Katie said, "And I think it was hard because like two of my pretty close friends in this class are of color and like I felt like, 'Oh my God, are they not going to want to be my friend if I say that.'" Her classroom behavior was affected by her fear of damaging relationships:

> I usually talk a lot [in] small classes, but . . . definitely, there was times when I like wanted to be like, "Whoa, I don't agree with that at all." But, I kind of just like sat back and . . . respected that that was their opinion.

White students also admitted to carefully choosing their words or making disclaimers like "I'm sorry if I'm offending anyone" and "I'm going to put out this disclaimer." Usually, though, Jenna said she would "whimper out my opinion and like hope that that's ok with everyone." These efforts were intended to avoid damaging relationships. As we noted in chapter 2, people with privilege often use disclaimers in an attempt to downplay the seriousness of their comments. However, disclaimers can actually compound the harm of a microaggression (Sue, 2010).

Women of color also described a fear of harming relationships. Even if they were not friends with particular peers, classroom relationships were important enough to warrant serious considerations about self-censorship. Jackie walked on eggshells because she feared having to do group work with peers whom she may have offended or disrespected during dialogues. Even though they were not close friends, she might have to depend on classmates to complete group assignments. She stated:

> So we didn't want to say anything that would upset someone because we know everyone has a different opinion about their race. So if we had said something that would spark something, that person wouldn't talk to us for probably the rest of the class. . . . To go and do a project we had little groups. It would feel uncomfortable sitting with the person.

Students of color discussed a tendency to remain quiet so they would not harm previously existing relationships. On a campus with relatively few students of color, Devon felt like she could not afford to alienate any potential friends or allies. Mindy said, "So even though [I] might feel something, it's not always necessary to say it because . . . you never know who you might offend." Regina also explained:

> There might have been some times where I didn't share because I was scared about how people would think about me. I mean even though I do talk a lot and I do speak my mind, there were times where I was like, I'm just going to step back and let someone else talk because I don't want someone to be like judgmental about me.

Angel, one of the graduate teaching assistants described witnessing students of color, especially women, hold back during conversations out of fear of harming relationships with peers of color. She explained:

> I know who is friends and I know who hangs out, outside of class . . . I noticed that one person wasn't willing to challenge her friend to think deeply. Because they [have relationships] outside of the classroom . . . they are not willing to push it. In particular, two of our students who [are] best friends, were not willing to question the other's approach or understanding. So yeah, I can definitely see how [silence and self-censorship] plays into the relationships that they have personally.

During a focus group with men of color, they discussed how a heated classroom debate could have dire consequences for personal relationships outside the classroom walls. A number of men admitted that they self-censored their perspectives because it was not "worth" the potential damage it could do to their relationships with women of color. For instance, Zuberi explained, "When you step outside that class, it's different. Alright, maybe he said this rude thing in class, but that doesn't mean he's a bad guy. . . . You don't want to be perceived wrong." Men of color worried that getting into heated classroom debate would harm important relationships with women of color. Most men agreed that sharing stories or opinions that would upset women of color were not worth it. In fact, they discussed how none of the topics were "important enough" to risk harming relationships by arguing about them. This was especially true when the topics related to beauty, body image, or women's wages. (See chapters 4 and 7 for lengthier discussions of these topics.) Diego shared how he did not want to "get into a heated debate on something that was still going to be a standstill at the end of the day." This was especially true since he would see women of color in extra-curricular settings after class. He admitted that he "just tried to keep my opinions to myself." Kalu concurred, saying, "I held back. I didn't want to get into a heated argument about something that's not serious enough to be argued about; that makes no sense." A critical race feminist lens can be used to interrogate men's perspective about what topics they deemed "serious enough" to warrant getting upset over. Kalu's comment suggested he felt justified in judging the "seriousness" of topics affecting women of color. By deeming certain topics as less serious or worthy, he invalidated the significance of those topics to women's lives. Such male privilege is precisely what critical race feminists critique (Wing, 2003).

IT'S NOT MY SPACE OR PLACE TO TALK

The course emphasis and foci about women of color was another reason why students self-censored or remained silent. Since Sister Stories centered the historical and contemporary experiences of women of color in the United States, White students and men of color understood their stories or opinions did not always belong. The course was a counterspace for and about women of color. So, they remained silent or limited their comments.

Most of the White students believed that their role in the classroom was to listen versus share. During the classroom conversations about racism, Kristin realized that she had nothing to contribute. Even when the instructor elicited student comments about racial microaggressions, she stayed silent. Kristin explained, "I kind of felt like I shouldn't say anything because I don't experience it. I don't really know what it's like." Conversely, Jenna, who identified as an immigrant, felt she had some valuable insight to share about discrimination. Yet, as a White woman, she felt her counterstory did not belong in the classroom. She lamented:

> I'm an immigrant. Some students [of color] in the class were talking about their accents. . . . And like I have the same experience too! Granted I'm not discriminated against. I'm not faced with [racial] prejudice, but like I've had the similar experience.

Even though Jenna felt she had a valuable story of immigration to share, she remained silent. Her tone and body language in the focus group conveyed resentment about being silenced.

John, a White man, seemed to understand that the classroom was designed to be a counterspace for women of color. He also acknowledged that every other space on campus was a place where he felt free to speak up and speak out. John explained:

> The class was for me to learn about women of color. I knew the class works if they speak more and I basically speak less, obviously because it's centered around them. So I kind of went in knowing to watch myself and to kind of make sure I'm not like infiltrating the class. . . . My perspectives were . . . the ones they didn't really want to learn about, which is fine, and I kind of went with it. I knew it was kind of centered around women of color. . . . You get the White perspective basically everywhere else in society.

John seemed to comprehend that most educational institutions were White spaces (Anderson, 2015) where the perspectives and opinions of White people are considered the norm. He also understood the importance of keeping Sister Stories centered on the counterstories of women of color instead of White perspectives like his.

Andrew, a White male from a different cohort, recognized that his personal narrative might not belong in the counterspace. However, he felt comfortable sharing his opinions about course topics. Andrew admitted that he tried not to get "huffy puffy" or resentful when it was time to remain quiet. Andrew would talk

> whenever I thought it was like kind of appropriate like for my two cents. If it was on the topic of women of color and . . . the image factor, I found myself kind of laid back because it's not like I can talk about how my hair curls or like everyone makes fun of my complexion or everyone dismisses me because of the way I dress . . . I didn't find myself really feeling it was appropriate for me to speak. But, I still participated . . . if it pertained to like a media type of thing or . . . the environment, that's when I would throw in my piece . . . I wasn't like huffy and puffy because I didn't get to talk.

We think it is interesting that Andrew seemed to recognize that his privileged experiences were not necessarily appropriate for Sister Stories conversations. Yet, he still participated in many conversations. In fact, he talked quite a bit during the course. Interestingly, the tone with which he expressed not being "huffy puffy" suggested Andrew may have indeed harbored a touch of resentment because his story was not always "appropriate" for class discussions. As a White man, Andrew's experiences, perspectives, and opinions were considered normative and valuable in most White educational spaces (Anderson, 2015). As such, he seemed to wrestle with curbing his privileged contributions so that the counterstories of women of color could take center stage. It was a new experience and took some adjustment for Andrew to accept that he was not the norm in the Sister Stories classroom.

Harry also recognized that there were times when it was not appropriate for men of color to share their perspectives in Sister Stories, even if they wanted to speak up. Harry said:

> I feel like we hit topics where there was nothing we could say. . . . Not because we don't want to, but just because the issues are more personal and you always gotta keep the boundaries. In the beginning, we were talking about more broad issues . . . but as soon as we started talking about body image, we don't know. To be completely honest, we don't know because we aren't women.

Research has shown the immense educational and psychological benefits of counterspaces where the counternarratives of people of color have center stage (Grier-Reed, 2010; Pérez Huber & Cueva, 2012; Solórzano, Ceja & Yosso, 2000; Solórzano & Villalpando, 1998; Yosso, 2006; Yosso, Smith, Ceja & Solórzano, 2009). We contend that there is also immense value in centering the lives of women of color in counterspaces like Sister Stories. If the narratives of White students and men of color had more prominence, it could have made Sister Stories no longer feel like a validating and affirming counterspace where the realities of women of color were the sole focus.

White students and men of color, however, were not the only ones who wondered if their stories belonged in the classroom counterspace. As we described in chapter 1, the Sister Stories curriculum was replete with counterstories about racism, resiliency, and leadership of women of color. Sometimes, these curricular counterstories did not align with the lived realities of women of color in class. So, they refrained from telling their stories. Becca had not experienced overt forms of racism and paid little attention to racial microaggressions on campus. So, she felt like she had nothing to contribute to that classroom discussion. She explained:

> I didn't really experience what they were experiencing. So, I . . . felt like I was in my own little world. You know? With the whole racism on campus—like I haven't really encountered that. When Bonnie spoke about [racism from her] film teacher, I had never experienced anything like that. So I'm just like "wow! That [kind of overt racism] exists?" I just see everyone as getting along. That stuff doesn't even come to my mind. So when she spoke about that I just, I felt uncomfortable and in a way in; just like, where am I? How come I'm not going through what other people are going through? It was a little challenging to under-

stand what they were going through. But after a while, I kind of started to notice [microaggressions on campus]. Yeah, now I can see it a little, but before I was so blinded by, I didn't know what it was.

By comparing her story to the overt oppression experienced by her peers, Becca felt her story was not appropriate for class. However, by reading course materials and hearing peers' experiences with subtle microaggressions, she began to realize that she, too, experienced them.

Rose was awed by the strength and resilience of women of color she learned about in class readings and panel presentations. When she compared her story to these historical and contemporary women of color, she worried that her story was less worthy. She explained, "I realized that the reason it was so hard for me to write the story of myself was I thought it was too boring and not interesting enough." Mindy talked about how her status as a middle-class woman of color made her feel like a "spoiled brat" in comparison to her peers of color and the poor and working-class women described in the Sister Stories curriculum. Her response was to remain silent out of fear of judgment regarding her class privilege.

The quotes in this section revealed how some students felt their story had no place in the Sister Stories counterspace. White students and men of color largely understood that their narratives might not belong in a counterspace focused on women of color. Quotes from select women of color also showed that they sometimes felt their counterstories were not always a perfect fit for counterspace discussions. Even though Rose, Mindy, and Becca identified as women of color, they felt their complex lived realities did not quite belong in the counterspace. Their concerns about not having experienced enough overt racism or social class privilege call attention to the importance of recognizing intersectionality in general (Choo & Ferree, 2010; Museus & Griffin, 2011) and in campus counterspaces, in particular.

THIS IS WHO I AM

Some students described how their lack of contributions to Sister Stories dialogue was a reflection on their personality. A few women of color explained how they were naturally quiet and rarely engaged in class discussions. They were "private" people who did not reveal emotions or personal matters freely. Ife described herself as a quiet person saying, "I just don't talk a lot in class." Hanna also explained, "It's just me. Sometimes I don't like to show my true emotions to people." Mindy shared her innermost thoughts and feelings with very few people. In her explanation of why she did not share personal stories with classmates, she said, "I'm a quiet person, so I tend not to talk if I really don't have to . . . even people in my family don't know stuff about me!" As the previous sections have shown, lack of sharing by students may be prompted by complex issues of race, ethnicity, class, gender, and intersectionality. However, student silence can also be related to personality and preferred styles of interaction. Jung (1923/1971), a pioneer of analytical psychology, explained how different individuals respond to the exact same environments (e.g., counterspace) differently because of varied interests, modes of information processing, and ideal learning styles. Ife, Hannah, and Mindy's quotes show that sometimes student silence may indeed be influenced by personality traits.

CONCLUSION

In this chapter, students shared a variety of reasons why they self-censored or remained silent in the Sister Stories counterspace. Contemporary higher education researchers have argued there are different reasons for silence and self-censorship among White students and students of color. Sister Stories students described complicated reasons for silence and self-censorship which did not always differ along race or gender lines. Certainly, some reasons for silence resonated more or less with particular groups (e.g., women of color, men of color), but most of the reasons transcended race and gender. In sum, student narratives shared in this chapter offered a more comprehensive understanding of silence and self-censorship in an academic counterspace than is presented in the literature (Fox, 2009; Goodman, 2011; hooks, 2003; Watt, 2007).

REFERENCES

Anderson, E. (2015). The white space. *Sociology of Race and Ethnicity, 1*(1), 10–21.

Bell, L. A. (2007). Theoretical foundations for social justice education. In M. Adams, L. A. Bell & P. Griffin (Eds.), *Teaching for diversity and social justice* (2nd ed., pp. 1–14). New York: Routledge.

Chang, M. J., Denson, N., Saenz, V., & Misa, K. (2006). The educational benefits of sustaining cross-racial interaction among undergraduates. *The Journal of Higher Education, 77*(3), 430–55.

Choo, H. Y., & Ferree, M. M. (2010). Practicing intersectionality in sociological research: A critical analysis of inclusions, interactions, and institutions in the study of inequalities. *Sociological Theory, 28*(2), 129–49.

Clark, R. (2004). Interethnic group and intraethnic group racism: Perceptions and coping in Black university students. *Journal of Black Psychology, 30*(4), 506–26.

Darder, A., Baltodano, M., & Torres, R. D. (2003). Critical pedagogy: An introduction. In A. Darder, M. Baltodano & R. D. Torres (Eds.), *The critical pedagogy reader* (pp. 1–21). New York: Routledge.

Delgado, R. (1989). Storytelling for oppositionists and others: A plea for narrative. *Michigan Law Review, 87*(8), 2411–41.

———, & Stefancic, J. (Eds.) (2000). *Critical race theory: The cutting edge.* Philadelphia: Temple University Press.

DuBois, W. E. B. (1903). *The souls of black folk.* New York: Oxford University Press.

Fox, H. (2009). *"When race breaks out": Conversations about race and racism in college classrooms.* New York: Peter Lang.

Goodman, D. J. (2011). *Promoting diversity and social justice: Educating people from privileged groups* (2nd ed.). Thousand Oaks, CA: Sage.

Grier-Reed, T. L. (2010). The African American student network: Creating sanctuaries and counterspaces for coping with racial microaggressions in higher education settings. *The Journal of Humanistic Counseling, Education and Development, 49*(2), 181–88.

Gurin, P. (1999). *Expert report of Patricia Gurin, in the compelling need for diversity in higher education. Gratz et al. v. Bollinger et al., No. 97-75321 (E.D. Mich.), Grutter et al. v. Bollinger et al., No. 97-75928 (E.D. Mich.)*. Ann Arbor, MI: University of Michigan.

hooks, b. (2000). *Feminist theory: From margin to center* (2nd ed.). Cambridge, MA: South End.

——— (2003). *Teaching community: A pedagogy of hope*. New York: Routledge.

Hu, S., & Kuh, G. D. (2003). Diversity experiences and college student learning and personal development. *Journal of College Student Development, 44*(3), 320–34.

Johnson, J. R., & Bhatt, A. J. (2003). Gendered and racialized identities and alliances in the classroom: Formations in/of resistive space. *Communication Education, 52*(3–4), 230–44.

Johnson-Bailey, J., & Cervero, R. M. (1996). An analysis of the educational narratives of reentry Black women. *Adult Education Quarterly, 46*(3), 142–57.

Jones, S. R. (2008). Student resistance to cross-cultural engagement: Annoying distraction or site for transformative learning. In S. R. Harper (Ed.), *Creating inclusive campus environments for cross-cultural learning and student engagement* (pp. 67–85). Washington, DC: NASPA.

Jung, C. G. (1971). *The Collected works of C. G. Jung* (Vol. 6). Princeton, NJ: Princeton University Press. (R. F. C. Hull, Ed., & H. G. Baynes, Trans.) (original work published in 1923).

Kelly, B. T., & Gayles, J. G. (2010). Resistance to racial/ethnic dialog in graduate preparation programs: Implications for developing multicultural competence. *College Student Affairs Journal, 29*(1), 75–85.

Laird, T. F. N., Engberg, M. E., & Hurtado, S. (2005). Modeling accentuation effects: Enrolling in a diversity course and the importance of social action engagement. *The Journal of Higher Education, 76*(4), 448–76.

Linder, C. (2011). Exclusionary feminism: Stories of undergraduate women of color. *NASPA Journal about Women in Higher Education, 4*(1), 1–25.

Martínez Alemán, A. M. (2000). Race talks: Undergraduate women of color and female friendships. *The Review of Higher Education, 23*(2), 133–52.

Maxwell, K. E., Nagada, B. A., & Thompson, M. C. (2011). *Facilitating intergroup dialogues: Bridging differences, catalyzing change*. Sterling VA: Stylus.

Museus, S. D., & Griffin, K. A. (2011). Mapping the margins in higher education: On the promise of intersectionality frameworks in research and discourse. *New Directions for Institutional Research,* (151), 5–13.

Myers, I. B. (1980). *Gifts differing*. Palo Alto, CA: Consulting Psychologists Press.

Nagada, B. A., & Zúñiga, X. (2003). Fostering meaningful racial engagement through intergroup dialogues. *Group Processes and Intergroup Relations, 60*(1), 111–28.

Pérez Huber, L. (2010). Using Latina/o critical race theory (LatCrit) and racist nativism to explore intersectionality in the educational experiences of undocumented Chicana college students. *Educational Foundations, 24*, 77–96.

———, & Cueva, B. M. (2012). Chicana/Latina testimonios on effects and responses to microaggressions. *Equity & Excellence in Education, 45*(3), 392–410.

Richeson, J. A., & Shelton, J, N. (2007). Negotiating interracial interactions: Costs, consequences, and possibilities. *Current Directions in Psychological Sciences, 16*, 316–20.

Richeson, J. A., & Trawalter, S. (2005). Why do interracial interactions impair executive function? A resource depletion account. *Journal of Personality and Social Psychology, 88*, 934–47.

Strayhorn, T. L. (2010). The influence of diversity on learning outcomes among African American college students: Measuring sex differences. *Journal of Student Affairs Research and Practice, 47*(3), 343–66.

Solórzano, D., Ceja, M., & Yosso, T. (2000). Critical race theory, racial microaggressions, and campus racial climate: The experiences of African American college students. *The Journal of Negro Education, 69*(1/2), 60–73.

Solórzano, D. G., & Yosso, T. J. (2002). Critical race methodology: Counter-storytelling as an analytical framework for education research. *Qualitative Inquiry, 8*(1), 23–44.

Solórzano, D. G., & Villalpando, O. (1998). Critical race theory, marginality, and the experience of students of color in higher education. In C. A. Torres & T. R. Mitchell (Eds.), *Sociology of education: Emerging perspectives* (pp. 211–24). Albany, NY: SUNY Press.

Sue, D. W. (2010). *Microaggressions in everyday life: Race, gender and sexual orientation.* Hoboken, NJ: Wiley.

———, Capodilupo, C. M., Torino, G., Bucceri, J. M., Holder, A., Nadal, K., & Esquilin, M. E. (2006). Racial microaggressions in everyday life: Implications for counseling. *American Psychologist, 62*(4), 271–86.

Tuitt, F. (2006). Afterword: Realizing a more inclusive pedagogy. In A. Howell & F. Tuitt (Eds.), *Race and higher education: Rethinking pedagogy in diverse college classrooms* (pp. 243–369). Cambridge MA: Harvard Educational Review.

U.S. Department of Education, National Center for Education Statistics (NCES) (2012). *Digest of Education Statistics, 2012* (NCES 2014–015).

Vaccaro, A. (2013). Building a framework for social justice education: One educator's journey. In L. Landreman (Ed.), *The art of effective facilitation: Reflections from social justice educators* (pp. 23–44). Sterling, VA: Stylus.

Watt, S. K. (2007). Difficult dialogues, privilege and social justice: Uses of privileged identity exploration framework in student affairs practice. *The College Student Affairs Journal, 26*(2), 114–26.

Williams, D. A., Berger, J. B., & McClendon, S. A. (2005). Toward a model of inclusive excellence and change in postsecondary institutions. *Association American Colleges and Universities,* 1–39.

Wing, A. K. (Ed.) (2003). *Critical race feminism: A reader.* New York: NYU Press.

Yosso, T. J. (2006). *Critical race counter-stories along the Chicana/Chicano educational pipeline.* NY: Routledge.

———, Smith, W. A., Ceja, M., & Solórzano, D. G. (2009). Critical race theory, racial microaggressions, and campus racial climate for Latina/o undergraduates. *Harvard Educational Review, 79*(4), 659–91.

Zúñiga, X., Nagada, B. A., Chesler, M., & Cytron-Walker, A. (2007). Intergroup dialogue in higher education: Meaningful learning about social justice. *ASHE Higher Education Report, 32*(4). San Francisco, CA: Jossey-Bass.

Zúñiga, X., Williams, E. A., & Berger, J. B. (2005). Action-oriented democratic outcomes: The impact of student involvement with campus diversity. *Journal of College Student Development, 46*(6), 660–78.

SIX

Learning about Identity

"Who am I?"

Who am I? What is my story? To answer tough questions like these, students often need a safe counterspace where they can make meaning of their life experiences, perspectives, and identities. As we described in chapter 1, engaging in deep self-reflection was one of the pedagogical strategies used in Sister Stories. During classroom discussions, in focus groups, and through assignments, students reflected deeply upon their racial and ethnic identity, noting how family socialization, culture, and experiences with oppression informed their meaning-making processes.

We begin this chapter with a brief overview of the extensive literature on psycho-social identity development. Then, we provide vignettes from students about both the processes and products related to learning about identity development. Since the Sister Stories curriculum required students to read and reflect upon racial and ethnic identity development models, student answers to the questions of "Who am I?" and "What is my story?" often revolved around their racial and ethnic identity as opposed to other social identities. Settles (2006) postulated that a Black woman's racial identity may take precedence in the presence of White people while her identity as a woman may become most salient when surrounded by men. We contend the Sister Stories curricular focus on racial and ethnic identity, combined with student feelings of marginalization at the predominantly White campus, prompted women (and men) of color to focus on racial and ethnic identities in course assignments. The focus of this chapter reflects this emphasis.

IDENTITY MODELS: UNDERSTANDING
SELF IN SOCIAL CONTEXT

Social identity refers to "the sense of group or collective identity based on one's perception that he or she shares a common . . . heritage with a particular reference group" (Helms, 1993, p. 4). Sometimes called social identity theories (Evans, Forney, Guido, Patton & Renn, 2010) or psycho-social identity theories, these writings describe the process by which individuals make meaning of particular social identities such as race, ethnicity, gender, or sexual orientation. The "social" aspect of these theories reflects the fact that self-understanding never happens in a vacuum. Societal messages about particular social identities (e.g., race, ethnicity, gender, sexual orientation) influence how people make sense of who they are. Social identity models focused on race and/or ethnicity (e.g., Cross, 1971; Ferdman & Gallegos, 2001; Hardiman & Jackson, 1992; Helms, 1993; Kim, 2012; Phinney, 1993; Torres, 2003) attempt to explain the complex psychological meaning-making process of understanding self in the context of a racially oppressive society.

Ortiz and Santos (2009) note a history of scholarly disagreements about the similarities, differences, and subsequent measurement issues related to racial and ethnic identity. They argued "racial issues are likely intertwined with ethnic identity" (Ortiz & Santos, 2009, p. 30), but they are not the same concept. Similarly, Kwan and Sodowsky (1997) explained:

> Members of a racial or ethnic minority group share an ethnic social and cultural heritage, such as language, family structure, religion, ethnic signs, symbols and artifacts, value orientations, and gender roles . . . that is passed on between generations, albeit with modifications influenced by intergenerational acculturation. Furthermore, the shared ethnic heritage includes individual members' sense of attachment to or identification with the ethnocultural group. (p. 51)

Racial identity is rooted in the socio-political context of racial oppression which is often based upon phenotype and biased assumptions about supposed biological underpinnings of race. Racial categorizations subsume various ethnicities. Therefore, racial identity models often purport to explain the racial identity journeys of individuals who may, or may not, share the same ethnic heritage, but who experience similar forms of racial oppression in U.S society. For instance, Asian American ethnic identity models attempt to explain racial identity realities of people from diverse ethnic backgrounds (e.g., Chinese, Vietnamese, Korean, Japanese, Filipino, etc.).

Ethnic identity development theories, on the other hand, tend to highlight topics like acculturation, sense of belonging, and identification with a particular ethnic group. We do not purport to reconcile these scholarly tensions in this chapter. As many scholars (Hill Collins, 1991, 2000; McCabe, 2009; Shah, 1997; Sue, 2010a, 2010b) have noted, contemporary oppression aimed at women of color stems from a host of racial *and* ethnic stereotypes. As such, we agree with Ortiz and Santos (2009), who argued distinctions between racial and ethnic identity development models are not always clear. As they described their life stories and identity journeys, students used race and ethnic terms separately *and* interchangeably.

The historical and socio-political context of oppression is different for each racial and ethnic group and changes over time. As such, models of racial and ethnic identity are also unique and have evolved over time. For instance, many early racial identity models were shaped by research with African Americans who were born in the United States. After the civil rights movement, a number of Black identity development models were published in the field of psychology (Cross, 1971; Jackson, 1975; Toldson & Pasteur, 1975). Those models reflected the socio-political context of racism in the 1960s and 1970s. Psycho-social identity models for Asian Americans, Latinos, and Native Americans (cf, Ferdman & Gallegos, 2001; Horse, 2012; Kim, 2012) as well as White Americans (Helms, 1993) emerged later. Additionally, a number of models were constructed to explain biracial (Kich, 1992; Poston, 1990; Renn, 2003, 2012) and multiracial identity (Wijeyesinghe, 2001).

A comprehensive review of racial and ethnic identity models is outside the scope of this chapter. However, many models include stages or phases that follow similar patterns. In line with CRT sentiments regarding the centrality of race and racism (Solórzano, 1997, 1998), recognizing, experiencing, reflecting upon, and responding to oppression are common elements of racial identity models. Hardiman and Jackson (1992, 1997) tapped into these common threads to construct their *Social Identity Development Theory* which purports to describe a generalized model of racial identity for everyone—people of color and White people. The *Social Identity Development Theory* contains five stages that all individuals go through, albeit slightly differently depending on whether they are a person of color or a White person. Those stages are titled: naïve, acceptance, resistance, redefinition, and internalization. It is not our intention to oversimplify racial and ethnic identity by focusing on this particular and highly generalized model. However, we felt it was important to offer a context to readers who have no familiarity with racial and ethnic identity development models. We chose this model because it aligns with our critical race perspectives that foreground power, privilege, and oppression. Hardiman and Jackson's model also highlights how dominant ideologies and structural inequities play a role in self-understanding and identity trajectories of people from privileged and minoritized social identity groups.

During the *Social Identity Development Theory* naïve stage (Hardiman & Jackson, 1992, 1997), very young children have not yet been socialized into dominant White culture, nor have they learned the history, values, or customs of their ethnic and/or racial heritage. The second stage, called acceptance, refers to passive or active, conscious or unconscious, acceptance of dominant ideologies about one's racial or ethnic group. As noted in prior chapters, dominant ideologies in the United States normalize Whiteness while portraying people of color through stereotypical and deficit lenses. Hardiman and Jackson (1992) argued that most White college students enter college in either active or passive acceptance. This means they accept dominant ideologies such as meritocracy, equal opportunity, and colorblindness and believe stereotypes and myths about people of color. Adoption of stereotypes and active engagement of overtly racist behavior during acceptance may manifest in microassaults (Sue, 2010a, 2010b). However, White people in passive acceptance usually do not see themselves as racist and may be unaware of the ways they unconsciously perpetuate racial microinvalidations and microinsults (Sue, 2010a, 2010b). In chapter 2, women of color shared a variety of stories about White peers whose behavior was reflective of the acceptance stage. Hardiman and Jackson (1992, 1997) explained people of color in acceptance may exhibit shame or other negative feelings about self because they have internalized dominant oppressive ideologies and view themselves through deficit lenses (David, 2013).

During the stage of resistance, individuals become much more aware and knowledgeable about oppression. Guilt and shame are common feelings for White people in resistance as they come to terms with racial privilege. Through college experiences, White students can move into the stage of resistance. However, this shift happens only if Whites learn that oppression and privilege are prevalent in society and that all White people contribute to oppressive systems. According to Hardiman and Jackson (1992), students of color often arrive at predominantly White institutions in resistance. In this stage, people of color question and challenge dominant ideologies, White normalcy, and inequality. Feelings typically associated with resistance are anger and frustration at systems of oppression.

The next stage of identity is called redefinition. It is a time when White people and people of color work to create new identities no longer rooted in oppressive dominant ideologies. The frustration of constantly challenging dominant paradigms eventually forces people of color to move into a place where they begin to redefine who they are. A redefined identity is often constructed within safe, racially homogeneous counterspaces, like Sister Stories, where students of color glean support from similar others. In counterspaces, students of color can also explore and express outward pride in their ethnic and/or racial heritage. White people in resistance begin to focus less on the oppression of others and, instead, explore what it means to have privilege.

Finally, during internalization (Hardiman & Jackson, 1992, 1997), all individuals incorporate their redefined identity into a more holistic sense of self—recognizing race and ethnicity are only portions of their holistic identity. They come to see intersectionality matters. Individuals in this stage also work toward social justice for all oppressed groups.

The *Social Identity Development Theory* (Hardiman & Jackson, 1992, 1997) provides useful information about racial identity. However, this model, as well as those cited earlier, are often insufficient for explaining the complex identity journeys of many people. First, single identity models often fail to capture the complicated identity journeys of mixed-race people. To fill this gap, psychologists and higher education scholars have crafted alternate models to describe biracial (Renn, 2003, 2012) and multiracial (Wijeyesinghe, 2001) identity development. Since a number of Sister Stories students self-identified as biracial or multiracial, we revisit these theories later in the chapter.

Second, single social identity models foreground one race or ethnicity, often at the expense of other important social identities such as gender, social class, religion, ability, or sexual orientation. While Hardiman and Jackson's (1992, 1997) *Social Identity Development Theory* suggested individuals begin to recognize and honor intersectionality in the final stage of racial identity development (internalization), many scholars suggest understanding multiple intersecting social identities is a process in and of itself (cf, Abes & Jones, 2004; Jones, 1997, 2009; Jones & McEwen, 2000; Jones, McEwen & Abes, 2007; Stewart, 2008, 2009).

Third, U.S.-based models of single racial and ethnic identity development often do not address the lived realities of immigrants or children of immigrants. Some scholars have emphasized the importance of acculturation in ethnic identity development (Berry, 1980, 1993; Berry, Phinney, Sam & Vedder, 2006; Chun, Organista & Marin, 2003; Phinney, 1993). The term *acculturation* describes the process whereby members of a cultural group come to know, and make meaning of, themselves in the context of dominant cultures that differ from their country of origin. We discuss some of this literature later in the chapter.

WHO AM I?

In this section, we draw from student papers, classroom discussions, and focus group conversations to offer a glimpse into the complex identity journeys of women of color, men of color, and White students. It is not our intention to categorize students into particular models, stages, or phases. Instead, we summarize recurrent identity-related themes that emerged from student narratives about "me."

I LEARNED SO MANY THINGS ABOUT MYSELF

Sister Stories was often the first academic counterspace where students were invited to reflect upon their identity journeys. Prose from assignments titled "My Story" and "I Am," as well as focus group conversations, show how powerful this educational strategy was for women of color. Victoria explained:

> I feel like [the instructor] wanted us to learn who we were. . . . It was different [than most classes] because you really got to learn . . . who it is that you are as a person and what you can do. You learn things about yourself that you'll never learn in any other class. I learned so many things about myself as a person . . . I never had a conversation like that [in a class]. I feel like for me, it was more of a learning experience . . . than I can even imagine. I really liked that class.

Becca concurred: "It was a great class like trying to find out your identity, you know, racial identity." Elsy also said, "learning about these theories, it helped me realize more about myself and where I came from."

Sia and Jewel found it affirming to read about racial and ethnic identity models and realize that other women of color experienced similar identity journeys. Sia said:

> When I think about this class, the first word that comes to mind is identity. Before I started this class, I was kind of quiet about what race I was. After taking this class, I came to terms with my racial identity . . . I realized a lot of people went through what I went through.

Similarly, Jewel assumed she was the only person who struggled to make meaning of her racial identity in a predominantly White world. As she read various racial and ethnic identity models, she learned she was not alone. She described how Sister Stories "validated a lot of the experiences that I had. Going through some of the identity development models definitely helped me come to understand what I'm going through or the things that I felt." When faculty focus on validation in their pedagogy, student learning about self can be enhanced. Rendón Linares and Muñoz (2011) explained how a validating classroom "invites students to explore the connections between their personal histories, group, and community contexts to allow students to affirm their own identities and create new knowledge" (p. 22).

Most students realized that to reap the full benefits of learning racial identity models, they had to apply the models to their lives and engage in deep self-reflection. By the end of the course, students like Elena came to realize that identity development was a life-long developmental process that would continue long after Sister Stories ended. Elena said:

> So as I continue to grow and mature and experience parts of my life that have not happened yet, my identity will continue to grow and

develop. Everyone should know the answer to the question "What is my identity." But, most of us have not taken the time to dig deep inside of ourselves for the true response. Finding your truth means really getting to know yourself. When you have full awareness of your identity, you don't have to rely on other things to define who you are.

As Elena suggested, identity development requires people to "dig deep inside." We contend such digging is not merely an internal process. Instead, it is an ongoing journey of simultaneously reflecting internally while situating oneself within larger societal contexts. Evans et al. (2010) suggest that moving through stages of social identity typically aligns with increasing cognitive complexity. Such cognitive complexity is required for individuals to understand themselves within ever-changing and complex historical, social, political, and personal contexts. Student narratives as well as our classroom observations revealed increasing cognitive complexity among Sister Stories students as they figured out who they were within the socio-political backdrop of oppression.

UNLEARNING OPPRESSIVE IMAGES

As we described in the opening section of this chapter, psycho-social identity models are situated within contexts of oppression. As such, early stages or phases of many identity models describe negative feelings about self. These result from learning and internalizing dominant ideologies and oppressive stereotypes about one's racial and ethnic group. In her book *Internalized Oppression,* David (2013) describes how adopting stereotypes about one's cultural group results in deep psychological harm. For instance, internalizing negative images about one's racial or ethnic group can lead to assimilation, stalled psycho-social identity development, low self-esteem, depression, and other negative mental health issues (David, 2013). The Sister Stories counterspace was designed to be a safe place where students could explore their social identities. Another goal of the counterspace was to mitigate the negative effects of internalized oppression by offering an affirming educational environment where students could unlearn oppressive ideologies and hopefully learn to express pride in their ethnic and racial backgrounds. During their journey toward racial and/or ethnic pride, students often reflected upon struggles with internalized oppression.

Most students of color talked candidly about internalizing negative images about people from their racial or ethnic group. Often, this process began when they were young children. Paul was taught to be ashamed of his Hmong heritage. He even wished he was White at some points in his life. Through affirmation received in Sister Stories, he learned to be proud of who he was.

Since I was young I wanted to leave the minority and join the White race. But, now I am finding that I need to be the minority. It is like walking around in a circle, but I am glad that I did because I feel like I have found myself again. I have found my purpose again. I am Paul, I am Hmong, and I want to be the change as much as I want to make it.

Mayra described a life-long history of internalizing oppressive messages about people of color as troublemakers and as lacking intelligence. She explained:

The course readings that were assigned had many overlapping themes that I could relate to over the track of my life. . . . The theme that resonated with me most was of acceptance, image, and fitting in. I went to a predominantly White elementary school with kids who did not look like me one bit. Although I excelled in all of my classes and my teachers complimented me on how smart I was, I truly did not feel as good as the other kids in my class.

Mayra's quote shows how oppressive images and stereotypes can shape the ways young people feel about themselves. Even though she excelled academically, Mayra still internalized negative stereotypes about people of color lacking intelligence. As CRT scholars have noted, Mayra was certainly not alone. Students of color often experience microaggressions rooted in deficit-laden stereotypes about their intelligence and academic ability (Dancy & Brown, 2008; Gildersleeve, Croom & Vasquez, 2011; Solórzano, 1998; Solórzano, Ceja & Yosso, 2000; Yosso, Smith, Ceja & Solórzano, 2009).

I AM STRONG, INVINCIBLE, EMPOWERED

While most identity development models include topics of internalized oppression, later stages and phases of those models highlight resistance, empowerment, and pride. By learning these identity models, women of color often recognized their own strength and began to exhibit identity pride. In a course paper, Mayra described how she was

the most proud I have ever been of who I am and where I come from. [Before] entering college I attended a predominantly White high school and I did not have the same pride I developed now for my culture, race, and identity. I have now found that pride because I have found a place where I can truly be myself and fit in. Still, attending a university that White people hold majority, I have found [counterspaces like Sister Stories that] have helped me shine in more ways I have ever shined before . . . I am in a room full of people that look like me, share common goals and values, and have similar beliefs as myself. I have witnessed firsthand how I, and some of my peers, have gone through [a racial identity] stage or who still are. I can definitely [identify] with this section of the theory.

It was invaluable for Camilla to work through her identity journey as a Black woman who also identified as a woman of color. During a focus group, she said:

> I can't be more proud of that, and just want to prove to myself that I can be successful regardless of my background or where I come from. . . . It's all about proving them wrong. And, I feel like women of color in general love to do that. 'Cuz I just feel like we are so *belittled* [said by another student in unison] and we feel we can't really set high goals or high standards. And like once we get there, it's like ok, I want to prove to this person that I got here without their help. And, I just feel like in general women of color have so much strength and I learned it in this class. . . . Women of color just go through so much and others don't really realize it, but I just feel like this class made us feel like, like we're important. . . . You know? They made us feel like we are worthy of being someone in life that is very successful . . . it gave me hope.

Camilla and Mayra's prose pulls together many of the concepts discussed in the literature. For example, Mayra contextualized her racial identity journey within oppression by referencing the White majority. Camilla and another student in the focus group simultaneously used the word "belittled" to describe their experiences with gendered racism (Essed, 1991). Camilla's quote also references the common racial microaggression taxonomy category whereby people of color are assumed be inferior (Sue, 2010a, 2010b).

Most models of social identity development include a stage or phase where members of minoritized social identity groups (e.g., women of color) resist oppression. Hardiman and Jackson (1992, 1997) even named their stage "resistance." During this part of their identity journey, people of color resist White normalcy and deficit-laden racial stereotypes. Often, they seek counterspaces where they can learn strategies for resistance and glean support from people who have already, or are concurrently, traveling on similar identity pathways. Sister Stories offered such a refuge for Mayra and other women of color. It was an academic counterspace where women of color could redefine (Hardiman & Jackson, 1992, 1997) their identity and become proud of their "culture, race, and identity" despite the oppressive messages that surrounded them. As Camilla so eloquently explained, learning about racial identity models—especially the stages where people of color show strength, resistance, and resiliency—gave her a sense of pride and "hope." We conclude this section with a powerful quote by Lucia, who came to see women of color, including herself, through a lens of resiliency, strength, and empowerment. Lucia said:

> Being a woman of color in today's society means being an invincible woman who accomplishes things despite socialized obstacles placed in her way. It means being a mentor and advocating for other women of

color, making sure they understand that they can achieve anything and
everything they want to and ensuring them that they always have an
advocate, someone to be there for them. . . . It also means networking
with other women of color and lifting each other up.

For Lucia, Sister Stories was a counterspace where she began to view
herself as a strong, invincible woman for the first time. She also became
committed to helping other women of color progress through their racial
and/or ethnic identity journeys, so they too would view themselves as
strong, invincible women.

FAMILY AND PEER CONTEXTS
FOR IDENTITY DEVELOPMENT

While Sister Stories offered an academic venue to reflect on racial and
ethnic identity, it is important to note that identity development begins at
birth. Throughout life, identity meaning-making processes are shaped by
family. Torres (2003) documented a number of influences on ethnic identity development of college students. First, the environment a child
grows up in, whether it be a predominantly White or ethnic community,
shapes how a young person feels about their culture, customs, and
norms. Second, generational status (e.g., first-, second-generation immigrant status), as well as the acculturation levels of close kin, influence
how an individual views their culture of origin as well as White spaces
(Anderson, 2015). Third, sense of self is shaped by perceptions of one's
group status in dominant White society. Such understandings can be
based upon perceived levels of respect for, prevalence of stereotypes
about, and microaggressions directed at ethnic group members. In alignment with this research, students in Sister Stories talked at length about
the ways family, peers, and oppressive societal messages shaped their
sense of self.

Diego's mother refused to teach him about his ethnic customs or language. He believed this lack of socialization shaped his ethnic identity in
negative ways. Diego's commentary also references contextual backdrops
of White normalcy and racial oppression that shaped how he, and his
mother, made meaning of their racial and ethnic identities:

> I don't know a lot of my heritage and a lot of the history in my cul-
> ture. . . . When I spoke to my mother about the issue of not knowing so
> much of my culture, she replied, "You're American," which put me in
> an awkward position because to some people, being American can
> mean White.

The refusal by Diego's mother to teach him about, or even acknowledge,
his ethnic heritage sent a powerful message about the value of his cultural background. He was confused with the label "American" because, to

him, the term meant Whiteness and implied assimilation. Lack of familial socialization about his ethnic heritage left him in an "awkward" position as a young person trying to figure out "Who am I?"

Diego's story is in direct contrast to Mayra whose family intentionally taught her about her cultural heritage. Mayra explained:

> I am the daughter of both a woman and man whom were born in Puerto Rico. I on the other hand was born and raised in the United States but also raised in the Puerto Rican culture. My parents introduced me into my culture at an early age. For example, the first language I learned to speak was Spanish. As I grew up my parents made sure to engrave their culture in me, and made sure that I learned about the food, music, holidays, religions, and traditions of Puerto Rico. I visit as much as I can and am very familiar with the streets of Puerto Rico. I do and will always identify myself as a Puerto Rican. . . . What I identify myself is not based on where I was born but instead what I was taught, the culture I learned, and simply what I feel most comfortable identifying myself as. I am Puerto Rican.

Mayra's pride in her ethnic heritage was influenced by positive images of her culture that were infused into her familial socialization.

While family socialization and messaging are essential pieces of racial and ethnic identity development, peers also play a large role. Brian was born in Nigeria and immigrated to the United States at an early age. He described family as "everything." Despite teachings about cultural roots from family, Brian resisted early familial teachings about his cultural roots. He did not embrace his Nigerian identity until he developed a friendship with PJ, who taught him about his culture, customs, and language. Brian stated:

> Family was everything. . . . My dad was quickly Americanized, while my mom stayed true to her culture. Specifically pertaining to foods, clothing, and her religion. A lot of people didn't understand me . . . I was never really interested or even paid attention to my culture or religion at all until my friend PJ moved to the U.S. from Nigeria when I was 10. . . . He was so cultured with the music he listened too and, things he ate and going to church every Sunday, it started to rub off on me. I started speaking with an accent sometimes. I wanted to learn more of my native language. I started attending church with him and listening to more Nigerian music. I thank him for that, because I used to say I was African, but now I see that ignorance isn't bliss when you're educated and know and now I say I am Nigerian. . . . At [my prior college] they thought I was just a Black American and I was quick to say that I'm African, better yet I'm Nigerian.

Torres (2003) found that one of the main reasons why college students change their ethnic identity is because of changing relationships within their home and/or collegiate environment. This was certainly the case for

Brian, whose relationship with PJ was the impetus for learning about his cultural heritage and ultimately his self-identification as Nigerian.

Berry (1980) described four acculturation strategies used by college students to traverse tensions between their cultures of origin and predominantly White higher education institutions. Individuals can: 1) assimilate into dominant White culture; 2) reject both cultures; 3) identify solely with one's ethnic culture and reject the dominant culture; or 4) become bicultural. People become bicultural when they integrate both their culture of origin and dominant White culture into their sense of self. Students of color in Sister Stories expressed a range of acculturation strategies used by themselves and their families. For instance, Brian's parents seemed to navigate the acculturation process differently, with his father assimilating and mother identifying solely with Nigerian culture. His quote also shows that identity development is a journey. At first, Brian leaned toward assimilation until he met a peer who encouraged him to learn more about Nigerian culture. Brian's rejection of the term *African American* and refusal to use Nigerian American suggests he identified solely with his ethnic culture and rejected dominant culture (Berry, 1980). Sister Stories helped Jackie adopt a bicultural identity. She explained:

> After reading the stories, watching the movies, and hearing people speaking, I feel like I can say that I am Cape Verdean and at the same time I am African American because they both link together so I feel like I was able to speak up about my identity.

Brian and Jackie's narratives show that Sister Stories afforded students a safe space to reflect upon their unique identity pathways.

DON'T MAKE ME PICK: BEING BI/MULTIRACIAL

As noted earlier, single identity perspectives are often insufficient for explaining the ways people from multiple racial and ethnic backgrounds come to understand themselves. Seven of the forty-nine students in Sister Stories self-identified as biracial or multiracial. Their narratives reflect more complicated identity realities than those portrayed in single identity models. These seven Sister Stories students expressed a range of opinions about the perceived applicability of biracial (Renn, 2003, 2012) and multiracial identity (Wijeyesinghe, 2012) (as well as single identity models) to their lives. Yet, they all agreed that they did not want to be forced to pick one identity. They desired wholeness. One student suggested that the single identity models could use some revisions to better reflect her complex biracial identity, saying, "Black identity development might need some upgrade." By contrast, Bonnie found Black identity models to be "pretty accurate" despite the fact that she was navigating the intersections of Latina and Black identities. Bonnie said:

I do feel like this model is pretty accurate, because I went through many stages before I found my Black identity. I went from Black being only based on the color of my skin, to Black being a part of who I am and wanting to find out more about it. My mother wasn't wrong for not teaching me about being Black, because she identifies as a Latina woman. She doesn't know how to incorporate the other part of me. That was something I would have learned from my father. Even if I did learn that from him, no one could teach me how to be both, except me. I will make sure that when I have children they will know what it is to be both Black and Puerto Rican. I will try my best to guide them, but their identity in the end is chosen by themselves . . . I do learn a lot in this class about myself and others, the readings really do address a lot having to do with identity. One thing that will definitely leave this class with me is the fact that I don't have to identify as just one thing. I've read many readings of women who either are biracial, or identify themselves with more than just their race. This challenged many of us in class to see that you may judge someone, but if you don't talk to them, you really don't know who they really are, or identify as. I am glad that this class is helping me grow as a person, because that's not something you learn about in any class in college.

As Bonnie expressed, it can be a challenge for young people to develop a holistic multiracial identity when families have not socialized them into all aspects of their cultural heritage. Bonnie's reality aligns with research by Nadal et al. (2011), who found individuals from multiracial heritage can experience isolation and exclusion from family members who have one race or ethnicity in common with their biracial or multiracial children.

According to Wijeyesinghe (2001, 2012), adopting a holistic sense of self as a multiracial person is dependent on eight factors, some that resonated with multiracial women of color, and some that did not. The eight factors in Wijeyesinghe's *Factor Model of Multiracial Identity* (FMMI) include: racial ancestry; early racial experiences and socialization; cultural attachment; physical appearance; social and historical context of racism; political awareness and orientation; spirituality; and other social identities such as gender, religion, or sexual orientation (Wijeyesinghe, 2001, 2012). After reviewing the model, Lacey said:

Growing up I struggled a lot with identifying myself. I would only claim to be Cape Verdean and not really say much about my Middle Eastern half only because I didn't feel like I was "Middle Eastern enough" to claim that nationality. Growing up people would always question why my eyes were so light, why my skin has a reddish tint to it, why my hair was so silky, and why I didn't look like the typical Black female. I would always find my way around answering those questions but eventually I knew I would have to explain myself. To this day I still struggle with identity issues, but I know where I came from even if I don't know specific facts and details about the Middle East. I still get that "Oh my god Lacey that's your dad?" question and "Why don't you look more like that?" question, but I learned that there is no such thing as not being good enough for your own race and nationality and that every race has a unique look to them. . . . On September 11th, 2001, a big event went down in history that I believe affects my identity and my ability to accept it. I feel this way because it was a terrorist attack and the people doing this were Middle Eastern (like my father) and it made me feel ashamed and embarrassed because growing up people would make jokes about it to me. Out of the eight factors [described by Wijeyesinghe] only those two that apply to me and my identity. . . . I see myself furthering my identity development by actually taking the time to engage and get to know both of my nationalities and not just one. I think it is important for me to know more about the Middle Eastern culture and lifestyle because it will help me discover who I am and where I came from. I could also learn more about my Cape Verdean culture.

Lacey felt she could only apply two of Wijeyesinghe's (2001, 2012) eight factors to her complicated life experiences and emerging multiracial identity. However, we noticed hints of many more of the eight FMMI factors embedded in her prose. Whether or not she applied the model appropriately, the take-away from her quote is that the Sister Stories assignment prompted Lacey to delve more deeply into what it means to be biracial. Sister Stories students like Lacey partook in complex meaning-making as they applied social identity models to their own lives. Sometimes the curriculum validated their experiences and gave them academic terms to express their lived realties. In other cases, the learning process was a little more challenging as they struggled to place themselves in models that did not quite fit.

WHAT DOES IT MEAN TO BE WHITE?

A total of eight White students enrolled in the Sister Stories during the five years we conducted the study. That small number, combined with the class emphasis on the historical and contemporary experiences of women of color, offered little classroom space for White students to wrestle with White racial identity development. I (Melissa) was very conscious of the dangers of focusing on Whiteness and White privilege in a counterspace designed to foster learning about, and support for, women of color. As such, evidence about White students' racial identity development was limited. The data we collected through course assignments and focus group conversations did, however, align well with many White racial identity development models (Helms, 1993; Hardiman & Jackson, 1992, 1997) as well as Hardiman and Jackson's (1992, 1997) *Social Identity Development Theory*.

Hardiman and Jackson (1992) argued that most White students begin college in acceptance. In this stage, they may engage in overt microassaults. However, it is more likely that they have internalized dominant ideologies and stereotypes about people of color and, in turn, unknowingly perpetuate microaggressions and microinsults (Sue, 2010a, 2010b). One of the racial myths inspired by dominant ideologies of equality and meritocracy is that of reverse discrimination. While people of color in positions of limited power (e.g., teacher, landlord, hiring authority) can certainly treat a White person unfairly, critical race scholars argue that systemic forms of race discrimination against White people is a myth that must be debunked (Harper, Patton & Wooden, 2009). Yet, White people in early stages of identity development (e.g., acceptance) (Hardiman & Jackson, 1992, 1997) believe myths (i.e., dominant ideologies) like reverse discrimination and feel anger about their supposed mistreatment by people of color. White people in acceptance will also claim they are "not racist." Fiona expressed frustration that her peers of color could not just "trust" that she is not racist. When they did not, she called it reverse racism. She explained:

> I think it's also frustrating because you don't want to be that person, but then like I felt like somehow we would read the quotes [in our course materials] and it's always like bashing White people and I would be like, "I'm not like that at all." And you can't even trust me right off the bat because that's what you're assuming; kind of goes back to the reverse discrimination thing.

Obviously, Fiona subscribed to the dominant ideologies and racial myths about reverse racism. Other aspects of White racial identity development include resistance to acknowledging privilege as well as the role White people play in perpetuating systemic racism. Such notions are apparent in Fiona's prose. Instead of exploring Whiteness, privilege, and her own racism, she resisted by saying "I'm not like that." Fiona also described course readings as "bashing White people" as opposed to recognizing them as important counter-narratives about systemic forms of racial oppression.

White students may move into later states of racial identity such as resistance (Hardiman & Jackson, 1992, 1997) when they learn about oppression and privilege and begin to unlearn dominant ideologies and racial myths. Students in resistance largely focus on the experiences of others instead of exploring who they are as White people. Kristen was beginning to understand the prevalence of oppression. She also came to see how her experiences as a White woman were different from her peers of color. She stated:

> I think in the work place . . . I have really high expectations of where I want to be in the future. I never really—I never took into account—that I might not get it because of my race or my gender for that matter. I

wanna work somewhere in politics so um being a woman of color could really influence whether you get the job or not especially in politics.

While Kristen expressed an increased awareness of oppression and privilege, she had not yet begun to reflect deeply into what it meant to be a White women with an oppressed (gender) and privileged (race) identity. Similarly, John's reflection paper also emphasized oppression faced by people of color instead of his own privileged White racial identity. He wrote:

I learned about feminism and racism. I . . . wasn't really focused around women of color and I didn't really know [much]. But, then this class kind of introduced me to [racism and feminism and] it kind of made me realize, like I said, how kind of male driven my racism was. . . . I never really thought about that before.

John had become aware of his "male-driven racism." However, in his paper he merely named the phenomenon and did not reflect deeply upon how "male-driven racism" shaped his sense of self. In essence, he was still focusing on others, instead of delving into his own racial identity.

One of the hallmarks of later stages of White identity development models is anger and frustration at systems of oppression. Anger can also be directed at White peers who knowingly or unknowingly perpetrate microaggressions, and perpetuate racist policies, practices, and systems. Sometimes individuals in later stages of development even try to disassociate themselves from other White people (Hardiman & Jackson, 1992, 1997; Helms, 1993). Andrew started to do this:

Overall, I still love this class, it has been one of the only ones during my college career that I get excited to go to in the morning. However, I always cannot shake this feeling of hate I have for other members of the White community. All this talk of racism and bigotry has really affected me at my core, to the point of me really changing how I act and treat men and women of color. The weird thing about this class is it really makes me resent the members of the White male community. I cannot fathom why there is so much hate.

Andrew clearly enjoyed the course, but he wrestled with the strong emotions engendered by Sister Stories. Andrew was not alone in his expression of deep emotions. Increased awareness of oppression and privilege is a natural part of the developmental process. In fact, strong emotions such as anger, shame, and guilt are often the impetus for progression into later stages of identity development where individuals begin constructing an anti-racist White identity (Hardiman & Jackson, 1992, 1997; Helms, 1993).

CONCLUSION

Sister Stories was a counterspace designed to offer a safe place for students to explore tough questions like "Who am I?" To facilitate academic and personal exploration of identity, students were asked to read and reflect upon a variety of racial and ethnic identity models. Most students of color found the curriculum, and counterspace discussions, about identity to be validating and empowering, saying things like: "I feel like finding your identity is a big part of life because there's nothing better than knowing yourself." However, a few students could not quite "fit" themselves into the identity development model phases or stages. Nonetheless, they still participated in deep reflection and, as a result, grew over the course of the semester. One student shared: "I never imagined that this class would change me as much as it did from the first class." Sister Stories was not designed to explore Whiteness. As such, our study yielded far less information about the identity journeys of White students. Our limited data suggested White students were in early stages of development where they focused more upon others rather than deeply reflecting on what it meant to be White within a society where racial oppression is pervasive.

REFERENCES

Abes, E. S., & Jones, S. R. (2004). Meaning-making capacity and the dynamics of lesbian college students' multiple dimensions of identity. *Journal of College Student Development, 45*(6), 612–32.

Anderson, E. (2015). The white space. *Sociology of Race and Ethnicity, 1*(1), 10–21.

Berry, J. W. (1980). Acculturation as varieties of adaptation. In A. Padilla (Ed.), *Acculturation: Theory, models and findings* (pp. 9–25). Boulder, CO: Westview.

——— (1993). Ethnic identities in plural societies. In M. E. Bernal & G. P. Knight (Eds.), *Ethnic identity: Formation and transmission among Hispanics and other minorities* (pp. 271–96). Albany, NY: State University of New York Press.

———, Phinney, J., Sam, D., & Vedder, P. (2006). *Immigrant youth in cultural transition: Acculturation, identity, and adaptation across national contexts.* Mahwah, NJ: Erlbaum.

Chun, K. M., Organista, P. B., & Marin, G. (Eds.) (2003). *Acculturation: Advances in theory, measurement and applied research.* Washington, DC: American Psychological Association.

Cross, W. E., Jr. (1971). The negro-to-black conversion experience: Toward a psychology of black liberation. *Black World, 20*(9), 13–27.

Dancy, T. E. E., & Brown, M. C. (2008). Unintended consequences: African American male educational attainment and collegiate perceptions after Brown v. Board of Education. *American Behavioral Scientist, 51*(7), 984–1003.

David, E. J. R. (2013). *Internalized oppression: The psychology of marginalized groups.* New York: Springer.

Essed, P. (1991). *Understanding everyday racism: An interdisciplinary theory.* Thousand Oaks, CA: Sage.

Evans, N. J., Forney, D. S., Guido, F. M., Patton, L. D., & Renn, K. A. (2010). *Student development in college: Theory, research, and practice.* San Francisco, CA: Jossey-Bass.

Ferdman, B. M., & Gallegos, P. I. (2001). Racial identity development in Latinos in the United States. In C. L. Wijeyesinghe & B. W. Jackson III (Eds.), *New perspectives on racial identity development: A theoretical and practical anthology.* New York: New York University Press.

Gildersleeve, R. E., Croom, N. N., & Vasquez, P. L. (2011). "Am I going crazy?!": A critical race analysis of doctoral education. *Equity & Excellence in Education, 44*(1), 93–114.

Hardiman, R., & Jackson, B. (1992, Winter). Racial identity development: Understanding racial dynamics in college classrooms and on campus. In M. Adams (Ed.), *Promoting diversity in college classrooms: Innovative responses for the curriculum, faculty, and institutions, 52,* 21–37.

Hardiman, R., & Jackson, B. W. (1997). Conceptual foundations for social justice courses. In M. Adams, L. A. Bell, and P. Griffin (Eds.), *Teaching for diversity and social justice. A sourcebook* (1st ed., pp. 16–29). New York: Routledge.

Harper, S. R., Patton, L. D., & Wooden, O. S. (2009). Access and equity for African American students in higher education: A critical race historical analysis of policy efforts. *The Journal of Higher Education, 80*(4), 389–414.

Helms, J. E. (1993). *Black and white racial identity: Theory, research, and practice.* Westport, CT: Praeger.

Hill Collins, P. (1991, 2000). *Black feminist thought: Knowledge, consciousness, and the politics of empowerment.* New York: Routledge.

Horse, P. G. (2012). Reflections on American Indian identity. In C. L. Wijeyesinghe & B. W. Jackson III (Eds.), *New perspectives on racial identity development: Integrating emerging frameworks* (2nd ed., pp. 108–20). New York: New York University Press.

Jackson, B. (1975). Black identity development. In L. Golubschick & B. Persky (Eds.), *Urban social and educational issues* (pp. 158–74). Dubuque, IA: Kendall Hall.

Jones, S. R. (1997).Voices of identity and difference: A qualitative exploration of the multiple dimensions of identity development in women college students. *Journal of College Student Development, 38*(4), 376–86.

——— (2009). Constructing identities at the intersections: An autoethnographic exploration of multiple dimensions of identity. *Journal of College Student Development, 50*(3), 287–304.

———, & McEwen, M. K. (2000). A conceptual model of multiple dimensions of identity. *Journal of College Student Development, 41,* 405–14.

———, McEwen, M. K., & Abes, E. S. (2007). Reconceptualizing the model of multiple dimensions of identity: The role of meaning-making capacity in the construction of multiple identities. *Journal of College Student Development, 48*(1), 1–22.

Kich, G. K. (1992). The developmental process of asserting a biracial, bicultural identity. In M. P. P. Root (Ed.), *Racially mixed people in America* (pp. 304–17). Newbury Park, CA: Sage.

Kim, J. (2012). Asian American racial identity development theory. In C. L. Wijeyesinghe & B. W. Jackson III (Eds.), *New perspectives on racial identity development: Integrating emerging frameworks* (2nd ed., pp. 138–60). New York: New York University Press.

Kwan, K. L. K., & Sodowsky, G. R. (1997). Internal and external ethnic identity and their correlates: A study of Chinese American immigrants. *Journal of Multicultural Counseling and Development, 25*(1), 51–67.

McCabe, J. (2009). Racial and gender microaggressions on a predominately White campus: Experiences of Black, Latina/o and White undergraduates. *Race, Gender and Class, 16,* 133–51.

Nadal, K. L., Wong, Y., Griffin, K., Striken, J., Vargas, V., Widemann, M., et al. (2011). Microaggressions and the multiracial experience. *International Journal of Humanities and Social Sciences, 1,* 36–44.

Ortiz, A. M., & Santos, S. J. (2009). *Ethnicity in college: Advancing theory and improving diversity practices on campus.* Sterling, VA: Stylus.

Phinney, J. S. (1993). A three-stage model of ethnic identity development in adolescence. In M. E. Bernal & G. P. Knight (Eds.), *Ethnic identity: Formation and transmis-*

sion among Hispanics and other minorities (pp. 61–79). Albany, NY: State University of New York.

———— (2003). Ethnic Identity and acculturation. In K. M. Chun, P. B. Organista & G. Marin (Eds.), *Acculturation: Advances in theory, measurement and applied research* (pp. 63–81). Washington, DC: American Psychological Association.

Poston, W. S. C. (1990). The biracial identity development model: A needed addition. *Journal of Counseling and Development, 69,* 152–55.

Rendón Linares, L. I. & Muñoz, S. M. (2011). Revisiting validation theory: Theoretical foundations, applications, and extensions. *Enrollment Management Journal, 2*(1), 12–33.

Renn, K. A. (2003). Understanding the identities of mixed-race college students through a developmental ecology lens. *Journal of College Student Development, 44,* 383–403.

———— (2012). *Mixed race students in college: The ecology of race, identity, and community on campus.* Albany, NY: SUNY Press.

Settles, I. H. (2006). Use of an intersectional framework to understand Black women's racial and gender identities. *Sex Roles, 54*(9–10), 589–601.

Shah, S. (Ed.) (1997). *Dragon ladies: Asian American feminists breathe fire.* Boston, MA: South End Press.

Solórzano, D. G. (1997). Images and words that wound: Critical race theory, racial stereotyping, and teacher education. *Teacher Education Quarterly, 24*(3), 5–20.

———— (1998). Critical race theory, race and gender microaggressions, and the experience of Chicana and Chicano scholars. *Qualitative Studies in Education, 11*(1), 121–36.

————, Ceja, M., & Yosso, T. J. (2000). Critical race theory, racial microaggressions, and campus racial climate: The experiences of African American college students. *The Journal of Negro Education, 69*(1/2), 60–73.

Stewart, D. L. (2008). Being all of me: Black students negotiating multiple identities. *Journal of Higher Education, 79*(2), 183–207.

———— (2009). Perceptions of multiple identities among Black college students. *Journal of College Student Development, 50*(3), 253–70.

Sue, D. W. (Ed.) (2010a). *Microaggressions and marginality: Manifestations, dynamics and impact.* Hoboken, NJ: Wiley.

———— (2010b). *Microaggressions in everyday life: Race, gender and sexual orientation.* Hoboken, NJ: Wiley.

Toldson, I., & Pasteur, A. (1975). Developmental stages of black self-discovery: Implications for using black art forms in group interaction. *Journal of Negro Education, 44,* 130–38.

Torres, V. (2003). Influences on ethnic identity development of Latino college students in the first two years of college. *Journal of College Student Development, 44*(4), 532–47.

Wijeyesinghe, C. L. (2001). Racial identity in multiracial people: An alternative paradigm. In C. L. Wijeyesinghe & B. W. Jackson, Jr. (Eds.), *New perspectives on racial identity development: A theoretical and practical anthology* (pp. 129–52). New York: New York University Press.

———— (2012). The intersectional model of multiracial identity. In C. L. Wijeyesinghe & B. W. Jackson, Jr. (Eds.), *New perspectives on racial identity development: Integrating emerging frameworks* (2nd ed., pp. 81–107). New York: New York University Press.

Yosso, T., Smith, W., Ceja, M., & Solórzano, D. (2009). Critical race theory, racial microaggressions, and campus climate for Latina/o undergraduates. *Harvard Educational Review, 79*(4) 659–69.

SEVEN

My Body, My Looks

"I'm never gonna look like that."

Interlocking race and gender oppressions were especially salient for women of color when Sister Stories conversations turned toward beauty and body image. As noted in chapter 1, I (Melissa) drew upon CRF perspectives to expose and critique oppressive beauty and body norms in the United States—norms that equate beauty with Whiteness (Frankenberg, 1993; Patton, 2006; Zinn & Dill, 1994). In this chapter, we share reflections from women of color about the impact of those oppressive aesthetic standards. We also highlight stories of resistance. In Sister Stories, many women learned how important it was to love their bodies. In turn, they became empowered to serve as role models to women of color who followed in their footsteps.

AESTHETIC OPPRESSION: A SHORT SUMMARY OF A LONG HISTORY

One of the ways oppression functions is through the perpetuation of hegemonic dominant ideologies such as equating beauty with phenotypic features associated with Whiteness (Bankhead & Johnson, 2014; Frankenberg, 1993; Johnson & Bankhead, 2014; Patton, 2006; Zinn & Dill, 1994). Rockquemore (2002) traced the long history of equating Whiteness to beauty in the United States:

> Dark skin increasingly symbolized lower status while light skin became even more associated with high status. . . . Because of the preference for all things that approximated whiteness, many Blacks longed for fair skin, white facial features, and straight hair. . . . Two categories

eventually emerged: (1) "good" (white) features—straight and/or long hair, a small nose, thin lips and light eyes and (2) "bad" (Black) features-short or kinky hair, full lips, and a wide nose. (p. 488)

Many writings critiquing White standards of beauty are by, and about, Black women. For instance, scholars have documented how Black women's skin color and hair is often used as a point of comparison to a White beauty standard of straight hair and White skin (Bankhead & Johnson, 2014; Capodilupo & Kim, 2014; Hall, 1995a; Johnson & Bankhead, 2014). A less voluminous, but growing, literature notes the ways women from other minoritized racial groups are also excluded from White standards of beauty. For instance, the shape of Asian American women's eyes is often contrasted with the ideal beauty norm of round eyes without an epicanthic fold (Hall, 1995b; Kim, 2012). Boisvert (2012) described how Native American women are stereotyped as, and shamed for, being fat. In sum, *any* woman who does not have typically White features (e.g., tall, thin, light skin, narrow nose, round eyes, straight—preferably blonde—hair) is deemed less attractive in dominant White U.S. culture.

In the later part of the twentieth century, writings by Black feminist, womanist, and CRF authors began to emerge critiquing oppressive beauty norms. In 1979, Wallace explained how Black women were constantly bombarded by exclusionary messaging regarding beauty.

The [B]lack woman had not failed to be aware of America's standard of beauty nor the fact that she was not included in it . . . but the [B]lack woman was only allowed entry if her hair was straight, her skin light, and her features European; in other words, if she was as nearly indistinguishable from a white woman as possible. (pp. 157–58)

Since then, many women writers have called attention to, and critiqued, dominant paradigms in the United States (and elsewhere around the globe) that portray Whiteness as the pinnacle of beauty (Frankenberg, 1993; Patton, 2006; Zinn & Dill, 1994). Such narrow and oppressive messages about aesthetics speak to the complicated intersections of sexism (e.g., women are judged by their appearance) and racism (e.g., people of color are not the "norm"). Quotes from Sister Stories students show that gendered racist messages about what is beautiful (or not) influence the way young women of color feel about themselves.

As we have noted throughout *Centering Women of Color in Academic Counterspaces*, dominant ideologies rooted in gendered racism perpetuate notions of Whiteness as normalcy. Twenge and Crocker (2002) further explained how dominant ideologies are often transformed into social stigmas that can be internalized by people from minoritized backgrounds:

The dominant or more powerful group defines what is valued in a culture as well as the specific forms those valued characteristics may take. Because these definitions almost always favor the attributes of the dominant group, the result is a generalized devaluation of subordinate minority groups. (p. 372)

How do hegemonic messages about aesthetics translate into feelings about self? In 1934, sociologist Herbert Mead described how perceptions of self can be shaped by the generalized other, or a person's socio-political and cultural contexts. More recently, Hardiman and Jackson (2007) explained how members of minoritized social identity groups can internalize and start to believe dominant societal messages about members of their social identity group. Harro (2013) proposed a detailed description of the cycle of socialization showing how oppressive messages are learned and internalized early in life. Messages from family, relatives, doctors, teachers, and the media bombard young children and shape the way they feel about themselves. Throughout life, oppressive messages are reinforced by individuals and social institutions (e.g., education, media, politics). People who challenge such notions can face ostracism, rejection, and outright violence from those who wish to maintain the oppressive status quo. Dominant ideologies are repeated from generation to generation, perpetuating oppression over time. The pervasiveness and similarities among standards of beauty throughout U.S. history show how deeply engrained oppression is, and how easily dominant ideologies are maintained over time (Patton, 2006).

There can be grave emotional costs associated with living in a body that is considered outside the norm. Rockquemore (2002) argued women of color, "held to a European standard of beauty, are socially and psychologically affected" (p. 489). Comparing oneself to an unattainable aesthetic standard can lead to negative mental health consequences such as low levels of self-esteem, self-concept, and self-acceptance. In one study, researchers found Black undergraduate women with greater appreciation for their bodies also reported higher self-esteem and body satisfaction (Cotter, Kelly, Mitchell & Mazzeo, 2013). Latinos, Asians, and American Indians in another study exhibited much lower self-esteem as compared to Whites (Twenge & Crocker, 2002). Low self-esteem and high public self-consciousness have been associated with greater levels body dissatisfaction and eating disorders for African American, Asian American, and White college students (Akan & Grilo, 1995). Scholars have also documented differences among women of color from different ethnicities, but the same racial group. For instance, one study of Black women found Afro-Caribbean women were more satisfied with their body shape than women who identified as African or African American (Mucherah & Frazier, 2013). In sum, literature suggests there are emotional ramifications for women of color whose bodies do not fit with normative standards of beauty and the impact of oppressive aesthetic standards can vary *among* women of color (Evans & McConnell, 2003).

We would be remiss if we did not conclude this section with a note about resistance. CRT and CRF scholars argue that despite the power of oppressive socialization, individuals resist dominant ideologies, and challenge the status quo. In an article about African American women's struggles with beauty and body image, Patton (2006) explained just how difficult it is to unlearn and challenge White-normed beauty standards. She called for women of color to engage in liberation instead of continuing on the path of internalizing and teaching future generations oppressive beauty standards.

> In order to be a liberated self, White hegemonic beauty needs to be challenged. Instead of succumbing to the White supremacist status quo, African American women need to continue to challenge the norm. We need to demand the same recognition of diversified Black beauty. . . . Through acknowledging and recognizing that other forms of beauty exist in the world beyond White supremacist definitions, we come to understand that there are different types of beauty in the world. (Patton, 2006, p. 45)

Empirical research suggests that challenging oppressive norms can have a positive influence on women's self concepts. For instance, Bankhead and Johnson (2014) found that women who resisted oppressive beauty standards and wore their hair in natural styles exhibited higher self-esteem than women who chemically or thermally straightened their hair. Sister Stories was designed as a counterspace where White supremacist notions of beauty could be debunked and challenged. Students were invited to interrupt the cycle of oppressive socialization and engage in resistance to craft more affirmational beauty and body counter narratives about women of color. In the following pages, student narratives explicate what this learning was like.

UNDOING A LIFETIME OF NEGATIVE
MESSAGES AND LOVING OUR BODIES

Through videos, readings, and assignments, I (Melissa) attempted to counter oppressive images of beauty with affirmational ones. As Harro (2013) noted, to stop oppression, individuals must interrupt the cycle of oppressive socialization. Sister Stories was a venue for students to talk candidly about, and learn to challenge, oppressive aesthetic messages. Students talked at length about how restrictive and unattainable images of beauty shaped the ways others viewed them, and in turn, how they felt about themselves. Such candid talk in Sister Stories was the first step in interrupting the cycle of socialization (Harro, 2013).

Throughout their lifetimes, women of color were bombarded with oppressive messages that their bodies were not good enough. Ife described some of those messages as: "My lips are too big. My eyes are too big. My nose is not bone shaped. My cheeks. . . . It's always something." Lucy also faced critiques of her body. She said, "Sometimes I'll hear things about my arms are too big or I'm too tall." Oppressive messaging about unobtainable beauty standards came from, and were reinforced by, a variety of people and social institutions. Lucy described how stereotypes about women of color were perpetuated by society in general, and the media in particular. She said, "In the media today . . . we're loud. We're ghetto. Our hair is crazy. Our nails are crazy. Our clothes are too tight. Our lips are too big. Butts are too big." Lena went on to explain the effects of narrow media images: "I just feel like all girls no matter what race or gender . . . they can relate to that because media puts . . . like society puts . . . a lot of pressure on girls." Bonnie concurred. She explained how media images created and perpetuated standards that others used to judged her. "That's been my issue is people telling me I need to look a certain way because my body type is not ok." Elena lamented the effects that narrow images of beauty had on women of color like herself. She said, "The things that women will do for beauty is absolutely ridiculous. Women of color will do anything from whitening their skin, to getting surgery to emphasize different body parts, just to be noticed. It is a sad reality."

Jocelyn's inability to fit into White standards of beauty was heightened at the predominantly White campus. Her presence in the White space drew extra attention to the fact that she did not look like White students or fit with White beauty standards. She explained:

> On top of being one of the only Black girls, I'm really dark skinned. So, I get put down a lot about my skin color. A double whammy on top of being, you know—I'm already not the norm. On top of that, I *can't* look like [the ideal White woman] and there's no way in hell I'm ever gonna look like [that] because this color.

While beauty standards are unobtainable for most women, Jocelyn's quote highlights the fact that women of color cannot achieve beauty standards because of the color of their skin. In the following section, narratives from women of color show how deeply engrained notions of beauty as Whiteness can be.

INTERNALIZING WHITENESS (AND LIGHTNESS) AS BEAUTIFUL

When standards of beauty are normed on Whiteness, women of color— especially those with darker phenotypes—are considered less attractive than their lighter-skinned peers (Awad et al., 2014; Patton, 2006). Many women of color in Sister Stories talked about beauty standards in the context of colorism (Hunter, 2005, 2007), which is discrimination based upon skin tone. In chapter 4, we addressed phenotype and colorism in the context of women's counterspace interactions. Here, we revisit phenotype and colorism to explicate the connections between skin tone, beauty standards, and women's feelings about self.

As noted earlier, oppression functions through the perpetuation of hegemonic dominant ideologies equating beauty with phenotypic features associated with Whiteness. Bell (2007) argued, "Through hegemony, a dominant group can so successfully project its particular way of seeing social reality that its view is accepted as common sense, as part of the natural order, even by those disempowered by it" (p. 10). Other scholars have noted how internalized oppression occurs when minoritized social identity groups accept and adopt dominant societal messages of inferiority about their group (David, 2013; Hardiman & Jackson, 2007; Harro, 2013). Many students admitted to accepting and internalizing oppressive images of beauty and body image. Their comments show how challenging it was to undo those deeply internalized messages about White standards of beauty. When beauty is equated with Whiteness, phenotype becomes a characteristic used to determine how closely (or not) women can come to achieving oppressive beauty standards.

Women of color judged themselves not only against White standards of beauty, but also against other women of color with different skin tones. Women of color with dark skin knew they could not achieve White beauty norms. Comparing themselves to an unobtainable beauty standard of White and/or lighter skin was painful for women like Regina. She said:

> I grew up in a predominantly White [community]. . . . It comes with the whole light-skinned, dark-skinned kind of thing . . . I have full lips. . . . You know, I have very Black features. So, I think for a long time that was looked down upon . . . I don't think you love yourself, I think you start looking at your skin tone, you want to be lighter. People don't want to go out in the summer because they don't want to get darker. And so, you know when you're a kid, you don't know any better.

As Regina's quote suggests, comparing herself to White standards had a negative effect on her self-esteem. She admitted to not loving herself because of the color of her skin. Yet, dark-skinned women were not the only ones who were taught they were not beautiful.

The following quotes suggest that women of color often applied oppressive standards of beauty to themselves and other women of color. The phenomenon of judging women's beauty by their skin tone is not a new phenomenon. Oppressive images about Whiteness and lightness as beauty date back to early American history (Bankhead & Johnson, 2014; Patton, 2006; Rockquemore, 2002). Patton (2006) explained:

> Since 1619, African American women and their beauty have been juxtaposed against White beauty standards, particularly pertaining to their

skin color and hair. During slavery, Black women who were lighter-skinned and had features that were associated with mixed progeny (e.g., wavy or straight hair, White/European facial features) tended to be house slaves and those Black women with darker-skin hues, kinky hair, and broader facial features tended to be field slaves. (p. 26)

During the alumni focus group, Regina and Nicole discussed debates among women of color about which was more beautiful—light skin or dark skin. They labeled these debates as "slave mentality." Hardiman and Jackson (2007) would likely describe them as a potential combination of internalized and horizontal oppression whereby people of color knowingly (or unknowingly) adopt oppressive ideologies and use them against other people of color.

> **Nicole**: I remember our first conversation was about being light-skinned and dark-skinned, and woo! Man, I got so heated. Aw man.
>
> **Regina**: I hate that.
>
> **Nicole**: I hate it too.
>
> **Regina**: Like I hate that hashtag too, #toolightskinned. Like, what are you, like, like what. . . . It's just slave mentality.
>
> **Nicole**: It's so true and it stinks because you know people really think that way.

Nicole's lamenting about how much "it stinks" that people still "think that way" points to the ways oppression is maintained and perpetuated over time. Contemporary Twitter conversations about beauty as Whiteness or lightness use and reinforce the same oppressive messages that were prevalent in colonial America.

As Regina and Nicole noted, instead of commiserating about, or collectively rejecting, narrow beauty standards, some women internalized and perpetuated oppression. Dark-skinned women of color were sometimes surprised (and irritated) when lighter-skinned women of color lamented oppressive beauty standards. This frustration stemmed from their belief that light-skinned women's phenotype allowed them to get closer to White beauty standards. Juba was irked by a light-skinned friend who complained about being marginalized for the color of her skin. Juba explained:

> One that shocked me the most was Nicole. She's Cape Verdean . . . I think she mentioned that she . . . was like the Black sheep of the family because she was the lightest . . . I would never in a million years think that her light skin would be a problem for her. Know what I'm saying? I'm sitting here thinking like: "Are you kidding me? Are you kidding

me? You fit the criteria [of beauty]. Society likes you. . . . Your face, everything!"

Juba was frustrated because "Society likes you. . . . Your face, everything!" Implied in her comment was that her friend more closely resembled "beautiful" (i.e., White) skin and facial features, while darker-skinned women, like herself, were not viewed as beautiful. Ife was also frustrated that her lighter-skinned friends had it better when it came to fitting into beauty norms. Ife said:

> From what I see they do have it easier. . . . My best friend, she's light skinned. She's the only light-skinned person in the group; she's gonna get all the attention in the world. *All* the attention. . . . She fails to realize that light-skinned people do have it better. I don't think there's any other way to say it, but it's true. . . . It's hard for them to believe because they have good hair, good curly, long hair and things like that.

Negative emotions directed toward other women of color seemed to be rooted in the ways students felt about their own bodies. For instance, Juba's resentment stemmed from the fact that she received less attention and was deemed less attractive because of her darker skin. Her internalization of White beauty norms was also apparent in her choice of words such as "good hair." Juba's comments align with decades of writings by women of color who discuss how ideas about good or beautiful hair result from socially constructed beauty standards normed on Whiteness (Patton, 2006; Wallace, 1979). Navigating gendered racist messages from society and White people is challenging. But, feeling horizontal oppression from other women of color who perpetuate versions of oppressive ideologies was sometimes even more challenging for women of color in Sister Stories.

OPPRESSIVE MESSAGES
FROM FAMILY AND MEN OF COLOR

In addition to horizontal oppression from other women of color, oppressive beauty standards were perpetuated and reinforced by those who women of color trusted the most—family and men of color. Harro (2013) explained how family and peers are crucial to our early and ongoing socialization. The implicit and explicit messages we get from loved ones influence our self-concepts and self-perceptions. When family socialization reinforced oppressive aesthetic standards, it negatively affected women's self-concept. Regina explained:

> Whatever younger age you are, you're very impressionable—especially when people of your own race [and your own family] are saying these things to you, so it's not just outsiders. . . . It's also very hard to have that self-confidence [when family says these things].

Regina was not alone. Many women of color received critiques from parents and extended kin about their weight, hair, and skin tone. When family members criticized their looks, women of color often internalized negative images and, in turn, felt badly about themselves. Sofia explained:

> My dad would be like, "Watch your weight or watch what you eat." A lot of times that just made me want to cry. It just really bothered me. I feel like it's something that Hispanic people, especially like in the family, always bring up—"You're gaining weight, you're losing weight." Something [from Sister Stories] that sat with me was appreciation for your body. . . . So, even though what they say is hurtful, I've learned how to address it or I tell them that it bothers me . . . I finally told my dad how much it bothers me and he was just like, "If it bothers you that much I won't mention it again." So now he addresses it nicer. He'll be like, "Oh, why don't you go walking with your sister." He addresses it nicer but my mom is still like, "Oh why don't you get like gastric bypass?"

Lucia was also criticized for her weight and phenotype. Her mother perpetuated colorism (Hunter, 2005, 2007) and Lucia internalized these messages. Constant reminders of thinness and Whiteness as beautiful took an emotional toll on Lucia. She explained:

> My mother valued thinness and made sure I knew that. Every time I would go home and visit my mom, she would say the same thing, "Lucia, you're gaining weight." This took a toll on how I saw myself. I thought that I had to be skinny in order to fit into my family. I became a vegetarian and started going to the gym. My mother also values light skin. I am the darkest one in my family and hear that all of the time. One time my mother offered me skin-bleaching cream, one that she personally uses herself. I did not understand what it was for and she explained that is was to lighten my face up. For my prom, my mother did not let me attend it with a dark-skin male. She said, "Lucia think about the picture, it'll come out so dark and you will have it forever." . . . [These conversations] made me think I was not pretty enough because my hair wasn't long enough and that dark skin was ugly.

Jewel also had family members who believed light skin was more beautiful. Because her mother lived in Nigeria, Jewel saw her infrequently. When she visited, Jewel noticed how much her mother had bleached her skin she said:

> The color complex plays so much into everything. Like it's so crazy . . . the fact like there's so many women bleaching their skin. Like, I sat down with my mother and was like, "You're a little lighter than I remember you." And she's just like, "You know I be mixing my stuff," and I'm just like, "You're crazy!" I just don't understand [the desire to bleach].

Women of color were critiqued for their hair. Jewel understood how "western" (i.e., White) influences played a role in how her Nigerian kin viewed beauty. She felt a constant pressure to relax her hair so she would be seen as "normal" by her own family, many of whom lived in Nigeria. Jewel said:

> Everybody was telling me—because they're trying to westernize—having thick, textured hair [was not attractive]. And, they would be like, "You need a relaxer." And, I'm just like, "No, I don't. Thank you." But if I didn't have the will power, by the end of my trip, I would have relaxed my hair because every single [relative] . . . my aunts, my cousins, my father, just everybody was telling me that [my hair was] not right. That it's not normal. That's not how I should be. How crazy is that? A culture that's supposed to be my own and still having that alienation. It's crazy.

While she was proud that she did not give in and relax her hair, Jewel also admitted family messages caused her to feel alienated from those she loved the most. While Sister Stories course materials largely focused on the United States, all societies construct aesthetic standards. Often, these norms are rooted in restrictive notions of beauty (Hall, 1995b; Rockquemore, 2002; Swami, Hwang & Jung, 2012). As Jewel noted, western influences on beauty as Whiteness have far-reaching effects in international communities. Researchers found South Korean university women reported high levels of acceptance of, and interest in, cosmetic surgery to obtain a White standard of beauty (Swami et al., 2012). In another study, U.S. Whites' perceptions of beauty were found to be almost identical to native Asians, Hispanics, and Taiwanese adults (Cunningham, Roberts, Barbee, Druen & Wu, 1995). In an Austrian study, men and women's attitudes about cosmetic surgery were shaped by restrictive notions of beauty and the importance of finding an attractive mate (Swami, Pietschnig, Stewart, Nader, Stieger, Shannon & Voracek, 2013). A more in-depth conversation about global aesthetic standards of beauty is outside the scope of this chapter. However, we felt it was important to note how prevalent, and similar, oppressive beauty standards are for women around the globe.

Like Nicole, Regina refused to treat her hair and experienced negative backlash from family. She recalled an incident where her grandfather suggested she was not dateable because of her hair. Regina described:

> So I went natural a year and a half ago. I had my hair out . . . I went to my grandparents' house. My grandfather is pushing 70. So, I was like, "Grandpa, I need a man!" I was just joking with him. And he's like "With your hair like that, you're not gonna get one." . . . He probably meant nothing by it. He probably thought it was a joke. But when it's a reoccurring theme, you're not just hearing it from the men your age, but you're hearing it from your grandfather, it can get [pause] disheartening. And it's generational too. [He's] probably teaching me some-

thing that was taught to him. . . . When you think about the fact that whoever the powers that be, however long ago it was, the things that they set in motion are still effective today. . . . It's almost to the point where I feel like as minorities we're doing it—we're doing the busy work of these people now. [Oppressive messages] have been so ingrained, that we're now feeding [those negative messages] on to our kids. We're feeding it on and on and on.

Regina's quote exemplifies many aspects of Harro's (2013) cycle of socialization. She noted how family members can consciously, or unconsciously, pass on oppressive standards of beauty to the next generation. Sometimes oppressive ideologies are all they know. Regina also noted that her grandfather was certainly not the only one who suggested her natural hair was not attractive. Oppressive beauty standards were harbored by men of color—leaving her few dating options. Juba also felt rejected by men of color who deemed her less beautiful because of her hair, skin color, and eye shape. Juba said:

I think what I struggled most with was when we talked about body image, the issue of body image . . . I'm struggling within myself. I am proud to be a woman of color, but I can't sit there, especially when I have a man of color telling me that: "You're afro is not what society's looking for. That's not the norm." [It makes me] upset. Certain perceptions of beauty were just really limited. All [men look for is] the long hair, the light skin, and the beautiful eyes. They don't pay attention to deeper. I don't know how to describe it. They are just very closed-minded sometimes.

Becca had an exchange with a White man that reinforced the oppressive ideology that only White women could achieve the pinnacle of beauty. His comment was deeply hurtful.

One of my best friends is White. He's always telling me, you're so pretty for a Black girl. . . . Just recently he's been saying that and all his fraternity brothers start saying it now. . . . So like when he said that to me, I kind of really took offense to it. I'm like, "What do you mean?" . . . I got really upset and I started crying. . . . It broke my heart.

As the prior quotes show, oppressive messages conveyed by family and peers can take a deep emotional toll. Instead of being supported, women of color were rejected by friends, family, and love interests who upheld gendered racism in the form of White beauty standards.

Women of color in Sister Stories were looking for support, solidarity, and sometimes love from men of color. Unfortunately, they were often painfully rejected because they did not meet White standards of beauty. These experiences are not novel. Hooks (2000) discussed the struggles faced by women of color who desired racial solidarity with men of color, but who experienced misogyny instead.

Peers and family can be essential elements to resilience for people of color (Garrett et al., 2014). Downey (1993) wrote of Native peoples: "We are told to be good to one another. Respect one another. Take care of each other, as well as ourself. These are some of our Instructions" (p. 3). Unfortunately, most women of color in Sister Stories conveyed stories whereby family and peers reinforced oppressive messaging instead of being "good to one another." Elena was one of the few exceptions:

> Sometimes it's your family telling you that you're not pretty enough, or that you need to lose weight to meet a man. . . . My grandmother always tells me that if someone can't accept me as I am, then they don't deserve me. But my family supports me one hundred percent, and family is also a big part of how you see yourself.

As Elena noted, family influenced how women of color saw themselves. Unfortunately, she was one of few women of color with a strong woman role model who interrupted the cycle of oppressive beauty socialization in order to teach her grandchild she was indeed beautiful.

I FELT REALLY VULNERABLE

Oppressive messages about beauty and body image left women of color feeling vulnerable when the topic came up in class. To be constantly objectified and compared to unobtainable standards of beauty is emotionally taxing. As such, talking about topics like beauty and body image in class was often emotional for women of color. Bonnie explained:

> I think body image was a hard day for everyone. I feel like that's the one that keeps coming up because it's just I feel like girls in general, we're all in that stage or are going through that stage where we're not comfortable with our body. I, personally was not comfortable with my body until I was probably 18 . . . I would look at myself in the mirror and just like look at all my flaws . . . I wouldn't go to the beach and wear a two piece . . . I did not like my body. . . . Body image—that's something I've just recently become comfortable with. So talking about it in class was still a little bit uncomfortable. . . . [But] I love to talk!

Even for a self-described extrovert who "loved to talk" in class, beauty and body image topics still caused Bonnie discomfort. Fola also found conversations about beauty to be difficult reminders of being objectified. Fola shared:

> This topic on body image really brought me back to my body issues and lack of confidence. When I was younger, I was known as the Black skinny girl who had long hair. People did not know my name, but as the girl with long hair. I did not want that to be my only worth, so I craved change.

Nicole actually broke down and cried during the conversation about body image. Nicole said:

> I definitely cried in class. It was pretty embarrassing . . . I feel like the girls in the room felt what I was saying, experienced what I experienced. It made me feel better about it and a lot more comfortable about it. I feel like [Melissa] validated the way I felt. She wasn't like, "No! You're wrong for feeling that way." She let me say what I had to say. I felt like I was heard and everything I said was important. I felt really vulnerable after I talked about my body image thing. I just thought people would think something of me because I got so emotional. I was nervous . . . about going to class again, if body image would come up . . . I feel like my body image is not something that I [usually] put out there for everyone to know. So, I was worried about that. . . . It was just really weird to cry about that in front of other people.

While Nicole felt validated by the instructor and women peers, conversations about body image were still difficult. Scholars have long written about the impact of oppressive beauty norms on women of color including: diminished self-esteem, eating disorders, and other mental health issues (Moradi, Dirks & Matteson, 2005; Wolf, 1991; Patton, 2006). Women's emotionally distressed responses to talking about beauty and body image speaks volumes about the deep and long-term impact of oppressive beauty standards.

RESIST OPPRESSION AND LOVE YOURSELF

Learning about and critiquing oppressive beauty standards in Sister Stories was often a catalyst for empowerment. Women of color were not merely passive recipients of oppressive beauty and body norms. They were active agents in their own lives and the lives of women friends and relatives. Anzaldúa (2015) wrote to women of color:

> The paths we've traveled on have been rocky and thorny and no doubt they will continue to be so. . . . But, instead of rocks and thorns, we want to concentrate on the rain and the sunlight and the spider webs glistening on both. . . . This land of thorns is not habitable. We carry this bridge inside us, the struggle, the movement toward liberation. (pp. xxvii–xxviii)

As a result of learning in Sister Stories, many women of color started to resist oppressive images and challenge those who perpetuated restrictive images of beauty. They began the movement toward liberation despite the rocky and thorny path of oppression. In reference to people commenting about how her body type was less than ideal, Bonnie responded, "Now, when they say things like that I do challenge them." When asked about the most moving aspect of the class, Becca responded:

I would say, the whole skin bleaching [topic] . . . I was born in Africa. Where I'm from we're like all different shades of colors. When I came to the United States, like, I saw like different skin colors and some people bleached. Even within my Liberian community some people like to bleach. So actually taking this course and learning about what skin bleaching does and how it lowers self-esteem [was powerful]. . . . My group, we actually did a presentation on that. I felt like that [topic] really moved me and influenced me to accept my skin complexion — actually love my skin complexion — instead of me not loving myself, or self-hate. So, the whole self-bleaching topic really touched me.

Like Becca, it was important for Fola to love herself while simultaneously fighting oppressive beauty ideologies that led women to alter their bodies. Fola said:

When I was younger, I went through this whole, like, era where I was not comfortable with my body and my shell. And I really tried to change it. But, as I got older, and as I educated myself [in classes like this one] I found out that I didn't really need to change myself . . . we need to eliminate those stereotypes [that make us feel badly about ourselves].

Earlier in this chapter, we noted how oppressive aesthetic standards can have grave psychological consequences. However, there are some studies that show the connections between oppressive beauty ideologies and self-esteem is complicated. In fact, two studies have noted that Black women have higher self-esteem than Whites and other minoritized racial groups (Gray-Little & Hafdahl, 2000; Twenge & Crocker, 2002). Twenge and Crocker (2002) suggest these findings might be explained by the presence of self-protective factors engendered in strong communities. Quotes from women of color in Sister Stories reinforce how women of color can feel good about themselves despite oppressive ideologies. Moreover, narratives from women like Becca, Fola, Jewel, and Nicole show that women of color were strong, resilient, and empowered to make change in the face of oppression.

As a result of their experiences in Sister Stories, many women of color were empowered to challenge not just friends and family, but also strangers. This type of behavior is indicative of critical race feminist praxis whereby women draw upon CRF perspectives to solve real-life problems (Wing, 2003). Women of color in Sister Stories felt it was crucial to interrupt the cycle of oppressive socialization whenever they saw it. Jewel and Nicole hoped that by challenging parents, less emotional harm might be done to girls of color in the future. In their opinion, perpetuating oppressive images of beauty manifested in self-hate and a corresponding lack of love for children. Jewel and Nicole believed children needed love, not self-hate, in order to thrive in a racist and sexist world.

Jewel: I had a conversation with a [pregnant woman who said,] "I hope my child, if it's a girl has black hair." And I was just like what kind of hair do you have cause you're clearly a Black woman? And she was just like, "Well um, I have real hair." And I was like, "okay." And then, I went on and I was just like, "I hope you would love your daughter unconditionally, regardless of the kind of hair that she has, because at the end of the day, you're hating yourself, or you're hating—

Regina: Your unborn child!

Jewel: Not only, but whoever is Black! You're hating them. And that self-hatred is gonna live on in her. And she was just like, "Yeah well I don't care," I was just like, "Oh I'm done!"

Regina: I just want a healthy baby cause look, I got bigger issues. I'd rather have nappy hair than a sickly kid [who needs to go to] St. Jude or something. So, you gotta pick your battles. I'll take the nappy-headed kid who is healthy. Like there's so many other bigger issues.

Nicole: It's a vicious cycle.

Regina: What do you do? I can stop it on my end, I can try to prevent my kids, but it's very disheartening [to see other people do it to their children].

Harro (2013) noted that "people who contradict the 'norm' pay a price for their independent thinking" (p. 49). When women of color resist oppressive standards of beauty and attempt to love their bodies, they sometimes experience backlash from Whites and other people of color. Sofia explained:

> When I was much younger my mother would relax my hair. . . . When I was old enough to know better I continued to relax my hair because I felt that slick straight hair was beautiful. In high school I struggled with having relaxed hair and always having to continue doing so in order to avoid my curly roots from showing. Eventually, I decided to embrace my curls. Growing my curls out was a process that lasted about 4 years and it is well worth it; I finally absolutely fell in love with my natural curly hair. When all my curls finally grew out and I began wearing it out more often I began getting questioned. Well, are you feeling wild? Are you untamable today? Look at the lioness! Is it fake hair? For so long I allowed people to question my hair . . . I also allowed them to try and define me by my hair.

Sofia engaged in a form of resistance by refusing to let others define her by her hair. As a result, she encountered negative responses from family and friends. Such responses are not uncommon. Women of color in Johnson and Bankhead's (2014) study revealed negative responses from friends and family when they wore their hair naturally. While resistance can make women feel good about themselves, the process is not always an easy one—especially when loved ones are not supportive.

Sister Stories offered women a venue to begin loving themselves. It also inspired women of color to become role models to others. In fact, a favorite class assignment was to write a letter to future women of color. Students like Jewel, Nicole, and Regina talked about the importance of feeling beautiful, worthy, and proud. They also felt a duty to help other women do the same. Jewel wished she had women role models to offer affirming and supportive messages. She intended to offer support and affirmation to young women who might also be lacking strong women of color role models. Her message to young women of color would be:

> I just remember growing up very angry, just angry at everything. I just always felt as though I was never enough, you know? So I think if I was to say something to my old self, or to younger women, I would say: "You're worthy. You are worthy of anything that you have coming toward you. You're worthy of the opportunities that will arise. You're worthy of life. Like, you're just worthy." Yeah.

Nicole also wished she could turn back the hands of time to tell her younger self she was beautiful, worthy, and amazing, despite oppressive messages that suggested otherwise. Nicole explained how important it was for women of color to understand that they were "enough" and what they had to say was important. Nicole explained:

> "You are enough." That's what I would tell myself. You are *more* than enough. I would tell myself. Well, I would tell any [woman of color], "If you have something important to say, say it. If you feel like someone needs to hear it, just say it. Even if it's just you who needs to hear it, just say it."

Nicole's quote was not just about body image. Her reference to being "enough" draws a connection between beauty, body image, and women's empowerment. Being objectified and judged against unattainable beauty standards can make women of color feel invisible. As noted in prior chapters, invisibility is a common form of microaggression for women of color (Nadal, 2010; Siesko & Biernat, 2010; Vaccaro & Mena, in press; Wing, 2003). Nicole wanted all women of color to know that they mattered and what they had to say was important. Regina summed up the sentiments of many of the women of color in Sister Stories. Her message to younger women of color was "love yourself . . . no matter what society says, love yourself."

CONCLUSION

Oppressive beauty standards normed on Whiteness were ever-present in the lives of women of color enrolled in Sister Stories. Women of color were socialized to accept and adopt restrictive aesthetic standards. These messages often came from those they trusted the most, including peers of color and family. This socialization prompted many women to feel badly about themselves. Yet, negative impacts on women's self-concepts are only part of the story. Women's voices also explicated the "rocky" and "thorny" (Anzaldúa, 2015, p. xxviii) path of liberation from oppressive beauty standards. As a result of their learning in Sister Stories, women of color were empowered to resist oppression and role model the way for women who came after them. In the next chapter, we share more insights from students about role modeling and enacting change in the context of leadership development.

REFERENCES

Akan, G. E., & Grilo, C. M. (1995). Sociocultural influences on eating attitudes and behaviors, body image, and psychological functioning: A comparison of African-American, Asian-American, and Caucasian college women. *International Journal of Eating Disorders, 18*(2), 181–87.

Anzaldúa, G. (2015). Acts of healing. In C. Moraga & G. Anzaldúa (Eds.), *This bridge called my back: Writings by radical women of color* (4th ed., pp. xviii–xviiii). Albany, NY: State University Press.

Awad, G. H., Norwood, C., Taylor, D. S., Martinez, M., McClain, S., Jones, B., & Chapman-Hilliard, C. (2014). Beauty and body image concerns among African American college women. *Journal of Black Psychology*, 1–25.

Bankhead, T., & Johnson. T. (2014). Self-esteem, hair-esteem and Black women with natural hair. *International Journal of Education and Social Science, 1*(4), 92–102.

Bell, L. A. (2007). Theoretical foundations for social justice education. In M. Adams, L. A. Bell & P. Griffin (Eds.), *Teaching for diversity and social justice: A sourcebook.* New York: Routledge.

Boisvert, J. A. (2012). Native American Indian women, fat studies and feminism. *Somatechnics, 2*(1), 84–92.

Capodilupo, C. M., & Kim, S. (2014). Gender and race matter: The importance of considering intersections in Black women's body image. *Journal of Counseling Psychology, 61*(1), 37.

Cotter, E., Kelly, N. R., Mitchell, K. S., & Mazzeo, S. E. (2013). An investigation of body appreciation, ethnic identity, and eating disorder symptoms in Black women. *Journal of Black Psychology, 41*(1), 3–25.

Cunningham, M. R., Roberts, A. R., Barbee, A. P., Druen, P. B., & Wu, C. H. (1995). "Their ideas of beauty are, on the whole, the same as ours": Consistency and variability in the cross-cultural perception of female physical attractiveness. *Journal of Personality and Social Psychology, 68*(2), 261.

David, E. J. R. (2013). *Internalized oppression: The psychology of marginalized groups.* New York: Springer.

Downey, V. (1993). Tewa tesque pueblo. In S. Wall (Ed.), *Wisdom's daughters: Conversations with elders of Native America* (pp. 2–21). New York: Harper Perennial.

Evans, P. C., & McConnell, A. R. (2003). Do racial minorities respond in the same way to mainstream beauty standards? Social comparison processes in Asian, Black, and White women. *Self and Identity*, 2(2), 153–67.

Frankenberg, R. (1993). *White women, race matters: The social construction of Whiteness*. Minneapolis MN: University of Minnesota Press.

Garrett, M. T., Parrish, M., Williams, C., Grayshield, L., Portman, T. A. A., Rivera, E. T., & Maynard, E. (2014). Invited Commentary: Fostering resilience among Native American youth through therapeutic intervention. *Journal of Youth and Adolescence*, 43(3), 470–90.

Gray-Little, B., & Hafdahl, A. R. (2000). Factors influencing racial comparisons of self-esteem: A quantitative review. *Psychological Bulletin, 126*, 26–54.

Hall, C. C. I. (1995a). Beauty is in the soul of the beholder: Psychological implications of beauty and African American women. *Cultural Diversity and Mental Health, 1*(2), 125.

——— (1995b). Asian eyes: Body image and eating disorders of Asian and Asian American women. *Eating Disorders, 3*(1), 8–19.

Hardiman, R., & Jackson, B. W. (2007). Conceptual foundations for social justice education. In M. Adams, L.A. Bell & P. Griffin (Eds.), *Teaching for diversity and social justice: A sourcebook* (2nd ed., pp. 35–48). New York: Routledge.

Harro, B. (2013). The cycle of socialization. In M. Adams, W. J. Blumenfeld, C. Casteñada, H. W. Hackman, M. L. Peters & X. Zúñiga (Eds.), *Readings for diversity and social justice* (3rd ed., pp. 45–52). New York: Routledge.

hooks, b. (2000). *Feminist theory: From margin to center* (2nd ed.). Cambridge, MA: South End Press.

Hunter, M. (2005). *Race, gender, and the politics of skin tone*. New York: Routledge.

——— (2007). The persistent problem of colorism: Skin tone, status, and inequality. *Sociology Compass, 1*(1), 237–54.

Johnson, T. A., & Bankhead, T. (2014). Hair it is: Examining the experiences of black women with natural hair. *Open Journal of Social Sciences*, 2, 86–100.

Kim, J. (2012). Asian American racial identity development theory. *New perspectives on racial identity development*. In C. L. Wijeyesinghe & B. W. Jackson III (Eds.), *New perspectives on racial identity development: Integrating emerging frameworks* (2nd ed., pp. 138–60). New York: New York University Press.

Mead, G. H. (1934). *Mind, self, and society*. Chicago, IL: University of Chicago Press.

Moradi, B., Dirks, D., & Matteson, A. V. (2005). Roles of sexual objectification experiences and internalization of standards of beauty in eating disorder symptomatology: A test and extension of Objectification Theory. *Journal of Counseling Psychology*, 52(3), 420–28.

Mucherah, W., & Frazier, A. D. (2013). How deep is skin-deep? The relationship between skin color satisfaction, estimation of body image, and self-esteem among women of African descent. *Journal of Applied Social Psychology*, 43(6), 1177–84.

Nadal, K. (2010). Gender microaggressions: Implications for mental health. In M. A. Paludi (Ed.), *Feminism and women's rights worldwide* (vol. 2, pp. 155–75). Santa Barbara, CA: Praeger.

Patton, T. O. (2006). Hey girl, am I more than my hair?: African American women and their struggles with beauty, body image, and hair. *NWSA Journal*, 18(2), 24–51.

Rockquemore, K. A. (2002). Negotiating the color line: The gendered process of racial identity construction among Black/White biracial women. *Gender & Society*, 16(4), 485–503.

Siesko, A. K., & Biernat, M. (2010). Prototypes of race and gender: The invisibility of Black women. *Journal of Experimental Social Psychology, 46*, 356–60.

Swami, V., Hwang, C. S., & Jung, J. (2012). Factor structure and correlates of the acceptance of cosmetic surgery scale among South Korean university students. *Aesthetic Surgery Journal*, 32(2), 220–29.

Swami, V., Pietschnig, J., Stewart, N., Nader, I. W., Stieger, S., Shannon, S., & Voracek, M. (2013). Blame it on patriarchy: More sexist attitudes are associated with stronger consideration of cosmetic surgery for oneself and one's partner. *International Journal of Psychology, 48*(6), 1221–29.

Twenge, J. M., & Crocker, J. (2002). Race and self-esteem: Meta-analyses comparing whites, blacks, Hispanics, Asians, and American Indians and comment on Gray-Little and Hafdahl (2000). *Psychological Bulletin, 128*(3), 371–408.

Vaccaro, A., & Mena, J. (in press). "I've struggled, I've battled": Invisibility microaggressions experienced by women of color at a predominately White institution. *The Journal About Women in Higher Education.*

Wallace, M. (1979). *Black macho and the myth of the superwoman.* New York: The Dial Press.

Wing, A. K. (2003). *Critical race feminism: A reader* (2nd ed.). New York: New York University Press.

Wolf, N. (1991). *The beauty myth: How images of beauty are used against women.* New York: William Morrow and Company.

Zinn, M. B., & Dill, B. T. (Eds.) (1994). *Women of color in U.S. society.* Philadelphia, PA: Temple University Press.

EIGHT

Becoming an Inclusive Leader

"Everyone has a voice."

What does it mean to be a leader? What are the most effective ways to train students to become inclusive leaders? For decades, scholars and practitioners have wrestled with questions like these. At the beginning of this chapter, we briefly summarize what experts think are key components of effective collegiate leadership development programs. We also analyze the small but growing body of critical race scholarship about leadership. Included in this review is a synopsis of different leadership theories, with emphasis on three models taught in Sister Stories: Servant Leadership (Greenleaf, 1977), the Relational Leadership Model (Komives, Lucas & McMahon, 2013), and the Social Change Model of Leadership Development (HERI, 1996). The heart of the chapter centers on student reflections about leadership. Through Sister Stories, students learned that critical race-inspired leadership meant: knowing and loving yourself, inclusively engaging others, being empowered to make change, and role modeling inclusive leadership. Moreover, as a result of the Sister Stories course, students began enacting positive change within their spheres of influence by using their voice to challenge others with grace and educate people about inequality.

DEVELOPMENT OF DIVERSE STUDENT LEADERS

Many higher education institutions claim that developing leaders of the future is central to their mission and purpose (Dugan, 2006). As such, fostering the leadership skills of college students has become a focus in higher education (Dugan & Komives, 2011; Komives, Longerbeam,

Owen, Mainella & Osteen, 2006). Across the country, the number of formal leadership development programs has proliferated. What are the
essential elements of these programs? Opinions vary, but some common
themes can be found in the literature. In general, literature suggests leadership development programs should include a focus on awareness
building, leadership theories, and skill development. A seminal work
from Roberts (1981) explicated three components of effective leadership
programs: training, education, and development. Training involved skill
building to enhance performance in leadership roles, such as effective
interpersonal communication, conflict management, and goal development. Education included knowledge of theory and leadership scholarship to inform leadership practice (Engbers, 2006). Developmental experiences allowed "for the refinement and internalization of core beliefs
related to leadership as well as the exploration of complex issues" (Dugan, Bohle, Gebhardt, Hofert, Wilk & Cooney, 2011, p. 67).

While critical race scholars might agree with these essential elements,
they might also contend that *critical* components are often missing from
leadership development literature and training programs. Chin (2010)
argued most leadership research is "silent on issues of equity, diversity,
and social justice" (p. 150). Similarly, Dugan, Kodama, and Gebhardt
(2012) lamented how literature on college student leadership has taken a
colorblind approach. As we noted in the Introduction, critical race theorists believe colorblindness is a dominant ideology that homogenizes
people and deflects attention away from the realities of pervasive and
systemic oppression. Critical race scholars seek to debunk colorblind approaches to leadership which have resulted in images of White people
and men as normative standards for great leadership. As we noted in
chapter 1, challenging the invisibility of women leaders of color was one
goal of the Sister Stories retreat. Students like Bonnie were frustrated that
they were unable to name many great women leaders of color during one
retreat activity. They could, however, name plenty of White men. As
critical race feminists have noted, women of color are often invisible despite their accomplishments (Wing, 2003). More specifically, Alston and
McClellan (2011) documented how the accomplishments of great women
leaders of color are regularly omitted from the leadership literature. Critical race perspectives on leadership teach us to recognize and celebrate
leaders of color who, despite their local, national, and international
achievements, are often overlooked. Correspondingly, the Sister Stories
curriculum consistently centered the accomplishments of women of color
who held formal and informal leadership positions.

Scholars using critical race paradigms contend that the purpose of
leadership development programs is to prepare socially just leaders
(Capper, Theoharis & Sebastian, 2006; Larson & Murtadha, 2002; López,
2003). Therefore, leadership development programs need to expose students to issues of power, privilege, and oppression. CRT authors like

López (2003) maintain that leadership development programs must rethink White and male-centric "knowledge base[s] and critically interrogate how race fits in to the larger discourse of what . . . leaders are supposed to know and be able to do" (p. 71). López (2003) even lobbied for an explicit use of CRT in leadership theory and leadership development programs, saying: "We cannot adequately prepare future leaders . . . if we avoid exposing them to issues of race, racism, and racial politics" (p. 70). We agree. As critical race feminists, we believe gender and intersectionality must *also* be staples of critical leadership development programs. If critical perspectives about social inequities like gendered racism are omitted, leadership development programs will likely produce leaders who perpetuate oppression through leadership practice.

Some critical race scholars recommend that leadership development programs teach students about racial identity and its influence on leadership styles (Capper et al., 2006; Solomon, 2001). Sister Stories accomplished this goal. In chapters 1 and 6, we explained how identity development was a central component of the Sister Stories curriculum. Critical race leadership scholars have also suggested that higher education institutions develop specific leadership programs for social identity groups (e.g., women of color), affording students an opportunity to explore how particular social identities inform leadership perspectives and practices (Capper et al., 2006; Solomon, 2001). This recommendation echoes that of Roberts and Ullom (1989), who argued that comprehensive leadership programs "should be designed and directed to meet the needs of various special populations that exist in a specific institution" (p. 69) such as students of color and others from historically marginalized backgrounds. Sister Stories was intentionally designed as a counterspace where women of color could explore leadership in the context of their intersecting social identities.

It is not merely the structure and content of leadership development programs that promote socially just leadership development, the pedagogy (i.e., method of teaching) is equally important. Jean-Marie, Normore, and Brooks (2009) argued that leadership development should be taught using tenets of critical pedagogy and a dialogical approach to give voice to learners while simultaneously raising their critical consciousness about oppression, power, and privilege. In their article about preparing future social justice leaders, Capper et al. (2006) suggested curriculum, assessment, *and* pedagogy in leadership programs must include: 1) an environment that promotes safety and risk taking; 2) an emphasis on the development of critical consciousness regarding power, privilege, and oppression; 3) knowledge of strategies that promote inclusion; and 4) the skill to enact their critical consciousness for socially just leadership. As noted in chapter 1, I (Melissa) draw upon these teaching strategies and perspectives in Sister Stories.

LEADERSHIP MODELS AND THEORIES

Most authors agree that leadership development programs should introduce students to leadership theories and models (Engbers, 2006; Roberts, 1981). Many leadership development models and theories exist, but which ones should be taught to undergraduates? Leadership theories that emerged between the mid-1800s and 1977 were based in industry and often portrayed leadership as hierarchical and bureaucratic, emphasizing tasks and productivity (Dugan & Komives, 2011). Some theories from this era included: great man theories, trait theories, behavioral theories, situational/contingency theories, and influence theories (Dugan & Komives, 2011; Komives, Lucas & McMahon, 2013). These theories typically emphasized leadership as power enacted through positions or traits—usually those held by White men. In the late 1970s, post-industrial approaches to leadership focused on reciprocity by emphasizing shared goals and mutual development among leaders and followers (Dugan & Komives, 2011; Komives et al., 2013). Leadership models from this era included: reciprocal, chaos/systems, and authentic approaches (Komives et al., 2013). These post-industrial approaches serve as the bedrock of many contemporary college leadership development programs. Three specific theories, rooted in post-industrial perspectives, are grounding theories for the university's Leadership Development Center (LDC), in general, and the Sister Stories course, in particular. Those are: Servant Leadership (Greenleaf, 1977), the Relational Leadership Model (Komives et al., 2013), and the Social Change Model of Leadership Development (HERI, 1996). Later in this section, we summarize these three models.

Critical scholars have lamented how traditional leadership theories, like those named above, were written by, and for, those in power. Yet, as Anzaldúa (1990) argued, "If we have been gagged and disempowered by theories, we can also be loosened and empowered by theories" (p. xxvi). To do this, oppressive theories need to be critiqued while new and more inclusive leadership theories, models, and perspectives are crafted (Jean-Marie et al., 2009; Larson & Murtadha, 2002; Young & López, 2005). For instance, Larson and Murtadha (2002) explained how feminist theories are useful for exposing the ways that traditional paradigms about leaders have "blocked researchers from envisioning theories of leadership that went beyond a White, middle-class, male standpoint" (p. 138). Similarly, Young and López (2005) described the benefits of using CRT to question hierarchical notions of leadership steeped in power and Whiteness. In the forthcoming pages, we show how the three traditional leadership theories adopted by the LDC (and required in Sister Stories) can be aligned with CRT and CRF perspectives to teach leadership that is socially responsible and socially just.

Servant Leadership

Servant leadership is based upon the notion that leaders should not be driven by power or position. Instead, servant leaders put the needs of others and their communities first (Greenleaf, 1977). Servant leadership highlights ten characteristics that define leadership: listening, empathy, healing, awareness, persuasion, conceptualization, foresight, steward-ship, commitment to the growth of people, and building community. Drawing upon these characteristics, servant leaders work collaboratively with others in hopes of creating a more caring and just world. While Greenleaf might not have been a critical race scholar, his focus on leaders collaborating with communities aligns with writings by women of color and CRT scholars who highlight the importance of recognizing people of color as experts about their lives and communities (Larson & Murtadha, 2002; Murtadha & Larson, 1999; Solórzano, 1997; Stovall, 2006). When leaders adopt a traditional hierarchical approach, they run the risk of speaking for and, in turn, further marginalizing the communities they hope to lead. Stovall (2006) explained:

> Countless communities of color continue to be "spoken for" by well-meaning Whites claiming to "understand" the struggles of communities of color. In response, CRT maintains that the communities of color in question remain and should be understood as the resident experts on their conditions. Any organizing effort that does not acknowledge and develop praxis on this level is doomed for failure. (p. 250)

CRT and CRF writings about leadership recommended that leaders develop trust and deep relationships with community members, validate community expertise, and work collaboratively with community members to enact change (Larson & Murtadha, 2002; Murtadha & Larson, 1999; Stovall, 2006).

Others argue servant leaders can come from within or outside a community as long as the focus is on doing with, not doing for, a community. Larson and Murtadha (2002) draw upon the writings of Freire to explicate the ways privileged people (e.g., men, Whites) can enact socially just leadership in collaboration with oppressed communities. They wrote:

> Freire contends that oppressed populations must pave the road to their own economic and educational empowerment. However, he is not suggesting that leadership is unnecessary; rather, he is arguing that if a developmental process of learning is to flourish—one that leads poor populations to their own liberation—leaders will have to reject . . . top-down, hierarchical theories of leadership. (Larson & Murtadha, 2002, p. 146)

In essence, those with privilege can be effective servant leaders if they engage in respectful, collaborative, and reciprocal relationships with minoritized communities.

Evans, Taylor, Dunlap, and Miller (2009) argued that people of color often serve as informal leaders through everyday actions within their communities. Moreover, these authors suggested that giving to one's community is "a natural part of cultural or familial legacy and survival" because people of color tend to draw upon "we are" our community leadership perspectives (Evans et al., 2009, p. 12). Therefore, people of color regularly engage in servant leadership by adopting a *do with* versus a *do for* leadership perspective within their own communities. In sum, by infusing critical race foci into traditional servant leadership perspectives, this theory has the potential to teach students from all racial and ethnic backgrounds to honor local community expertise and foster socially just community change.

Relational Leadership Model

In the Relational Leadership Model, leadership is viewed as "a relational and ethical process of people together attempting to accomplish positive change" (Komives et al., 2013, p. 33). The model suggests leadership has five main characteristics: purposeful, inclusive, empowering, ethical, and process oriented. There are three ways to enact effective relational leadership, often referred to as know-be-do (Komives et al., 2013). Relational leaders must *know* self and have an understanding of others' perspectives. They must *be*, in other words, embody attitudes and perspectives of effective leaders (e.g., ethical, thoughtful, inclusive). Finally, as relational leaders develop and hone key skills (e.g., communication, listening, group facilitation) they can *do* effective leadership.

Using CRT and CRF lenses, we can see how the Relational Leadership Model has the potential to be enacted for social justice. Critical race writings on leadership would suggest that effective leaders *know* themselves in the context of racially oppressive systems (Jean-Marie et al., 2009). This is not always easy, but essential. As hooks (2000) noted, the "heart of justice is truth telling, seeing ourselves and the world the way it is, rather than the way we want it to be" (p. 33). Leaders can envision a better and more just world. However, they must first examine themselves, their beliefs, and their surroundings through a critical lens (Jean-Marie et al., 2009). In line with the Relational Leadership Model concept of *being* a leader who embodies certain attitudes and perspectives, Jean-Marie et al. (2009) explained, "it is incumbent upon leadership preparation programs to teach, model, and cultivate the necessary behaviors, attitudes, and knowledge to help shape the social justice value stances and skills of practicing and future [leaders]" (p. 11). Being a socially just leader requires individuals to embody values of equity, fairness, and justice. In sum, by taking a critical race approach to the Relational Leadership Model, individuals can *be* social justice leaders who *do* the work of challenging inequities, creating inclusive environments, and leading through reciprocal and validating relationships.

Social Change Model of Leadership Development

The Social Change Model of Leadership Development (HERI, 1996) was created specifically for college students who seek to create social change. As such, it aligns with much of the CRT leadership literature that presumes the goal of leadership is to achieve social justice outcomes (Capper et al., 2006; Jean-Marie et al., 2009; Larson & Murtadha, 2002; Murtadha & Larson, 1999; López, 2003). In fact, Capper et al. (2006) explained, "effective social justice leaders empower others to enact change" (p. 216).

The Social Change Model is values based and assumes that leadership is not a position—but rather a collaborative process that is socially responsible and accessible to everyone (Cilente, 2009). The model includes seven values, known as the seven C's, that are grouped into three dimensions: society/community, group, and individual—reflecting various spheres of influence. Societal/community values include Citizenship. Group values include Collaboration, Common Purpose, and Controversy with Civility. Individual values include Consciousness of Self, Congruence, and Commitment. Each of these values are connected, meaning growth in one value can impact growth in others (Cilente, 2009). The Social Change Model focuses on making "a better world and a better society for self and others" by encouraging student leaders to take action (HERI, 1996, p. 21). As such, it aligns well with CRT perspectives on leadership.

WHAT STUDENTS LEARNED ABOUT LEADERSHIP

Sister Stories was a venue where undergraduate students learned three leadership models—Servant Leadership (Greenleaf, 1977), the Relational Leadership Model (Komives et al., 2013), and the Social Change Model of Leadership Development (HERI, 1996)—through critical lenses. They were also provided the space to reflect upon what leadership meant to them. The remainder of this chapter is dedicated to student perspectives on leadership. We include a few comments from men of color alongside leadership prose from women of color. In the final section of the chapter, we offer a CRT/CRF analysis of leadership quotes from White students. While we dedicate most of the chapter to women of color, we included selected quotes from men of color and White students, because we agree with critical race leadership authors who contend that individuals with privilege *can* become socially just leaders (Larson & Murtadha, 2002).

LEADING MEANS KNOWING AND LOVING YOURSELF

Critical race perspectives on leadership, as well as the three foundational leadership theories used in Sister Stories, stress the importance of self-awareness. Individuals cannot lead effectively if they do not know themselves as racial and gendered beings who live within systems of power, privilege, and oppression. As noted in chapter 1, a major pedagogical strategy used in Sister Stories was reflection. Through Sister Stories assignments, and during individual and focus group interviews, students were invited to reflect upon the ways their identities, experiences, and values shaped their leadership perspectives and behaviors. Students emphasized self-awareness as critical to effective leadership. Fola explained, "After taking this class, I learned that the first step in becoming a great leader is to understand myself." Elsy concurred, saying, "To be a leader you should understand yourself." Some men of color, like Kalu, reflected on their increased awareness. He noted how reflections upon his values prepared him to be a more effective leader:

> [The Sister Stories] class was an eye-opening experience. Prior to this [course] I was not aware of what values and standards I held high. After [doing] assignments, I have found the things I hold high are my family values, safety, loyalty, and creativity. [Sister Stories] brought me to a new level of understanding about myself.

As discussed in chapters 1 and 4, identity development was a main area of emphasis for the Sister Stories counterspace. Throughout the semester, students began to see how their social identities shaped not only their sense of self, but also their leadership perspectives. Lucia noted the connection between social identities and leadership:

> It is very important to know and understand yourself. Knowing yourself is not a concrete thing or explanation. Knowing yourself is something that you gradually learn. There are many different aspects of a person's self, such as race, ethnicity, gender, sexual identity, intersectionality.

Increasing her leadership awareness required Lucia to delve into her intersecting social identities. As noted throughout the book, intersectionality is a hallmark of CRT and CRF theories (Solórzano, 1997; Wing, 2003). We contend intersectionality is also an important aspect of leadership development and Lucia agreed.

Notions of self-love also shaped women's perspectives on leadership. Hanna explained that effective leaders did not merely know themselves, they loved themselves. She said:

> My mother always tells me to love yourself before you love anyone else. So for me to become a leader to others, I have to love who I am from the outside and inside and accept the flaws that I carry in order to show people how to love themselves.

Hanna believed leaders must teach others to love themselves. While some might be skeptical of using the term *love* in regard to leadership, Larson and Murtadha (2002) showed ethics of care and notions of spiritual love have historically served as important foundations of leadership for women of color. Similarly, Keyes, Capper, Hafner, and Fraynd (2000) explicated how women of color engaged in leadership for social justice by taking risks, building trust, and fostering love in their communities. Relatedly, hooks (2000) equated love and leadership for social justice when she claimed "all the great movements for social justice in our society have strongly emphasized a love ethic" (p. xix). Women of color in Sister Stories seemed to agree.

LEADERSHIP IS INCLUSIVELY ENGAGING OTHERS

Leaders do not exist in a vacuum. As critical race writers and some post-industrial leadership theories suggested, leadership requires collective, reciprocal, non-hierarchical leader involvement with groups or communities (Dugan & Komives, 2011; Evans et al., 2009; Komives et al., 2013). All three grounding theories for Sister Stories—Servant Leadership (Greenleaf, 1977), the Relational Leadership Model (Komives et al., 2013), and the Social Change Model of Leadership Development (HERI, 1996)— emphasize working collaboratively with others. In Sister Stories, students learned that leadership was about fostering connections and a sense of community with others. For instance, Jocelyn said, "That's what I learned from being in this class—you can be the leader, but the group leader won't be anything without the group."

Through Sister Stories, women of color learned how important it was for leaders to interact with others in a respectful and inclusive manner. Students talked about becoming more open-minded, developing patience, and respecting other people's worldviews. They also learned how to speak up and challenge others with grace and compassion. Many of these inclusive social justice skills are hallmarks of the three Sister Stories grounding theories. For instance, being open to differences and valuing others' perspectives is an essential element of *being* a relational leader (Komives et al., 2013). Three of the ten characteristics of servant leaders are listening, empathy, and persuasion (Greenleaf, 1977). Also, one of the seven C's in the Social Change Model is the ability to deal with controversy with civility (HERI, 1996). Sister Stories prompted Elsy to be open-minded and learn about the worldviews of others. Elsy said:

I feel like the course helps you have an understanding of other peoples' lenses and helps you want to understand people more in a leadership position. To be a leader you should . . . be open-minded to understand other people's perspectives and understanding who they are as a person.

Komives et al. (2013) explained that being an inclusive relational leader means "having the skills to develop the talent of members so they can be readily involved" (p. 109). Leadership is not just about individual growth, it is about increasing the talent and skills of every person involved in a group or community. Unfortunately, critical race critiques of leadership lament how leaders often inhibit growth by viewing people and communities of color through stereotypical and deficit-laden lenses (Larson & Murtadha, 2002). Many women of color in Sister Stories understood that being an effective leader meant honoring other people's perspectives. It also meant not interpreting their experiences through a lens of deficiency. Jocelyn explained, "you have to learn to take the positives from your group members and work with them." During Sister Stories, Nicole began to value the ideas and experiences of others. By getting to know her peers' perspectives and strengths, she could help them develop into great leaders. She shared:

I feel like if you want to be a leader, you need to learn about other people—so you can serve them better. You can understand where they are coming from and you can help them grow and develop as members and develop into leaders. I think that [Sister Stories] should definitely be required for everyone . . . in the whole world.

Nicole believed Sister Stories should be a required course so that *everyone* could learn respectful and inclusive leadership. As a result of the Sister Stories course, Pamela began to respect different worldviews and adapt her leadership strategies to include everyone. Pamela explained, "Everybody had their own personal stories and everyone is different. So I just want to take different approaches depending on the person." To successfully meet everyone's needs and diversify her approach, she had to first understand them. The quotes from Jocelyn, Nicole, and Pamela suggest learning critical race perspectives on leadership inspired them to become social justice leaders who "recognize rather than ignore the life world of the [individuals they] serve" (Larson & Murtadha, 2002, p. 145).

Getting to know the perspectives of others often required effective and sustained communication. Vera found that she could start and maintain meaningful conversations when she approached people with patience and thoughtfulness. Before enrolling in Sister Stories, she often avoided conflict by disengaging from conversations when she disagreed with someone or was offended by their comments. Inclusive leadership requires not only skill, but also resilience and the ability to respond to oppression with grace. As we note throughout *Centering Women of Color in Academic Counterspaces*, Sister Stories students learned the importance of responding to oppression with grace and compassion. They also applied these lessons to leadership. For instance, Vera began asking questions to facilitate sustained communication. Instead of telling people they were wrong or closed-minded, Vera became a leader who opened lines of communication instead of shutting down tough conversations and walking away. Vera said:

> I really am more patient and I think before I speak. I also think about what somebody has told me . . . I question people now. I used to be very passive and be like, "Okay whatever, whatever—it doesn't matter." But now I really do think [about other people's comments]. Like, I let it sink in. Then I ask: "Can you please explain that?" I feel like that's helped a lot. Cause that's how a conversation can start.

Sofia and Brian also mentioned how important it was to be open-minded and actively listen to other people. By being open and listening, leaders conveyed the message that everyone's opinions and perspectives mattered. Sofia's newfound capacity to listen to others helped her be a better leader. She said:

> I learned how to be open-minded. Before [Sister Stories], I would just be like whatever I say *is*. If you didn't agree, I would just shut down. So that helped me to be a little bit more open-minded and to actually consider what other people have to say.

Brian found openness and reflective listening helped people feel valued and respected. He shared, "it taught me to basically hear out others and to show them that I notice that they have a voice . . . [and they] would be listened to." As critical race feminists have argued, such leadership perspectives are especially important for men of color and Whites, who often treat women of color as if they are voiceless and invisible (Wing, 2003).

Merely listening to others did not necessarily mean interpersonal communications went smoothly. Conflict happens in all groups. In Sister Stories, students came to see that conflict and controversy were not always bad things. In fact, they began to develop a capacity to handle controversy with civility, a central tenet of the Social Change Model of Leadership Development. Alvarez (2009) explained that controversy with civility

> requires the belief that there is not just one "right" point of view, but that everyone will see an issue slightly different, depending on his or her background and previous experiences. Civility does not require the group to agree with every opinion that is raised, but each opinion should be listened to with respect and taken under consideration while considering the issue or making the decision. (p. 270)

Through sometimes heated Sister Stories conversations, students developed the skill to challenge others with grace and compassion. Sister Stories students also learned that everyone had the capacity to grow as a result of healthy controversy and disagreement. Becca recounted a conversation where she disagreed with the parenting style of a classmate:

> In the moment I kind of challenged her . . . but after hearing her reasoning it basically kind of made me realize that: "Ok, maybe that's how she wants to raise her child. I can't tell her what to do." My opinion was just different from hers and I had to respect that and she had to respect that.

While she initially approached the conversation with strong opinions about parenting, Becca left the interaction with a broader worldview and respect for her classmate's right to raise her child as she saw fit. In sum, Sister Stories helped students see that inclusively engaging others required openness to difference, respect for diverse worldviews, effective communication, and the ability to challenge others with grace.

EMPOWERED TO LEAD AND MAKE CHANGE

CRT and CRF scholars critique and aim to dismantle systematic forms of oppression. As such, leaders using critical race- inspired paradigms contend:

> Traditional hierarchies and power structures must be deconstructed and reconfigured, thereby creating a new social order that subverts a longstanding system that has privileged certain students while oppressing or neglecting others . . . leaders must increase their awareness of various explicit and implicit forms of oppression, develop an intent to subvert the dominant paradigm, and finally act as a committed advocate for . . . change that makes a meaningful and positive change in the . . . lives of traditionally marginalized and oppressed students. (Jean-Marie et al., 2009, p. 4)

Seeing oneself as an agent of change is not always an easy process, especially for women of color who have experienced a lifetime of disempowering oppression. Nonetheless, Solórzano and Bernal (2001) suggested that by engaging in transformational resistance, people of color can be part of individual and systemic-level change.

The Sister Stories counterspace empowered women of color to become agents of change. Drechsler and Jones, Jr. (2009) argued: "A first step to becoming a change agent is to claim the personal empowerment to recognize oneself as a leader" (p. 401). Through Sister Stories, many women of color began to see themselves as leaders—whether or not they had a formal leadership title or position. Women of color learned that they could make large and small-scale changes within their family, campus, and community spheres of influence. While fighting systems of oppression can feel daunting, women of color understood that challenging inequities within their spheres of influence was an invaluable form of leadership. Sister Stories taught Elena that all types of action were important and that "one person can make a difference, no matter how big or small." Before enrolling in Sister Stories, Camilla would ignore or try to "brush off" microaggressions. After spending a semester in the Sister Stories counterspace, she felt empowered to speak up and challenge gendered racism. Camilla explained:

> In general, the [Sister Stories] readings, guest student panels, and movies . . . brought up . . . many important topics [for me to reflect upon]. . . . It was usually things I have not said . . . even though I should have. I am a woman of color and have actually thought of times where someone has said a racial comment toward me. But, I would just brush it off without really thinking about how serious I should take it. No person of color should allow that kind of behavior and just brush it off. Instead, I need to stand up for what is right for not only myself, but also for other people of color.

As Camilla assumed the identity of leader, she began to view leadership as an opportunity to resist microaggressions, educate perpetrators, and support other people of color. Camilla was not alone. Many women of color came to see that they were already leaders within their spheres of influence, even if they did not have a formal leadership title or position. Jocelyn realized that she regularly assumed leadership in informal settings like classroom project groups. She explained:

> I always get put in positions where—like when I do group projects—I always end up being either told that I'm the group leader, or end up taking upon that role. I learned from this class how to be a leader without being a boss. People might not understand what I mean by that. Sometimes I might come off as bossy because I like to speak my mind, [but] I don't want to hurt people's feelings. I feel like this gave me the opportunity to learn different lenses. Sometimes you have to put yourself in people's shoes and see people's strengths and weaknesses within the group.

Through Sister Stories, Jocelyn learned that being an effective leader meant honoring the perspectives of others, speaking her mind without being bossy, and drawing upon the strengths and skills of group members to achieve a goal. Leading a group project may not come with a formal leadership title (e.g., secretary, vice president), but in informal venues, like group projects, Jocelyn was indeed a leader.

Through Sister Stories, Lauren learned about the often hidden forms of systemic oppression and everyday manifestations of microaggressions. The course opened her eyes, and as a result, she hoped to open the eyes of her peers. She found herself serving as a leader by educating her peers about critical race topics covered in Sister Stories. Lauren stated:

I feel like before taking the course . . . I would know some things [about privilege, power, and oppression], but I wouldn't say anything. But then after the course, I found myself explaining things more to people. And like, if they wouldn't understand something . . . my thing is I like to have people just read the articles I read and [laughter] [ask them to] "Tell me what you think about this." . . . So, I feel like that class just really helped me go beyond more than just sitting in my head thinking about [challenging inequality]. I speak more on it.

For students like Lauren, leading by challenging oppression meant educating others about the pervasiveness of inequality. Clearly, Lauren (and many of her peers of color) were empowered by Sister Stories to lead for change though informal interactions and educational conversations.

ROLE MODELING INCLUSIVE LEADERSHIP

The Sister Stories curriculum emphasized how leadership happens in all types of settings, including schools, families, and communities. Such perspectives align with writers of color who contend that collaborative and communal leadership is often enacted by women of color who see these forms of leadership as essential to "cultural or familial legacy and survival" (Evans et al., 2009, p. 12). For women of color in Sister Stories, leadership often manifested through positive role modeling for peers and siblings. Role modeling critical social justice leadership is an important way to debunk deficit notions about women of color and combat their invisibility (Wing, 2003) in society.

Hanna was very involved in extra-curricular programs and earned high grades. Through formal and informal leadership positions, she served as a role model and source of encouragement for other women of color. She explained:

Now, I am viewed as a leader to some people such as my friends. I had some of them coming up to me and telling me how—because of me—I make them get involved in organizations, take their work more seriously, and reach for different opportunities that the university has to offer.

Peers became more active and successful as a result of their interactions with, and observations of, Hannah.

Many students enacted change through their most intimate sphere of influence—family. Ana and Fola taught about respect and role modeled inclusion for siblings. Fola wanted to help her younger brother grow into a respectful and inclusive young man. Fola said:

I have a younger brother. I try [to role model inclusion]. I don't want to make him a stereotypical African American male—or have the values that I see some of these boys have that make no type of sense. [laughter] I want him to treat people as equal and have respect for all types of people—just try to make him a better person.

When Fola referred to values that "make no type of sense," she was using her CRF lens to critique misogynist perspectives harbored by her brother and his friends. As a CRF leader, she felt a responsibility to role model inclusion in hopes that her brother would learn to treat everyone (especially women) with respect and equity. Ana also modeled inclusion for her siblings. Ana explained:

> At this point in my life I consider myself a leader because I am a role model for my young siblings and other younger family members as well. I believe that knowing about the socialization process and other oppression makes me a better leader. It allows me to be more aware and conscious [and] understand the root of some of the problems we face today.

Ana and Fola were just two of the many Sister Stories students whose learned leadership included "model[ing] the way" by serving as a role model for inclusion (Kouzes & Posner, 2012, p. 3).

As we alluded to in chapter 7, women of color wanted to be role models and positive influences on young women who came after them. While that chapter was about beauty and body image, here we show that women of color also felt a responsibility to support young people by leading for social justice and role modeling inclusion. Lena explained:

> I got a lot more than I bargained for from [Sister Stories]. I never expected to feel as empowered as I did . . . I was affected by the words of many [women of color]. More importantly, I was reminded of the impact that my voice can have if I just speak up. If there was one thing that I learned overall, it was that I can make a difference—if not in the world, perhaps just in the life of a young woman of color like myself.

As we noted in chapter 1, mentoring was an important focus of Sister Stories. Throughout *Centering Women of Color in Academic Counterspaces*, student narratives affirmed the importance of finding, and serving as, role models. Women of color came to understand that leadership meant role modeling empowerment and resistance. Fola said, Sister Stories "made me realize how important it is to reach out and mentor young women of color so that they can use our knowledge to their advantage in the future." Women of color drew upon their leadership learning in Sister Stories to role model inclusion. Through their efforts, they helped other women of color find the courage to resist oppression and lead for social justice.

WHITE STUDENTS ON LEADERSHIP

We would be remiss if we did not mention how Sister Stories inspired social justice action in all students—including White men and women. Critical race scholars have argued that people with privilege can lead for social justice *if* they: develop critical consciousness; acknowledge their own power, privileges, and biases; and develop an understanding of, compassion for, and commitment to minoritized communities (Murtadha & Larson, 1999). If students do not engage in these processes, they run the risk of enacting socially unjust leadership whereby they speak for the needs of people of color and/or minoritized communities.

People with privilege may participate in leadership activities, not because it is the right thing to do, but because it benefits them. Critical race scholars call attention to the notion of interest convergence (Bell 1980; Milner, 2008). "Interest convergence stresses that racial equality and equity for people of color will be pursued and advanced when they converge with the interests, needs, expectations, and ideologies of Whites" (Milner, 2008, p. 333). For White people, some benefits of doing leadership can include: feeling like a savior, building a leadership accomplishment resume, and alleviating White guilt. From the short time we spent with the eight White students in Sister Stories, we cannot know their motivations. Therefore, it is unclear if interest convergence played a role in their reflections on leadership. But, as critical race scholars, we feel obligated to mention interest convergence as we present White students' desires to rethink their leadership styles. It is important to note that with one exception (Emily), the following quotes reflect a *desire* to be more inclusive leaders in the future instead of demonstrating changes to current leadership behavior. We also acknowledge that White students' desired behavior changes may have resulted from Sister Stories pressure to "do the right thing" or interest convergence. Nonetheless, we felt it was important to include the leadership narratives of White students to show how White students benefitted from learning the three leadership models—Servant Leadership (Greenleaf, 1977), the Relational Leadership Model (Komives, Lucas & McMahon, 2013), and the Social Change Model of Leadership Development (HERI, 1996)—through a critical race lens.

Most White students described increased awareness of injustices (i.e., racism) as a result of Sister Stories. This new knowledge informed the ways they thought about themselves as leaders. Jenna was intimidated by the topic of oppression and was sometimes uncomfortable during Sister Stories discussions about racism. However, that discomfort fueled a desire to lead in more socially just ways. She said:

> This class is great because it definitely did make me think. . . . It really got me thinking about [inequality] and more so why [society is] like that. And then, what can we do about it? So I want to thank the class

for bugging my brain and like making me uncomfortable—making me uncomfortable for change . . . you know?

John also appreciated how the course prompted him to think about challenging systems of oppression. He said:

> This class will be my most memorable, and probably one of the most important classes, I take in my college career. I will never forget the experience I had in this class. I will apply this knowledge to my future—taking action against racism and sexism so that I can be as effective [a leader] as possible.

While Jenna and John spoke generally about challenging oppression in the future, Allie and Emily described more specific actions they took (or hoped to enact) as a result of their learning in Sister Stories. Emily was so moved by the counterstories of her Sister Stories classmates of color, that she began challenging White peers when they acted in exclusionary ways. She explained:

> I actually banned a person from coming to my house because of racial slurs that they said to one of my brother's friends. And it started almost a riot in my house this year. . . . But, I just think back in my head of people's stories and people in my class—I felt I [had to do something].

CRT and CRF scholars describe counterstories as essential components in the struggle for racial justice (Delgado, 1989; Delgado and Stefancic, 2000; Pérez Huber & Cueva, 2012; Solórzano & Yosso, 2001). As Emily's quote suggests, the counterstories of women of color had a deep impact on her leadership perspectives. Those powerful classroom counterstories stayed with Emily and prompted her to challenge oppression in her personal sphere of influence.

During Allie's Sister Stories class, women of color talked at length about feeling excluded from predominantly White sororities on campus (see chapter 2). Their counterstories influenced the ways Allie thought about leadership. She explained her plan for enacting more socially just leadership to make her sorority more inclusive:

> [I was just] elected Vice President of my sorority next year. There's no diversity in Greek life. I think that last year there was one Black girl who rushed and she didn't even want our house. . . . Just like listening to people's opinions in Sister Stories, I realized—okay, there's a reason that girl doesn't want [to rush our sorority]. I wish I could do something about that. [pause]. I mean I *will* definitely be able to have a say about pretty much everything—like picking new girls. I also think that I can hopefully bring some open-mindedness into the house.

Allie's quote brings us back to the notion that students can enact change on large and small scales. At first, Allie wondered if there was anything she could realistically do to change the lack of diversity in the whole Greek system on campus. However, she realized recruiting diverse pledges into her specific sorority and fostering "open-mindedness" among her White sisters were two ways she could be an inclusive leader within her sphere of influence. Of course, we cannot know if the sorority would be a welcoming environment, or if the new recruits of color might end up feeling like tokens. (See chapter 3 for a discussion of tokenization.) Nonetheless, Allie was taking a step in the right direction toward inclusive leadership by rethinking her role in future recruitment efforts.

In sum, the Sister Stories experience prompted White students to think differently about leadership. While we cannot know their motivations, or if they followed through on their plans, student narratives suggest they were beginning on a path toward more inclusive and socially just leadership.

CONCLUSION

In this chapter, we reviewed some of the seminal and critical perspectives on leadership and leadership development programs. Those writings suggest that effective programs teach awareness, perspective taking, theoretical foundations, and skill development. Student narratives showed the Sister Stories counterspace did just that. Women of color learned that to be effective leaders they had to know (and love) themselves. They also needed to be open-minded, respect diverse worldviews, and learn by listening to the perspectives of others. Sister Stories students were empowered to lead change through advocacy, education, and role modeling inclusion within their spheres of influence—whether it was in their families, classrooms, peer groups, or sororities. Throughout this chapter, we centered the leadership perspectives of women of color. However, we also included selected leadership prose from men of color and White students to show that all students—even those with privilege—can learn to enact socially just leadership.

REFERENCES

Alston, J. A., & McClellan, P. A. (2011). *Herstories: Leading with the lessons of the lives of Black women activists.* New York: Peter Lang.

Alvarez, C. (2009). Controversy with civility. In S. R. Komives, W. Wagner & Associates (Eds.), *Leadership for a better world: Understanding the social change model of leadership development* (pp. 263–92). San Francisco, CA: Jossey-Bass.

Anzaldúa, G. (1990). *Haciendo caras/making face, making soul: Creative and critical perspectives by women of color.* San Francisco, CA: Aunt Lute Press.

Bell, D. A. (1980). Brown v. Board of Education and the interest convergence dilemma. *Harvard Law Review, 93*(3), 518–33.

Capper, C. A., Theoharis, G., & Sebastian, J. (2006). Toward a framework for preparing leaders for social justice. *Journal of Educational Administration, 44*(3), 209–24.

Chin, J. L. (2010). Introduction to the special issue on diversity and leadership. *American Psychologist, 65*(3), 150–156.

Cilente, K. (2009). An overview of the social change model of leadership development. In S. R. Komives, W. Wagner & Associates (Eds.), *Leadership for a better world: Understanding the social change model of leadership development* (pp. 43–78). San Francisco, CA: Jossey-Bass.

Delgado, R. (1989). Storytelling for oppositionists and others: A plea for narrative. *Michigan Law Review, 87*(8), 2411–41.

———, & Stefancic, J. (2000). *Critical race theory: The cutting edge.* Philadelphia, PA: Temple University Press.

Drechsler, M. J., & Jones, Jr., W.,A. (2009). Becoming a change agent. In S. R. Komives, W. Wagner & Associates (Eds.), *Leadership for a better world: Understanding the social change model of leadership development* (pp. 397–443). San Francisco, CA: Jossey-Bass.

Dugan, J. P. (2006). Explorations using the social change model: Leadership development among college men and women. *Journal of College Student Development, 47*(2), 217–25.

———, Bohle, C. W., Gebhardt, M., Hofert, M., Wilk, E., & Cooney, M. A. (2011). Influences of leadership program participation on students' capacities for socially responsible leadership. *Journal of Student Affairs Research and Practice, 48*(1), 65–84.

———, Kodama, C. M., & Gebhardt, M. C. (2012). Race and leadership development among college students: The additive value of collective racial esteem. *Journal of Diversity in Higher Education, 5*(3), 174.

———, & Komives, S. R. (2011). Leadership theories. In S. R. Komives, J. P. Dugan, J. E. Owen, C. Slack, W. Wagner & Associates (Eds.), *Handbook for student leadership programs* (pp. 35–58). San Francisco, CA: Jossey-Bass.

Engbers, T. A. (2006). Student leadership programming model revisited. *Journal of Leadership Education, 5*(3), 1–14.

Evans, S. Y., Taylor, C. M., Dunlap, M. R., & Miller, D. S. (2009). Community service, volunteerism and engagement. In S. Evans, C. Taylor, M. Dunlap & D. Miller (Eds.), *African Americans and community engagement in higher education* (pp. 11–15). Albany, NY: SUNY Press.

Greenleaf, R. K. (1977). *Servant leadership: A journey in the nature of legitimate power and greatness.* New York: Paulist.

Higher Education Research Institute (HERI) (1996). *A social change model of leadership development: Guidebook version III.* College Park, MD: National Clearinghouse for Leadership Programs.

hooks, b. (2000). *All about love: New visions.* New York: William Morrow & Company.

Jean-Marie, G., Normore, A. H., & Brooks, J. S. (2009). Leadership for social justice: Preparing 21st century school leaders for a new social order. *Journal of Research on Leadership Education, 4*(1), 1–31.

Keyes, M., Capper, C., Hafner, M., & Fraynd, D. (2000, October). *Spiritual justice histories: The lives of two womanist leaders.* Paper presented at the annual meeting of the University Council of Educational Administration, Albuquerque, NM.

Komives, S. R., Longerbeam, S. D., Owen, J. E., Mainella, F. C., & Osteen, L. (2006). A leadership identity development model: Applications from a grounded theory. *Journal of College Student Development, 47*(4), 401–18.

Komives, S. R., Lucas, N., & McMahon, T. R. (2013). *Exploring leadership: For college students who want to make a difference* (3rd ed.). San Francisco, CA: Jossey-Bass.

Komives, S. R., Wagner, W., & Associates (Eds.) (2012). *Leadership for a better world: Understanding the social change model of leadership development.* Hoboken, NJ: Wiley.

Kouzes, J. M., & Posner, B. Z. (2012). *The leadership challenge: How to make extraordinary things happen in organizations* (5th ed.). San Francisco, CA: Jossey-Bass.

Larson, C. L., & Murtadha, K. (2002). Leadership for social justice. *Yearbook of the National Society for the Study of Education, 101*(1), 134–61.

López, G. R. (2003). The (racially neutral) politics of education: A critical race theory perspective. *Educational Administration Quarterly, 39*(1), 68–94.

Milner, H. R. (2008). Critical race theory and interest convergence as analytic tools in teacher education policies and practices. *Journal of Teacher Education, 59*(4), 332–46.

Murtadha, K., & Larson, C. (1999, April). *Toward a socially critical, womanist theory of leadership*. Paper presented at the annual meeting of the American Educational Research Association, Montreal, Canada.

Pérez Huber, L., & Cueva, B. M. (2012). Chicana/Latina testimonios on effects and responses to microaggressions. *Equity and Excellence in Education, 45*(3), 392–410.

Roberts, D. (1981). *Student leadership programs in higher education*. Carbondale, IL: Southern Illinois University Press.

———, & Ullom, C. (1989). Student leadership program model. *NASPA Journal, 27*(1), 67–74.

Solomon, R. P. (2001). School leaders and anti-racism: Overcoming pedagogical and political obstacles. *Journal of School Leadership, 12*, 174–97.

Solórzano, D. (1997). Images and words that wound: Critical race theory, racial stereotyping and teacher education. *Teacher Education Quarterly, 24*, 5–19.

———, & Bernal, D. D. (2001). Examining transformational resistance through a critical race and LatCrit theory framework: Chicana and Chicano students in an urban context. *Urban Education, 36*(3), 308–42.

———, & Yosso, T. J. (2001). Critical race and LatCrit theory and method: Counter-storytelling. *International Journal of Qualitative Studies in Education, 14*(4), 471–95.

Stovall, D. (2006). Forging community in race and class: Critical race theory and the quest for social justice in education, *Race, Ethnicity and Education, 9*(3), 243–59.

Wing, A. K. (2003). *Critical race feminism: A reader* (2nd ed.). New York: New York University Press.

Young, M., & López, G. R. (2005). The nature of inquiry in educational leadership. In F. W. English (Ed.), *The Sage handbook of educational leadership: Advances in theory, research, and practice* (pp. 337–61). Thousand Oaks, CA: Sage.

Conclusion

In the following pages, we offer insight into key themes that emerged from the Sister Stories student narratives. This chapter, however, does not repeat the key findings from prior chapters; our end-of-chapter conclusions do that. Instead, we discuss five concepts that represent overarching takeaways from *Centering Women of Color in Academic Counterspaces*. Those include: oppression exists and counterspaces matter; everyone needs a sense of community; transformative learning through critical reflection; students and educators naming and sharing power; and education is empowerment. Using CRT and CRF lenses, we analyze each of these five themes through macro- and micro-level perspectives. This dual analytic lens aligns with CRF and CRT theories that center the lives of marginalized people through personal (micro) counterstories in hopes of drawing attention to systemic (macro) forms of oppression and privilege in social institutions like higher education.

Pervasive forms of gendered racism woven throughout the U.S. educational system cannot be dismantled quickly or by a single institution or individual. However, every student, educator, and higher education institution can be part of the process of change by focusing on their particular spheres of influence. By offering small- and large-scale recommendations to students, educators, and higher education institutions, we emphasize the many ways readers can work toward combating systemic forms of oppression (macro) by engaging in social justice action within their local spheres of influence (micro). We acknowledge, however, macro- or micro-level change is not an easy endeavor.

If ending systemic forms of oppression were easy, activists would have eradicated it long ago. Challenging and extinguishing pervasive and systemic forms of oppression is a time-consuming endeavor that requires commitment, resources, and persistence. More specifically, critical race scholars argue that ending discrimination has historically required interest convergence—which is the notion that those with power only act in socially just ways when it suits their interests (Bell, 1980). Higher education institutions may espouse the values of diversity and equity, but do little to enact structural change to combat oppression, privilege, and unwelcoming campus climates for women of color. López (2003) argued that discourses on diversity have not been successful in penetrating the pervasiveness of racism in education, likely because institutions have not yet been persuaded it is in their best interest to do so.

With the United States in general, and school systems in particular, becoming increasingly racially diverse, higher education institutions will need to position themselves as inclusive spaces for women of color. Drawing upon the notion of interest convergence, higher education institutions may work to dismantle gendered racism *if* the interests of women of color (e.g., safety, inclusion, validation, belonging) converge with university interests—possibly in the form of increased enrollment, persistence, and graduation rates. We offer a variety of macro-level suggestions for change at the institutional level throughout this chapter, not because it is in our interest to do so, but because we believe it is the right thing to do.

Throughout the chapter, we invite individuals to consider a variety of micro-level questions such as: What can students and educators learn from the literature, counterstories, and critical race analyses presented throughout *Centering Women of Color in Academic Counterspaces*? How can educators (i.e., professors, administrators, trainers) use student stories to create more inclusive learning environments? What can students do to find validation, deep learning, and empowerment on campus? We also acknowledge that activism, advocacy, and allyship can take a personal and professional toll on faculty, staff, and students. However, we believe the demands of doing social justice work pale in comparison to the cost of doing nothing. Therefore, we recommend a variety of actions—big and small—that individuals can take to enact change within their spheres of influence. Our CRT and CRF roots prompted us to write *Centering Women of Color in Academic Counterspaces* in hopes of sparking change at the personal, professional, and institutional level. In the following pages, we offer tangible suggestions so that institutions, educators, and students can do just that.

OPPRESSION EXISTS AND COUNTERSPACES MATTER

Throughout *Centering Women of Color in Academic Counterspaces*, student narratives explicated regular occurrences of gendered racism on campus, at home, and in their communities. Oppression typically manifested as microaggressions, which are subtle forms of exclusion, often committed without conscious awareness. In order to combat oppression, higher education institutions must "develop antiracist educators who recognize the reproductive functions of schooling and have the courage to envision different possibilities for schooling—particularly for our most marginalized . . . communities" (López, 2003, p. 71). However, López also argued "very few individuals have had a critical dialogue about the role of racism in society—and more specifically, racism in our beliefs, ideas, practices and knowledge bases" (p. 76). University administrators, professors, and student affairs staff must be aware of the prevalence of systemic (macro) oppression as well as interpersonal (micro) microaggressions in higher education. Most importantly, they need to develop the awareness, knowledge, and skills to combat exclusion and create inclusive courses, programs, and services (Pope, Reynolds & Mueller, 2014).

Much empirical research has shown microaggressions are often perpetrated by instructors who harbor low academic expectations, assume deficits, tokenize students, or treat individuals as if they were invisible (Harris, Haywood, Ivery & Shuck, 2015; Gildersleeve, Croom & Vasquez, 2011; Solórzano et al., 2000; Suarez-Orozco, et al., 2015). In chapter 2, we detailed the ways other university employees also engaged in exclusionary behaviors. Higher educators and trainers must do the tough self-work of determining if, and how, they perpetuate microaggressions against students from minoritized social identity groups. We recommend campuses offer regular professional development workshops about gendered racism and microaggressions. Such training must emphasize both individual manifestations (micro) of gendered racism as well as the structural (macro) roots of oppression. Beyond the ivory tower, there are a plethora of professional development opportunities (e.g., workshops, conferences, certificate programs) where practitioners can increase their awareness, knowledge, and skills such as: the Social Justice Training Institute, National Coalition Building Institute, White Privilege Conference, and National Conference on Race and Ethnicity in Higher Education (NCORE). Fostering the development of anti-oppressive educators cannot be the *only* way higher education institutions acknowledge and challenge systemic oppression. Other structural changes are needed.

As we noted in the Introduction, one of the goals of critical race theory is to expose and challenge dominant ideologies such as meritocracy, race neutrality, colorblindness, and equal opportunity (Bergerson, 2003; Harper, Patton & Wooden, 2009; Solórzano, 1997; Solórzano & Yosso, 2001). Unfortunately, schools often operate in ways that reflect tacit acceptance of oppressive dominant ideologies like colorblindness. Moreover, school leaders who have been socialized to believe these oppressive ideologies perpetuate them through their practice. Larson and Murtadha (2002) noted:

> School leaders who believe that their schools are equitable . . . enact programs and policies that they assume are fair and serve the academic and social interests of all students. But many are misguided, in part, because they are not sufficiently aware of the differences [inequities] that limit [students'] and their families' freedoms to achieve.

One step toward ending this oppressive cycle is for educators and school leaders to critically examine policies, practices, and curriculum to determine if, and how, they perpetuate dominant ideologies. During that review, educators must also consider how policies, practices, and curriculum confer dominance to White people and men while disenfranchising women of color. López (2003) explained how critical policy reviews should focus on formal, as well as informal, policies that manifest in common practices and customs. As we saw in chapter 2, predominately White sororities and campus police did not have formal policies excluding women of color, but informal policy was created through consistently exclusionary practices. In a chapter about the history of multicultural student services on campus, Lupo (2011) explained that despite the passage of civil rights legislation to protect the rights of people of color, "invisible systems of privilege, prejudice, and oppression were not addressed, manifesting themselves through professional practices, attitudes and curriculum and perpetuated through campus culture and traditions" (p. 25). In short, informal policies matter and oppressive ones must be exposed and abrogated by educational leaders.

Institutions can also create structural change by tackling the environmental microaggression of invisibility of women of color in higher education. Colleges and universities can do this by addressing the severe under-representation of women of color in faculty and administration by recruiting, hiring, *and* retaining women of color in positions of power and authority. As part of this process, institutions must take measures to legitimize (Bernal & Villalpando, 2002) and honor their knowledge and expertise so women of color feel like valued members of the university community. If they feel excluded, disrespected, or invisible, they will seek employment elsewhere. To create environments where women faculty and staff of color want to work, institutions must combat formal and informal practices such as double standards in tenure and promotion (Villalpando & Bernal, 2002) and cultural taxation on faculty and staff of color (Baez, 2000; Joseph & Hirshfield, 2011).

In higher education, environmental microaggressions also manifest through invisibility and/or deficit images of women and people of color in curriculum (Vaccaro, 2016). Infusing counterstories from women of color throughout the curriculum is an important first step toward combatting curricular exclusion (Solórzano & Yosso, 2002). Inclusive curriculum must be built upon literature that includes non-deficit experiences of women of color. As López (2003) noted, critical race paradigms should be infused throughout the curriculum, not merely in special topics courses. Classes emphasizing manifestations of, as well as strategies for challenging, gendered racism should be required for all students through general education and major requirements. For example, critical accounts of U.S. history that emphasize the pervasiveness of gendered racism and privilege in politics, education, and law must be staples of higher education curriculum.

Critical race feminists and other women writers of color explain how imperative it is to address intersectionality (Carbado, Crenshaw, Mays & Tomlinson, 2013; Crenshaw, 1989; Wing, 2003), and we contend it is especially important in curriculum. As Sister Stories students learned, women of color are not a monolithic group and they should not be treated as such in curriculum. Addressing intersectionality means courses on race, racism, or ethnic studies cannot gloss over the contributions of women of color (Alston & McClellan, 2011), as they often do. Nor can women's studies courses perpetuate hegemonic Whiteness, by excluding the counterstories of women of color or selectively including them as tokens (Zinn, Cannon, Higginbotham & Dill, 1986). If curriculum ignores intersectionality by focusing on single identities, it renders women of color invisible.

In order to create inclusive curriculum that represents the lived realities of women of color, disciplines need empirical work that reflect diverse women's lives. Unfortunately, CRT and CRF scholars have long argued empirical research is often informed by deficit paradigms, misrepresents the experiences of people of color, or excludes them altogether (Bernal, 2002; Parker & Lynn, 2002; Vaccaro, 2016). In response, CRT scholars call for the use of critical race methodology, which is a "theoretically grounded approach to research that . . . foregrounds race and racism in all aspects of the research process" (Solórzano & Yosso, 2002, p. 24). While studies using these methods are increasing in number, more must be done.

Until universities accurately represent women of color in research, curriculum, and staffing, counterspaces like Sister Stories will be among the few places where women of color feel validated on campus. Indeed, students lamented how Sister Stories was the *only* class of its kind on campus. We contend counterspaces should be infused throughout the campus—not just in special programs like women's or ethnic studies. As Diana noted in chapter 3, Sister Stories was an exceptionally affirming "out of body experience." All students deserve to learn in spaces where their lived realities are validated. Educators can do their part to ensure women of color have curricular and extra-curricular counterspace options on campus. Instructors should offer departmental and general education courses like Sister Stories and encourage colleagues to do the same. They can also serve on curriculum committees where they lobby for the creation of, and on-going support for, existing counterspace courses.

Administrators and student affairs professionals can support extra-curricular counterspaces such as student organizations, campus events, and living and learning communities for women of color. Educators play an important role in making sure that counterspaces are fully supported by their university. Backlash against campus diversity efforts is an ever-present reality. In tough fiscal times, the relevance of, and need for, gender, multicultural, and other identity-based campus centers and programs is often questioned. Those who do not understand the need for campus counterspaces suggest funding for multicultural and women's centers, as well as race/ethnic student organizations, be diverted to other areas of the university. Sometimes public demands result in exclusionary policy decisions that have a detrimental effect on people of color. For instance, some campuses have been pressured to close cultural centers, eliminate women's studies programs, or cancel course offerings about privilege and racism. CRT scholars argue it is paramount to "critically confront racism and racist educational polic[ies]" and actions such as these (López, 2003, p. 72). All campus employees have a role to play in challenging oppressive policies and actions that threaten to defund, close, or otherwise restrict academic and extra-curricular counterspaces. Too often, people of color—and especially women of color—are expected to lead these fights, or fight alone. Women of color need allies (i.e., White people, men of color) to help defend existing counterspaces and to create new ones. In sum, everyone has a role to play in challenging oppression on campus.

Most students found refuge from oppression in the Sister Stories counterspace. Specifically, they felt a reprieve from the White normalcy and dominant ideologies embedded throughout the rest of the predominately White campus. The Sister Stories counterspace was a unique environment where women of color built social capital and gleaned validation from peers and faculty of color. We encourage students to seek counterspaces on their campuses. If none exist, students can petition to create them. While each campus has unique procedures for creating new student organizations, the process typically involves an application, a list of interested members, and approval from the student senate or student activities office. A good place to start the process of creating an extra-curricular counterspace is by talking to a trusted student affairs professional who can explain, and offer suggestions for navigation of, complex university systems.

EVERYONE NEEDS A SENSE OF COMMUNITY

As we discussed in chapter 3, students who experience a sense of belonging and sense of community are more likely to achieve academic success (Freeman, Anderman & Jensen, 2007; Strayhorn, 2012), persist (Hausmann, Schofield & Woods, 2007; Hoffman, Richmond, Morrow & Salomone, 2002/2003), and experience healthy psychological adjustment (Pittman & Richmond, 2008). Feeling a sense of community in predominately White higher education institutions may be challenging for women and people of color who encounter oppression in the form of microaggressions and hostile campus climates (Howard-Hamilton, Morelon-Quainoo, Johnson, Winkle-Wagner & Santiague, 2009; Hurtado, 1992; Hurtado & Guillermo-Wann, 2013; Vaccaro, 2010, 2012, 2014). Recent campus climate literature describes how formal and informal institutional policies, practices, and curriculum shape the campus climate in profound ways (Hurtado & Guillermo-Wann, 2013). As we noted earlier, higher education institutions must address gendered racism embedded in these structural areas. One way for campuses to expose and address inhospitable and unwelcoming climates is to engage in formal climate assessment and planning. Due to the historical and structural nature of oppression (Lupo, 2011), climate change needs to be part of comprehensive and systematic change efforts that include combatting oppression at the individual, group, and institutional level (Pope, Reynolds & Mueller, 2014) and in all functions of a university such as enrollment, hiring, policies, and curriculum (Hurtado & Guillermo-Wan, 2013; Williams, Berger & McClendon, 2005). A plethora of research papers and assessment tools are available to schools interested in improving campus climate. One recent example of how to use research to improve climate is described in the Ford Foundation report, *Diverse Learning Environments: Assessing and Creating Conditions for Student Success* (Hurtado & Guillermo-Wann, 2013).

As we have argued throughout *Centering Women of Color in Academic Counterspaces*, creating counterspaces is an important way to foster a sense of validation and community in an otherwise exclusionary educational environment. However, campus counterspaces should not be the ultimate macro-level goal—widespread inclusion, validation, and empowerment of women of color should be. At present, students need counterspaces (e.g., Sister Stories, multicultural centers) to find reprieve from microaggressions. Stewart (2011) argued that counterspaces, such as multicultural student services offices can "compel colleges and universities to 're-vision' or redefine what makes a community" (p. 3) by offering social justice education and community development programs for the entire campus. Until such re-visioning happens, and women of color feel validated, affirmed, and empowered in all sectors of campus, counterspaces like Sister Stories are important community-building venues for women of color. We contend educators from all campus units (not just multicultural affairs) have a responsibility to develop a sense of community among women of color in department or unit-specific workshops, classes, and programs.

Developing a sense of community requires trust. Educators can foster community by utilizing icebreaking activities in curricular and extra-curricular settings where students learn basic information about each other and begin to develop a sense of trust. Those surface-level activities should be followed by more in-depth team builders whereby students share deeper information in a structured, well-facilitated environment. For the first few years, I (Melissa) conducted icebreakers at the beginning of Sister Stories class periods. However, a half-day retreat proved to be more effective at building a sense of community. It afforded a longer period of time where students could engage in intensive activities and build trust. Following the retreat, class sessions began to feel more like a community. We acknowledge that not all instructors have the skill or confidence to facilitate difficult dialogues and the intense emotions that can emerge during trust-building exercises—especially community-building conversations about race and gender. In fact, Sue, Torino, Capodilupo, Rivera, and Lin (2009) found White faculty worried that they did not have the skill to appropriately intervene when student dialogues about race turned heated or emotional. Developing skills to effectively navigate difficult interpersonal interactions can be done through formal professional development activities (e.g., conferences, workshops) or through guidance, observation, and feedback from seasoned colleagues.

Community-building exercises are only successful if students engage. We encourage students to actively participate in "get to know you" activities. These activities and conversations might feel uncomfortable or awkward, but the benefits can be immense. The validation, affirmation, and sense of community that comes from connecting with peers only happens if students commit to the trust-building process. We are not suggesting students share their deepest darkest secrets. Those do not necessarily have a place in a classroom. However, connections and camaraderie can be fostered when students share non-threatening information about themselves. Once trust is built, in-depth sharing can happen. Sister Stories students were not always comfortable sharing their counterstories, even in a counterspace designed to foster trust and sharing. In chapter 5, Mindy and Becca explained how they did not trust Sister Stories classmates with their most personal stories. Living within oppressive systems can foster a lack of trust in people from minoritized populations. Sue (2010) also documented how emotionally exhausting it can be for people of color to talk about racism. Moreover, secondary harm can occur (and trust can be threatened) when Whites question the legitimacy of counter narratives of people of color. Women writers of color have also suggested a common form of oppression is for women of color to be silenced when they try to speak up (Domingue, 2015; Hill Collins, 1991, 2000; Wing, 2003). Given these realities, it is understandable why some women of color might decide to keep personal information to themselves or disengage from trust-building exercises altogether.

The loss of a sense of community can be devastating for students of color—especially those who have found meaningful connections in validating classrooms, programs, or student organizations. As Lena noted at the end of the Sister Stories course, "I am . . . sad that I am no longer able to meet with a group of amazing people twice a week." She mourned the loss of the Sister Stories community. Educators should seek venues whereby students can retain community connections after a course, workshop, or program concludes. Teachers and trainers can encourage students to continue to meet in person or online. Educators do not necessarily need to be active members of these ongoing communities, but they play an important role in setting them up. To reap the benefits of an ongoing sense of community, students must do their part. They must make an effort to maintain connections with peers outside a counterspace. This means responding to electronic messages, suggesting community activities, and showing up to community get-togethers.

As we noted in chapter 4, differences among women of color can cause tension in a supposedly safe counterspace. When entering a counterspace, students must realize that finding a sense of communal support and validation means honoring the experiences and perspectives of people who—despite a shared social identity—differ from them. Some Sister Stories students expected peers to adopt particular perspectives, or to act in prescribed ways. They conflated camaraderie and support with sameness. We hope students will not expect sameness or pressure their peers to prove they are worthy of a counterspace community based upon narrow notions of how women of color *should* act. As Sister Stories students noted, "women going against other women" was never helpful. Students should honor, and learn from, the diversity among women of color. If they do, they have an opportunity to gain authentic support and in turn, glean a sense of community and belonging (Vaccaro & Newman, in press).

Faculty who hope to foster community in a counterspace must recognize that merely putting students of the same race or ethnic background together does not necessarily result in a safe counterspace or immediately foster a sense of community. As we noted in chapter 4, one semester, the Sister Stories counterspace was rife with gendered racism perpetrated by men of color. Educators and trainers have a responsibility to confront exclusion when it emerges in a counterspace. Naming the offense and educating people about harm is tantamount to healthy counterspace dynamics and the development of a sense of community among women of color.

TRANSFORMATIVE LEARNING
THROUGH CRITICAL REFLECTION

Students are not blank slates, nor are they receptacles for academic content (Freire, 1970/2006). Students come to educational environments with a lifetime of experiences with power, privilege, and oppression. CRT and CRF educators recognize the inherent value, strength, and power in each student's rich history. They also contend the most valuable and transformative learning happens when students make meaning of course concepts in the context of real-life experiences (Brookfield, 1995, 2000; Dirkx, 1998; Mezirow, 1991; Parker & Stovall, 2004; Stovall, 2006; Vaccaro, 2013).

Learning about self is an essential element of human growth and development and a foundation of transformational learning. Until students delve deeply into who they are, it is challenging to make meaning of the world around them. CRT and CRF perspectives explicate how self-understanding is always framed within the context of oppression and privilege. Critical race educators invite students to critically reflect upon their lived experiences and to acknowledge the range of emotions associated with the learning process (Sue, Torino, Capodilupo, Rivera & Lin, 2009). Critical reflection is the process whereby students make meaning of the world by analyzing and synthesizing their lived experiences within manifestations of power, oppression, and privilege in society. Learning about self was a critical component of the Sister Stories curriculum. Students were invited to ponder tough questions: Who am I? What do I stand for? How do I make meaning of, and respond to, issues of power, privilege, and oppression?

Educators must recognize that students are on various developmental trajectories. Some students will be excited to explore the ways their personal experiences connect to larger systems of power, oppression, and privilege, but others might not be ready for that type of critical reflection. While collecting stories from diverse working-class women, Wong (1998) realized that her positionality as a critical researcher led her to look for (and be disappointed by the lack of) critical stories from her participants. Wong wanted her participants to "be perfect critics—able to pierce through the veil of hypocrisy and hegemony" (p. 185). To her dismay, many women were "terribly inarticulate about the political . . . [and] did not connect the macro structural shifts with their familial, social and personal lives" (p. 185). In fact, participant responses suggested they believed dominant ideologies, deficit notions, and stereotypes about women from minoritized backgrounds. In essence, participants were unwilling (or unable) to engage in the kind of deep critical reflection Wong hoped for. Higher educators must remember that some college students are ready and excited about engaging in critical reflection and counter storytelling, while others are not.

Critical reflection can be hard. Nonetheless, we encourage students to take the risk, because the benefits are boundless. Sister Stories students were often pleasantly surprised by the results of deep and critical reflection. Victoria said, "It was more of a learning experience than I can ever imagine." Opportunities for critical reflection should not be limited to academic counterspaces. Some campuses offer extra-curricular programs and events specifically designed to help students critically reflect. Multicultural offices, women's centers, student activities offices, and intergroup dialogue programs are good places to find such opportunities. Critical reflection can also be done independently through journaling or blogging. Examples of critically reflective blogging can be found on the website Black Girl Dangerous (www.blackgirldangerous.org). Students who need more structured guidance to critically reflect can connect with faculty and staff who are interested in engaging students in reflective dialogue, possibly through independent study.

EDUCATORS AND STUDENTS
NAMING AND SHARING POWER

Naming and critiquing macro and micro power differentials by race and gender (as well as other social identities) are at the heart of critical race and critical race feminist perspectives. By using CRT and CRF as analytic tools in higher education, conferred dominance can be exposed and addressed. As we discussed in chapter 3, conferred dominance refers to the systemic advantages that can be gleaned by men and White people without them doing anything at all (Johnson, 2006; McIntosh, 1988). Faculty and staff can expose and eradicate conferred dominance embedded in student handbooks, judicial policies, student programs, admissions processes, and curriculum. One example of how CRT perspectives can be used to challenge conferred dominance is Bondi's (2012) analysis of a student affairs graduate preparation program. Bondi exposed the ways individuals and institutions protected and perpetuated Whiteness as property and offered tangible suggestions for change in a particular academic program. Similar analyses can be completed with programs, services, policies, and curriculum at any university.

At a more micro level, power differentials emerge between faculty and students. These teacher-student power differences stem from not only differences in position, but also social identities like race and gender. One way to decrease power differentials is for educators to share power with students by inviting them to provide input into the content and delivery of a course, program, or workshop. Sharing power can be as simple as inviting students to co-construct behavioral expectations for the classroom, workshop, or extra-curricular event. Power sharing with students is not always comfortable for educators because it means letting go of control (Sue, Torino, Capodilupo, Rivera & Lin, 2009). However, through the process, educators can increase trust and buy-in from students who are rarely asked for such input.

Students can do their part by offering candid and thoughtful contributions when they are invited to share power. We always begin courses or training sessions by asking participants to co-construct ground rules. Some students offer thoughtful expectations of peers and us. However, there are some students who chose not to engage in expectation conversations. Maybe this is because they are disinterested or skeptical. Given volumes of literature about hostile and unwelcoming campus climates, as well as research showing faculty often perpetrate microaggressions, we understand why women of color might be suspicious about the notion of sharing power. After being socialized in educational systems where power is held, and sometimes abused, by privileged faculty, it makes sense that some learners might be hesitant to believe offers to share classroom power are genuine, or even possible.

Ongoing student feedback about the process and product of education can be invaluable for educators and another way to share power. Instructors and trainers should regularly ask for anonymous student feedback *and* honor it. As noted in chapter 1, I (Melissa) collected feedback from students at the end of every class period. Students offered insightful information regarding their questions, struggles, and interests, which were used to adjust weekly lesson plans. Feedback from course evaluations, focus groups, and student assignments were also used to improve the course from year to year.

Educators should offer both closed-ended and open-ended options for student feedback. Anonymous questionnaires with Likert-scale response options offer helpful statistical data. Qualitative data from open-ended questions, interviews, or focus groups provide rich information about student perspectives and experiences. Partnerships with faculty, staff, and graduate students can make the collection, analysis, and application of qualitative data manageable. As we found, our Sister Stories research was more enjoyable and fruitful when we collaborated. Here, we must revisit our earlier point about the long history of racism in research. Instructors must be cautious about not allowing deficit notions of women of color to shape the wording of evaluation questions or the interpretation of results. Otherwise, the intention to share power via assessment can become yet another instance of oppressive educational practice.

Evaluation data is only useful if students are thoughtful with their feedback. We urge students to be candid and explicit on counterspace evaluations. Ongoing assessment of a counterspace is not merely an opportunity to express opinions that a space is "great" or an educator "really sucks." Such glib responses are rarely useful. Students are the experts about their classroom experiences. Only students can describe their perceptions of the classroom climate and whether or not power has truly been shared. When completing evaluations, students should seriously consider what they need to succeed and offer specific recommendations for improvement. What exactly would make the counterspace more engaging? What can instructors, trainers, or college administrators do to make students feel more included and validated? Students should remember that evaluation is not just about finding out what is wrong. Evaluation is also intended to determine what aspects of a course, program, or event were effective. We encourage students to offer thoughts about what worked well in a counterspace so those things can continue.

Another way educators can share power is by taking risks in the classroom and telling their own counterstories. Specifically, Tuitt (2006) argued educators should "be willing to demonstrate their humanity by identifying weaknesses and sharing personal accounts" (p. 255). It can be an important life lesson for students to recognize educators are also on a life-long journey of understanding what power, privilege, and oppression mean in their everyday lives. Of course, such teacher-student interactions can feel risky and spark educator fears of being exposed as something other than an expert who holds power in the form of knowledge. Research shows that faculty from marginalized social identity groups can find this type of disclosure and risk taking emotionally taxing (Sue, Rivera, Watkins, Kim, Kim & Williams, 2011). Such fears are compounded by systemic racism faced by faculty of color whose credibility is often questioned by disrespectful students (Constantine, Smith, Redington & Owens, 2008; Patton & Catching, 2009). We acknowledge these challenges and encourage educators to decide for themselves which counterstories are appropriate to share with students, if at all.

Students need to realize that when educators share their stories, they are taking risks, being vulnerable, and sharing power. Some students might consider admission of life challenges and mistakes from educators to be taboo. We encourage students to honor the risks taken by educators and recognize sharing is not a sign of personal weakness. Instead, it is intended to role model openness to learning and growth. Sometimes the most powerful learning comes from recognizing and acknowledging mistakes. If educators can do it, so can students.

Educators can share power by role modeling a willingness to grow and learn. Sister Stories students described how educators were often the perpetrators of microaggressions. The nature of many microaggressions is that they are committed without intent. Naming and critiquing researcher identities, biases, assumptions, and privileges is paramount for socially just inquiry (Jones, Torres & Arminio, 2013; Parker & Lynn, 2002; Solórzano & Yosso, 2002). Inclusive educators suggest that teachers must do the same in the classroom (Tuitt, 2006; Vaccaro, 2013). Educators have to be hyper-vigilant about the impact of their facilitation style, informal interactions with students, and curricular choices on not only women of color, but all students from minoritized social identity backgrounds (Capper, Theoharis & Sebastian, 2006). When confronted with, or accused of, microaggressions, educators should not dismiss student concerns. This is an abuse of power that can cause additional harm to students. Rather, educators must role model a willingness to accept responsibility and learn from the experience. Again, we recognize this type of power sharing can be personally and professionally risky. However, we contend that social justice education and real inclusion requires educators and students to not merely talk about the idea of naming and challenging power inequities, but to actually do it.

EDUCATION IS EMPOWERMENT

Fostering resiliency and empowerment is a challenging but essential job for higher educators. Critical race scholars like Villalpando (2003) noted, students of color "live in a society and go to school in an environment that operates in contradictory ways, by both oppressing and marginalizing [student of color] while offering . . . the potential for empowerment and emancipation" (p. 636). Villalpando (2003) also offered the following advice to students: "Try to maintain your focus on your resiliency and agency in helping to bring about social justice and direct improvements in the conditions of [y]our communities" (p. 636). Sister Stories was a venue for students to develop social capital, learn how to pick their battles, advocate for self, challenge oppression, and become inclusive leaders. Students resisted oppression, exhibited agency and empowerment, and role modeled strength and inclusive leadership skills in the face of campus exclusion. As critical race feminists, we contend there is much to be learned about empowerment and emancipation from women of color.

Universities must create programs, services, and curriculum that empower women of color to thrive—not merely survive in the face of gendered racism. Examples include student organizations and leadership development programs that foster resilience and inspire women of color to succeed despite systemic and interpersonal oppression. Creating credit-bearing courses like Sister Stories is another way to provide empowering educational experiences for women of color.

Sister Stories students consistently reported guest speakers and panel presentations from women of color to be a highlight of the course. Inspirational stories of success, resiliency, and activism from successful women of color empowered students to believe they could also succeed. Educators should consider ways to tap into the wealth of empowering resources on their campuses and surrounding communities. Introducing students of color to prosperous professionals who look like them is a priceless resource (Capper et al., 2006; Mena & Vaccaro, 2014).

Sister Stories students developed invaluable networks with peers and guest speakers. To derive the full benefits of social capital, students had to foster those relationships. As Suzanna noted in chapter 3, guest speakers could provide her with essential career support, like letters of recommendation. However, Suzanna understood it was her responsibility to keep in touch with faculty and staff. We encourage students to take active steps to build connections with role models and mentors on campus—identify admirable faculty, staff, and student leaders and make an effort to build relationships with those people. A first step is introducing oneself in person or via email. Students can also make an appointment to meet with professionals whom they admire. As we noted in chapter 3, due to their small numbers, women of color in academe are often overwhelmed by the volume of requests for such support. Knowing this, students should not take it personally if a particular staff or faculty member does not have time to meet.

Another option for building social capital, fostering support, and empowering women of color is through formal mentoring programs. Many campuses have free peer-peer or faculty-student mentoring programs.

We encourage students to take advantage of these programs. In some instances, it is beneficial for students to go off campus to expand their social networks and find inspiration. Higher education institutions sometimes sponsor students to attend national programs such as: the National Conference for College Women Student Leaders, the Social Justice Training Institute, the NASPA Undergraduate Fellows Program, and the Campus Pride Summer LGBTQ Leadership Academy. There are also a host of state and regional conferences, workshops, and events where women of color can develop and hone their skills and, in turn, feel empowered to enact change. Students should learn more about these opportunities through websites and then approach student affairs staff members about potential grants to cover the cost of attendance. In sum, we encourage women of color to take advantage of the variety of empowering campus and community opportunities available.

CONCLUSION

We crafted this book to be an in-depth exploration of the experiences of students in a unique counterspace designed by, and for, women of color. Because the voices of women of color are often marginalized (Wing, 2003), it was important for us to center and share the powerful narratives of women of color in Sister Stories. We hope this book, however, goes beyond the mere sharing of voices. Women's stories offer precious insight to students and educators who want to make micro- and macro-level changes on campus, at home, and in their communities. Just as women of color in Sister Stories were empowered to incite change, we hope readers are motivated to enact change in their spheres of influence.

REFERENCES

Alston, J. A., & McClellan, P. A. (2011). *herstories: Leading with the lessons of the lives of Black women activists.* New York: Peter Lang.

Baez, B. (2000). Race-related service and faculty of color: Conceptualizing critical agency in academe. *Higher Education, 39*(3), 363–91.

Bell, D. A. (1980). Brown v. Board of Education and the interest convergence dilemma. *Harvard Law Review, 93*(3), 518–33.

Bergerson, A. A. (2003). Critical race theory and white racism: Is there room for white scholars in fighting racism in education? *Qualitative Studies in Education, 16*(1), 51–63.

Bernal, D. D. (2002). Critical race theory, Latino critical theory, and critical raced-gendered epistemologies: Recognizing students of color as holders and creators of knowledge. *Qualitative inquiry, 8*(1), 105–26.

———, & Villalpando, O. (2002). An apartheid of knowledge in academia: The struggle over the "legitimate" knowledge of faculty of color. *Equity &Excellence in Education, 35*(2), 169–80.

Bondi, S. (2012). Students and institutions protecting Whiteness as property: A critical race theory analysis of student affairs preparation. *Journal of Student Affairs Research and Practice, 49*(4), 397–414.

Brookfield, S. D. (1995). *Becoming a critically reflective teacher.* San Francisco, CA: Jossey-Bass.

————— (2000). The concept of critically reflective practice. In A. L. Wilson & E. R. Hayes (Eds.), *Handbook of adult and continuing education* (pp. 33–49). Hoboken, NJ: Wiley.

Capper, C. A., Theoharis, G., & Sebastian, J. (2006). Toward a framework for preparing leaders for social justice. *Journal of Educational Administration, 44*(3), 209–24.

Carbado, D. W., Crenshaw, K. W., Mays, V. M., & Tomlinson, B. (2013). Intersectionality. *Du Bois Review: Social Science Research on Race, 10*(02), 303–12.

Constantine, M. G., Smith, L., Redington, R. M., & Owens, D. (2008). Racial microaggressions against Black counseling and counseling psychology faculty: A central challenge in the multicultural counseling movement. *Journal of Counseling & Development, 86*(3), 348–55.

Crenshaw, K. (1989). Demarginalizing the intersection of race and sex: A Black feminist critique of antidiscrimination doctrine, feminist theory and antiracist politics. *University of Chicago Legal Forum,* 139.

Dirkx, J. M. (1998). Transformative learning theory in the practice of adult education: An overview. *PAACE Journal of Lifelong Learning, 7,* 1–14.

Domingue, A. D. (2015). "Our leaders are just we ourself": Black women college student leaders' experiences with oppression and sources of nourishment on a predominantly white college campus. *Equity & Excellence in Education, 48*(3), 454–72.

Freeman, T. M., Anderman, L. H., & Jensen, J. M. (2007). Sense of belonging in college freshmen at the classroom and campus levels. *The Journal of Experimental Education, 75*(3), 203–20.

Freire, P. (1970/2006). *Pedagogy of the oppressed.* New York: Continuum Press.

Gildersleeve, R. E., Croom, N. N., & Vasquez, P. L. (2011). "Am I going crazy?!": A critical race analysis of doctoral education. *Equity & Excellence in Education, 44*(1), 93–114.

Harper, S. R., Patton, L. D., & Wooden, O. S. (2009). Access and equity for African American students in higher education: A critical race historical analysis of policy efforts. *The Journal of Higher Education, 80*(4), 389–414.

Harris, J. C., Haywood, J. M., Ivery, S. M., & Shuck, J. R. (2015). "Yes, I am smart!": Battling microaggressions as women of color doctoral students. In J. L. Martin (Ed.), *Racial battle fatigue: Insights from the front lines of social justice advocacy* (pp. 151–62). Santa Barbara, CA: Praeger.

Hausmann, L. R. M., Schofield, J. W., & Woods, R. L. (2007). Sense of belonging as a predictor of intentions to persist among African American and White first-year college students. *Research in Higher Education, 48*(7), 803–39.

Hill Collins, P. (1991, 2000). *Black feminist thought: Knowledge, consciousness, and the politics of empowerment.* New York: Routledge.

Hoffman, M., Richmond, J., Morrow, J., & Salomone, K. (2002/2003). Investigating "sense of belonging" in first-year college students. *Journal of College Student Retention, 4*(3), 227–56.

Howard-Hamilton, M. L., C. L. Morelon-Quainoo, C. L., Johnson, S.D., Winkle-Wagner, R., & Santiague, L. (Eds.) (2009). *Standing on the outside looking in: Underrepresented students' experiences in advanced degree programs.* Sterling, VA: Stylus.

Hurtado, S. (1992, September/October). The campus racial climate: Contexts of conflict. *Journal of Higher Education, 63*(5), 539–69.

—————, & Guillermo-Wann, C. (2013). *Diverse learning environments: Assessing and creating conditions for student success—Final Report to the Ford Foundation.* University of California, Los Angeles: Higher Education Research Institute.

Johnson, A. G. (2006). *Privilege, power and difference* (2nd ed.). Boston, MA: McGraw Hill.

Jones, S. R., Torres, V., & Arminio, J. (2013). *Negotiating the complexities of qualitative research in higher education: Fundamental elements and issues* (2nd ed.). New York: Routledge.

Joseph, T. D., & Hirshfield, L. E. (2011). "Why don't you get somebody new to do it?" Race and cultural taxation in the academy. *Ethnic and Racial Studies, 34*(1), 121–41.

Larson, C. L., & Murtadha, K. (2002). Leadership for social justice. *Yearbook of the National Society for the Study of Education, 101*(1), 134–61.

López, G. R. (2003). The (racially neutral) politics of education: A critical race theory perspective. *Educational Administration Quarterly, 39*(1), 68–94.

Lupo, V. L. (2011). Remembering our past to shape our future. In D. L. Stewart (Ed.), *Multicultural student services on campus: Building bridges, re-visioning community* (pp. 13–28). Sterling, VA: Stylus.

McIntosh, P. (1988). *White privilege and male privilege: A personal account of coming to see correspondences through work in women's studies. Working Paper No. 189.* Wellesley, MA: Wellesley Centers for Women.

Mena, J., & Vaccaro, A. (2014). Role modeling community engagement for college students: Narratives from women faculty and staff of color. In S. K. Iverson & J. A. James (Eds.), *Feminist Community Engagement: Achieving Praxis* (pp. 53–74). New York: Palgrave Macmillan.

Mezirow, J. (1991). *Transformative dimensions of adult learning.* San Francisco, CA: Jossey-Bass.

Parker, L., & Lynn, M. (2002). What's race got to do with it? Critical race theory's conflicts with and connections to qualitative research methodology and epistemology. *Qualitative Inquiry, 8*(1), 7–22.

Parker, L., & Stovall, D. O. (2004). Actions following words: Critical race theory connects to critical pedagogy. *Educational Philosophy and Theory, 36*(2), 167–82.

Patton, L. D., & Catching, C. (2009). "Teaching while Black": Narratives of African American student affairs faculty. *International Journal of Qualitative Studies in Education, 22*(6), 713–28.

Pittman, L. D., & Richmond, A. (2008). University belonging, friendship quality, and psychological adjustment during the transition to college. *Journal of Experimental Education, 76*, 343–61.

Pope, R. L., Reynolds, A. L., & Mueller, J. A. (2014). *Creating Multicultural Change on Campus.* San Francisco, CA: Jossey-Bass.

Romney, P. (2008). Consulting for diversity and social justice: Challenges and rewards. *Consulting Psychology Journal: Practice and Research, 60*(2), 139–56.

Solórzano, D. G. (1997). Images and words that wound: Critical race theory, racial stereotyping, and teacher education. *Teacher Education Quarterly, 24*(3), 5–20.

———, Ceja, M., & Yosso, T. J. (2000). Critical race theory, racial microaggressions, and campus racial climate: The experiences of African American college students. *The Journal of Negro Education, 69*(1/2), 60–73.

———, & Yosso, T. J. (2001). Critical race and LatCrit theory and method: Counter-storytelling. *International Journal of Qualitative Studies in Education, 14*(4), 471–95.

———, & Yosso, T. J. (2002). Critical race methodology: Counter-storytelling as an analytical framework for education research. *Qualitative inquiry, 8*(1), 23–44.

Stewart, D. L. (Ed.) (2011). *Multicultural student services on campus: Building bridges, re-visioning community.* Sterling, VA: Stylus.

Strayhorn, T. L. (2012). *College students' sense of belonging: A key to educational success for all students.* New York: Routledge.

Stovall, D. (2006). Forging community in race and class: Critical race theory and the quest for social justice in education, *Race, Ethnicity and Education, 9*(3), 243–59.

Suarez-Orozco, C., Casanova, S., Martin, M., Katsiaficas, D., Cuellar, V., Smith, N., & Dias, S. (2015). Toxic rain in class: Classroom interpersonal microaggressions. *Educational Researcher, 44*(3), 151–60.

Sue, D. W. (2010). *Microaggressions in everyday life: Race, gender and sexual orientation.* Hoboken, NJ: Wiley.

————, Rivera, D. P., Watkins, N. L., Kim, R. H., Kim, S., & Williams, C. D. (2011). Racial dialogues: Challenges faculty of color face in the classroom. *Cultural Diversity and Ethnic Minority Psychology, 17*(3), 331.

————, Torino, G. C., Capodilupo, C. M., Rivera, D. P., & Lin, A. I. (2009). How White faculty perceive and react to difficult dialogues on race implications for education and training. *The Counseling Psychologist, 37*(8), 1090–15.

Tuitt, F. (2006). Afterword: Realizing a more inclusive pedagogy. In A. Howell & F. Tuitt (Eds.), *Race and higher education: Rethinking pedagogy in diverse college classrooms* (pp. 243–369). Cambridge, MA: Harvard Educational Review.

Vaccaro, A. (2010). What lies beneath seemingly positive campus climate results: Institutional sexism, symbolic racism, and male hostility toward equity initiatives. *Equity and Excellence in Education, 43*(2), 202–15.

———— (2012). Campus microclimates for LGBT faculty, staff, and students: An exploration of the intersections of social identity and campus roles. *Journal of Student Affairs Research and Practice, 44*(4), 429–46.

———— (2013). Building a framework for social justice education: One educator's journey. In L. Landreman (Ed.), *The art of effective facilitation: Reflections from social justice educators* (pp. 23–44). Sterling, VA: Stylus.

———— (2014). Campus climate for diversity: Current realities and suggestions for the future. *Texas Education Review, 2*(1), 129–37.

———— (2016). Strategies for teaching multicultural psychology: Who, what, and how. In K. Quina & J. Mena (Eds.), *Teaching a multiculturally-informed psychology of people.* Washington, DC: American Psychological Association.

————, & Newman, B. M. (in press). The development of a sense of belonging for privileged and minoritized students: An emerging model. *Journal of College Student Development.*

Villalpando, O. (2003). Self-segregation or self-preservation? A critical race theory and Latina/o critical theory analysis of a study of Chicana/o college students. *Qualitative Studies in Education, 16*(5), 619–46.

————, & Bernal, D. D. (2002). A critical race theory analysis of barriers that impede the success of faculty of color. In W. A. Smith, P. G. Altbach & K. Lomotey (Eds.), *The racial crisis in American higher education: Continuing challenges for the twenty-first century* (rev. ed., pp. 243–69). Albany, NY: SUNY Press.

Williams, D. A., Berger, J. B., & McClendon, S. A. (2005). *Toward a model of inclusive excellence and change in post-secondary institutions.* Washington, DC: AAC&U.

Wing, A. K. (2003). *Critical race feminism: A reader* (2nd ed.). New York: New York University Press.

Wong, L. M. (1998). The ethics of rapport: Institutional safeguards, resistance, and betrayal. *Qualitative Inquiry, 4*(2), 178–99.

Zinn, M. B., Cannon, L. W., Higginbotham, E., & Dill, B. T. (1986). The costs of exclusionary practices in women's studies. *Signs, 11*(2), 290–303.

Appendix

Table A.1. Sister Stories Participants

Pseudonym	Year Enrolled	Class Standing	Gender	Own words that describe students' race	Race/ Ethnicity Selected from List
Abe	4	Sophomore	Man	No answer	Black, Bi/ Multiracial— Nigerian/ American
Allie	1	Sophomore	Woman	White	Caucasian
Ana	5	Senior	Woman	Dominican	Latina
Andrew	4	Junior	Man	Greek, American, Western European	Caucasian
Becca	5	Sophomore	Woman	African American	Black
Bonnie	5	Junior	Woman	Bi/multiracial Latina & Black	Biracial
Brandon	2	Junior	Man	African American and Italian American	Bi/Multiracial
Brian	5	Junior	Man	Specifically Nigerian American, but I am African American	Black
Camila	4	Sophomore	Woman	Colombian	Latino/ Latina
Carla	4	First-year	Woman	Puerto Rican	Latino/ Latina
Carmen	3	Sophomore	Woman	Hispanic	Latino/ Latina

Pseudonym	Year Enrolled	Class Standing	Gender	Own words that describe students' race	Race/ Ethnicity Selected from List
Carolina	5	Sophomore	Woman	Guaterican American	Latino/ Latina
Chrissy	4	Sophomore	Woman	African	Black
Claire	3	First-year	Woman	No answer	Black
Diana	2	Senior	Woman	Biracial, Indian and Portuguese	Bi/Multiracial
Diego	2	Junior	Man	Hispanic American	Latino/ Latina
Dominic	1	Senior	Man	Ghanaian, Native American	Black
Eddie	4	First-year	Man	Cape Verdean/ African American	Black
Elena	4	Sophomore	Woman	Latina	Latino/ Latina
Elsy	5	Junior	Woman	Latina	No answer
Emily	3	Sophomore	Woman	Caucasian (White)	Caucasian
Fiona	1	Junior	Woman	White	Caucasian
Fola	5	First-year	Woman	Black	No answer
Hanna	5	First-year	Woman	African American & part Cuban	Black
Harry	2	Sophomore	Man	African American	Black
Ife	2	Senior	Woman	Nigerian	Other, Brown skinned
Jackie	1	Sophomore	Woman	Cape Verdean	Black
Jenna	1	Junior	Woman	White Scandina-vian	Caucasian
Jewel	1	Sophomore	Woman	Nigerian American	Black

Pseudonym	Year Enrolled	Class Standing	Gender	Own words that describe students' race	Race/ Ethnicity Selected from List
Jocelyn	3	Sophomore	Woman	Haitian and Cape Verdean American	Bi/Multiracial
John	5	Junior	Man	Caucasian	White
Juba	2	Sophomore	Woman	Nigerian	Black, Other, Nigerian
Juliana	3	Senior	Woman	Dominican/ Hispanic	Latino/ Latina
Kalu	2	Junior	Man	African American	Black
Katie	1	Sophomore	Woman	White— Non-Hispanic	Caucasian
Kendra	3	Senior	Woman	Multiracial— Syrian, Italian, and Jamaican	Bi/Multiracial
Kristin	3	Junior	Woman	Caucasian	Caucasian
Lacey	4	First-year	Woman	Middle Eastern and Cape Verdean	Bi/Multiracial
Laura	2	Senior	Woman	Cape Verdean & Native American	Black
Lauren	4	First-year	Woman	Cape Verdean & Senegalese	Black
Lena	4	First-year	Woman	Cape Verdean	Black
Liza	4	First-year	Woman	No answer	Asian American/ Pacific Islander
Lucia	5	Junior	Woman	Dominican American/ Latina/ Hispanic	Latino/ Latina

Pseudonym	Year Enrolled	Class Standing	Gender	Own words that describe students' race	Race/ Ethnicity Selected from List
Lucy	3	Senior	Woman	African American	Black
Malcolm	1	Sophomore	Man	Black— African American	Black
Maria	1	First-year	Woman	Puerto Rican	Latino/ Latina
Mayra	4	Sophomore	Woman	Cape Verdean because it is a mixed race/ ethnicity	Bi/ Multiracial— Cape Verdean/ Native American Indian
Mindy	1	Sophomore	Woman	Colombian	Latino/ Latina
Nicole	2	Senior	Woman	Cape Verdean/ African	Black
Pamela	3	Junior	Woman	Purebred Puerto Rican and American citizen	Latino/ Latina
Paul	4	Senior	Man	Asian (Hmong)	Asian American/ Pacific Islander
Regina	1	Sophomore	Woman	African American	Black
Rose	4	First-year	Woman	West African	Black
Ruben	4	First-year	Man	Cape Verdean	Black
Sarah	2	First-year	Woman	No answer	Caucasian
Sia	1	First-year	Woman	Liberian American	Black
Sofia	5	Senior	Woman	Latina	No answer
Suzanna	3	First-year	Woman	Cape Verdean	Black

Pseudonym	Year Enrolled	Class Standing	Gender	Own words that describe students' race	Race/ Ethnicity Selected from List
Vera	3	First-year	Woman	American-born woman of Cape Verdean descent	Black
Victoria	2	Junior	Woman	Puerto Rican and Dominican	Latino/ Latina
Zuberi	2	Sophomore	Man	Black/ African descent	Black

Note: Table created by Annemarie Vaccaro and Melissa J. Camba-Kelsay.

Index

Abes, E. S., 115
acculturation, 112, 115, 120, 122
Ackelsberg, M., 35
Adams, M., xxvi
aesthetics, 73, 95, 131, 132, 133, 134, 138, 140, 144, 147
Akan, G. E., 133
Alston, J. A., 152, 175
Alvarez, C., 161
Anderson, E, 51, 52, 61, 105, 106, 120
Anzaldúa, G., xx, 70, 143, 147, 154
Arminio, J., xx
Arthur, C. J., 50
Atkinson, D. R., 9
attribution, 31, 32, 33, 42; ambiguity, 31, 33, 42; primary, 30, 31, 42; secondary, 30, 31, 42
Awad, G. H., 135

Baez, B., 174
Bankhead, T., 73, 131, 132, 134, 136
Bankston, C. L., 56
Barnes, K., 5
Bell, D. A., xxvi, 166, 171
Bell, L. A., xviii, xix, xxii, 50, 99, 136
Bergerson, Amy Aldous, xiv, xxvi, xxviii, 49, 50, 84, 173
Bernal, D. D., xxvi, 162, 174, 175
Berry, J. W., 115, 122
Bhatt, A. J., 102
Bhopal, R., xviii
Biernat, M., 146
Billig, M., 34
Blume, A. W., 30
body image, xxx, 95, 104, 131, 134, 136, 142–143, 146
Boisvert, J. A., 132
Bondi, S., 181
Bonilla-Silva E., 36
Bourdieu, P., 60

Brayboy, B. M. J., 10
Bridges, B., 54
Broido, E. M., 84
Brookfield, S. D., 8, 179
Brown v. Board of Education, 54
Brown, M. C, xxviii, 118
Bryan, M. L., 85
Buescher, D. T., xxiii
Burdsey, D., 35
Butler, J. E., xxix, 55, 69

Capodilupo, C. M., xxi, xxii, xxiii, 28, 29, 39, 40, 42, 69, 132
Capper, C. A., 152, 153, 157, 159, 183, 184
Carbado, D. W., 174
Carter, D. F., 58
Carter, R. T., 30
Case, K. A., xiii, 50
Castagano, A. E., 10
Catching, C., 183
Cervero, R. M., 91
Chang, M. J., 90
Charleston, L. J., xxviii, 42, 51, 52, 61
Chesney-Lind, M., xxii
Chin, J. L., 152
Cho, S., xix, xx, xxi
Choo, H. Y., 70, 107
Chun, K. M., 115
Cilente, K., 157
Clark, R., 99
Cole, E. R., xiii
College Opportunity, Campaign for, 51
colorblindness, xxi, xxv, xxvi, xxvii, 50, 114, 152, 173
colorism, 73, 136, 139
Combahee River Collective, xix, xx, 70
community, sense of, 159, 171, 176, 177, 178, 179
conferred dominance, 49, 181

consciousness, double, 53
Constantine, M. G., xxi, 183
Cotter, E., 133
Crawford, J. B., 52, 53
Crenshaw, K., xix, xx, xxvii, 4, 28, 70, 174
critical race theory (CRT), xiv, xvii, xxv, xxvi, xxvii, xxviii, xxix, xxx, 1, 4, 5, 49, 50, 59, 70, 84, 95, 113, 134, 152, 153, 154, 155, 158, 162, 173, 175, 179, 181
Crocker, J., 132, 133, 144
Cross, W. E., 9, 112, 154
CRT. *See* critical race theory
Cueva, B. M., xxvii, xxviii, xxix, 54, 55, 69, 94, 97, 106, 167
Cullen, M., 35, 36
Cunningham, M. R., 140

Dancy, T. E. E., xxix, 118
Darder, A., xxvi, xxvii, xxix, 5, 89, 94
David, E. J. R., 40, 114, 117, 136
Delgado, R., xxvii, xxviii, 94, 167
DiCaprio, N. S., 10
Dill, B. T., 71, 75, 131, 132
Dirkx, J. M., 8, 179
Domingue, A. D., 28, 29, 30, 40, 42, 56, 79, 178
Downey, V., 142
Drechsler, M. J., 162
DuBois, W. E. B., 53
Dugan, J. P., 10, 151, 152, 154, 159

Engbers, T. A., 152, 154
Engels, Fredrick, 50
equal opportunity, xxvi, xxvii, xxviii, 50, 75, 114, 173
Essed, P., xxi, 72, 77, 119
ethnic identity development, 111, 112, 113, 115, 121
ethnic studies, xxix, 55, 175, 176
Evans, N. J., 112, 117
Evans, P. C., 133
Evans, S. Y., 156, 159, 164

family dynamics, 6, 75, 97, 111, 112, 120, 121, 133, 138, 139, 140, 141, 142, 145, 162, 168
Feagin, J. R., xxiii, 45

Ferdman, B. M., 9, 112, 113
Ferree, M. M., 70, 107
Fhagen-Smith, P., 9
Fincher, J., 7
Fleming, J., xxiii, 45
FMMI. *See* Multiracial Identity
Folkman, S., 30–31, 33, 42
Ford, K. A., 64
Ford, T., 35
Fox, H., 16, 90, 91, 99, 101, 108
Frankenberg, R., 132
Frazier, A. D., 133
Fredrickson, B. L., xxii, 29, 30, 77
Freeman, T. M., 58, 176
Freire, P., 8, 155, 179
Freyd, J. J. 2014, xxiv

Gallegos, P. I., 9, 112, 113
Garrett, M. T., 142
Gayles, J. G., 85, 91, 97
gender expression, 75
Gildersleeve, R. E., xxviii, 28, 118, 173
Goodman, D. J., xiii, 51, 53, 91, 99, 101, 108
Goto, S., 28, 37
Gray-Little, B., 144
Greenleaf, R. K., 151, 154, 155, 157, 159, 166
Greenman, E., 56
Grier-Reed, T. L., xxix, 97, 106
Griffin, K. A., 70, 107
Grilo, C. M., 133
Guillermo-Wann, C., xx, xxiii, xxiv, 176, 177
Gurin, P., 90

Hafdahl, A. R., 144
Hall, C. C. I., 132, 140
Hall, R. M., xxiii, 45, 52, 58
Harbour, C. P., 52, 61
Hardiman, R., 112, 113, 114, 115, 119, 124, 125, 126, 133, 136, 137
Harley, D. A., 64
Harper, S. R., xix, xxiii, xxvi, 45, 54, 75, 125
Harris-Perry, M. V., xxii, 29, 44
Harris, J. C., xxviii, 173
Harris, K. L., 36
Harro, B., 9, 133, 134, 136, 138, 141, 145

Hausmann, L. R. M., 58, 176
hegemony, 50, 136, 180
Helms, J. E., xiv, 9, 112, 113, 124, 126
HERI. *See* Higher Education Research Institute
Higher Education Research Institute (HERI), 8, 151, 154, 157, 159, 166
Hill Collins, P., xix, xx, xxii, xxiii, 11, 28, 29, 44, 51, 56, 70, 79, 81, 112, 178
Hirshfield, L. E., 174
Hoffman, M., 58, 176
hooks, b., xx, xxi, xxii, xxvii, 28, 29, 44, 52, 70, 71, 81, 90, 98, 108, 142, 156, 159
Horse, P. G., 9, 113
Howard-Hamilton, M. L., xxiii, 45, 176
Hu, S., 90
Hunter, M., 73, 136, 139
Hurtado, S., xx, xxiii, xxiv, 45, 54, 58, 90, 176, 177
Hwang, W. C., 28, 37
hypervigilance, 94, 97

identity development, 9, 10, 111, 112, 113, 114, 115, 116, 117, 118, 119, 120, 121, 124, 125, 126
ideologies, dominant, xxvi, xxvii, xxviii, 40, 50, 55, 73, 75, 94, 99, 113, 114, 117, 125, 131, 132, 133, 134, 136, 173, 176, 180
inferiority, assumptions of, xxii, 28, 40
intergroup relations, 90
internalized oppression, 117, 118, 136
invisible, 29, 42, 51, 146, 152, 161, 173, 174; invisibility, xxii, xxiv, 29, 40, 146, 152, 164, 174

Jackson, B., 112, 113, 114, 115, 119, 124, 125, 126, 133, 136, 137
Jean-Marie, G., 153, 154, 156, 157, 162
Johnson-Bailey, J., 91
Johnson, A. G., xix, 49, 181
Johnson, D. R., 58
Johnson, J. R., 102
Johnson, T. A., 73, 131, 132, 134, 136
Jones, Jr. W. A., 162
Jones, S. R., 17, 18, 91, 99, 115, 183
Joseph, T. D., 174
Jung, C. G., 108

Kaiser, C. R., 30
Kanjorski, J., 35
Kanter, R. M., 57
Kelly, B. T., 85, 91, 97
Keyes, M., 159
Kich, G. K., 113
Kim S., 132
Kim, J., 9, 112, 113, 132
Kolb, D. M., 52, 54
Komives, S. R., 10, 151, 154, 156, 157, 159, 160, 166
Kouzes, J. M., 13, 165
Kuh, G. D., 90
Kwan, K. L. K., 112

Laird, T. F. N., 90
Larson, C. L., 152, 154, 155, 157, 158, 159, 160, 166, 173
Lazarus, R. S., 30, 31, 33, 42
leadership, 9, 10, 60, 106, 151, 152, 153, 154, 155, 156, 157, 158, 159, 160, 161, 164, 165, 166, 168, 184; critical race leadership, 33, 153; relational leadership model, 151, 154, 156, 157, 159, 166; servant leadership model, 151, 154, 155, 156, 159, 166; social change model, 8, 151, 154, 157, 159, 161
Lewis, J. A., 30, 77, 79
Locks, A. M., 58
López, G. R., 152, 153, 154, 157, 171, 172, 174, 176
López, V., xxii
Lorde, A., 11, 29
Love, B. J., xxvi, xxviii, 49
Lupo, V. L., 174, 177
Lynn, M., xxvi, 175, 183

Maramba, D. C., 10
Martin, D. B., 28
Martínez Alemán, A. M., 85, 91, 97
Marx, Karl, 50
masculine discourse, 52, 53, 55
Maxwell, K. E., 90
McCabe, J., xxii, 28, 29, 113
McCall, L., xix, xxvii
McClellan, P. A., 152, 175
McConnell, A. R., 133
McGee, E. O., 28

McGlynn, A. P., 5
McIntosh, P., xix, 49, 60, 181
Mead, G. H., 133
Mena, J., 10, 53, 146, 184
meritocracy, xxii, xxvi, xxvii, 50, 75, 114, 125, 173
Merriam, S. B., 18
Meyerson, D. E., 52, 54
Mezirow, J., 8, 179
microclimate, 35, 45
Miller, C. T., 30
Mills, A. J., 52
Milner, H. R., xxvi, 166
Minikel-Lacocque, J., 28
Moradi, B., 143
Moraga, C., xx, 70
Mucherah, W., 133
multicultural centers, xxix, 54
Multiracial Identity (FMMI), 9, 123, 124
Muñoz, S. M., 58, 59, 116
Murtadha, K., 152, 154, 155, 157, 158, 159, 160, 166, 173
Museus, S. D., 70, 73, 107

Nadal, K. L., xxi, xxii, 28, 29, 30, 123, 146
Nagada, B. A., 90
Nagasawa, R., 56
National Center for Education Statistics (NCES), 51, 89
National Science Foundation (NSF), 51
NCES. *See* National Center for Education Statistics
Newman, B. M., 179
normalcy, white, 53, 55, 59, 64, 76, 114, 119, 176
NSF. *See* National Science Foundation
Nuñez, A. M., xxix, 55, 58, 69

objectification, xix, xxii, 27, 28, 29, 30, 77
Ono, K. A., xxiii
Ornelas, A., xxvi
Ortiz, A. M., 10, 112, 113

Palmer, R. T., 10, 11
Parker, L., 5, 6, 8, 175, 179, 183
Pasteur, A., 113
Patton, L. D., 183

Patton, T. O., 73, 75, 131, 132, 133, 134, 135, 136, 138, 143
pedagogy, 5, 6, 7, 8, 9, 11, 93, 116, 153; critical, 5, 6, 7, 8, 9, 11, 93, 153; inclusive, 7, 8, 93
Perez Huber, L., xxvii, xxviii, xxix, 49, 50, 54, 55, 69, 94, 97, 106, 167
Perna, L. W., 35
Phelps, A. D., 51, 52, 53, 58
phenotype, 72, 73, 112, 135, 136, 137, 139
Phinney, J. S., 112, 115
Pichardo-Diaz, D., 10
Pierce, C., xxi, 30
Pittman, L. D., 58, 176
Pope, M. L., 10
Pope, R. L., xiv, xx, 10, 173, 177
Posner, B. Z., 13, 165
Poston, W. S. C., 113
praxis, 5, 6, 8, 155
Putnam, R. D., 60

Rankin, S., xxiv
Reason, R., xxiv, 84, 122
Reason, R., xxiv, 122
Reason, R. D., 84
Rendón Linares, L. I., 58, 59, 116
Rendón, L., 58, 59
Renn, K. A., 10, 73, 113, 115
Richeson, J. A., 91
Richmond, A., 58, 176
Roberts, D., 152, 153, 154
Roberts, T. A., xxii, 29, 30, 77
Rockquemore, K. A., 73, 131, 133, 136
role modeling, 151, 164, 165, 168, 183
Rowe, W., 9
Ryan, K. M., 35

Sadker, D., 52, 61
Sadker, M., 52, 61
Sandler, B. R., xxiii, 45, 52, 58
Santos, S. J., 112, 113
Sartre, J. P., 34
Schwartz, S. J., 56
self-censorship, xxx, 91, 92, 96, 97, 108
Settles, I. H., 111
Shah, S., xxii, 29, 113
Shelton, J, N., 91
Shields, S. A., xxvii, 70

Shuford, B. C., 54
Siesko, A. K., 146
Smith, C. P., xxiv
Smith, D. G., 55
Smith, W., xxviii, 28, 30, 49
social identity development theory,
    114, 115, 119, 124
socialization, 9, 10, 99, 111, 121, 123,
    133, 134, 138, 142, 144, 147, 165;
    familial/family, 120, 121, 156, 164,
    180; Harro's Cycle of, 9, 133, 134,
    141; oppressive, 50, 59, 62, 71, 73, 75,
    112, 117, 118, 120, 133, 134, 136, 137,
    138, 141, 142, 144
Sodowsky, G. R., 112
Solomon, R. P., 153
Solórzano, D. G., xix, xx, xxv, xxvi,
    xxvii, xxviii, xxix, 4, 6, 49, 50, 70, 75,
    81, 84, 94, 97, 106, 113, 118, 155, 158,
    162, 167, 173, 174, 175, 183
Solórzano, D. J., xxviii, xxix, 5, 28, 30,
    37, 54, 69, 97, 106, 118, 173
Stefancic, J., xxvii, 94, 167
Stewart, D. L., xxix, 18, 33, 115, 177
Stovall, D. O., 5, 6, 8, 9, 11, 155, 179
Strayhorn, T. L., 28, 58, 90, 176
Suarez-Orozco, C., 173
Sue, D, 9
Sue, D. W., xxi, xxii, xxiii, xxiv, xxv, 9,
    28, 30, 31, 32, 33, 36, 37, 38, 39, 40,
    42, 56, 60, 69, 70, 81, 84, 93, 94, 97,
    103, 113, 114, 119, 125, 178, 180, 181,
    183
Swami, V., 140

Tatum, B. (1994)., 84
taxonomy, microaggression, xxi, xxii,
    xxiii, 28, 39, 119
tokenization, 57, 58, 91, 168, 173
Toldson, I., 113
Torres, V., 112, 120, 121
transformational education/learning, 8,
    9, 89, 179
trust building, 14, 18, 92, 94, 178
Tuitt, F., 8, 13, 18, 94, 102, 182, 183

Twenge, J. M., 132, 133, 144

U.S. Census Bureau, xviii
Ullom, C., 153

Vaccaro, A, xxiii, 10, 13, 28, 29, 30, 35,
    40, 45, 51, 52, 57, 58, 94, 146, 174,
    175, 176, 179, 183, 184
validation, 49, 58, 59, 64, 71, 75, 82, 85,
    97, 116, 172, 177, 178, 179
Van Dijk, T.A., 36
Villalpando, O., xxix, 97, 106, 174, 183,
    184

Wallace, M., 132, 138
Walter, J. C., xxix, 55, 69
Watson,L., xxiii, 45
Watt, S. K., xiii, 16, 90, 91, 99, 101, 108
white identity development, 125, 126
white spaces, 51, 52, 54, 61, 105, 120
Wijeyesinghe, C. L., 9, 113, 115, 122,
    123–124
Williams, D. A., 177
Wing, A. K., xix, xx, xxvi, xxvii, 4, 5, 6,
    27, 29, 40, 51, 53, 56, 70, 76, 81, 98,
    99, 104, 144, 146, 152, 158, 161, 164,
    174, 178, 185
Wise, T., xx, 50
Wolf, N., 29, 30, 143
Wolgemuth, J. R., 52, 61
women's studies. *See* ethnic studies
Wong, G., 70
Wong, L. M. (1998), 180

Xie, Y., 56

Yin, R. W., 15, 17, 18
Yosso, T. J., xxvi, xxvii, xxviii, xxix, 28,
    30, 49, 54, 55, 61, 69, 75, 94, 95, 97,
    106, 118, 167, 173, 174, 175, 183
Young, M., 154

Zhou, M., 56
Zinn, M. B., 71, 75, 131, 132, 175
Zúñiga, 90

About the Authors

Annemarie Vaccaro is an Associate Professor and the Graduate Program Director for the College Student Personnel Program at the University of Rhode Island. She earned her PhD in Higher Education and Master's in Sociology from the University of Denver. She also has a Master's in Student Affairs in Higher Education from Indiana University of Pennsylvania. Her scholarship examines social justice issues in higher education and has been published in a variety of higher education journals. She is also the co-author of two books: *Safe Spaces: Making Schools and Communities Welcoming to LGBT Youth* (Praeger) and *Decisions Matter: Using a Decision Making Framework with Contemporary Student Affairs Case Studies* (NASPA).

Melissa J. Camba-Kelsay is a coordinator for student leadership and instructor in the minor in Leadership Studies in the Center for Student Leadership Development at the University of Rhode Island. Prior to that, she served as assistant director in the Marshall Center for Intercultural Learning at Wheaton College in Massachusetts. She received her Master of Science degree in Student affairs in Higher Education from Colorado State University, and her Bachelor of Arts in English, with a minor in Human Development, from the State University of New York at Geneseo. Melissa's professional expertise includes leadership development, inclusion, and social justice.